'This practical handbook, combining contemporary management theory with very practical suggestions, is an indispensable tool for any manager involved in change processes. And aren't we all ...'
Adriaan Vollebergh, Managing Director, Tata Steel Plates, Tata Steel Europe

'This is a book which lives up to its title. By combining a guide to the ideas of key thinkers on change and useful tips for making change happen, it really does provide a toolkit to help us to make sense of change. It is useful to see a focus on the individual, team and organizational levels, and in particular, on the role of the leader in the change process. It is written in a way that makes the book interesting to read both at length as well as to dip into.'
Dr Richard McBain, Head of Postgraduate Post Experience Programmes, Henley Business School

'Surprisingly relevant to my role – a very readable and helpful insight into how to manage change today, with some teasers as to what to expect as the world evolves.'
David Owen, Senior Enterprise Architect, Oil and Gas Industry, Canada

'A comprehensive guide on the topic of change management. What stands out is its wide coverage of the underpinning theories on change management as well as practical applications of these theories on different types of change. This makes the book a fantastic resource not just for field practitioners like me, but also for students studying the topic of change management.'
Chris Chew, Head of Organization Development, IMC Pan Asia Alliance Pte Ltd

'This book serves as an easily readable, un-intimidating, and comprehensive guide on understanding the complexities of various change projects. It provides advice and many a useful model to structure and manage a wide range of change initiatives. A practical toolkit on change management, both for students as well as practicing management professionals.'
George Philip, Principal Consultant, The Performance Factory, Oman

'I use MSoCM as a desktop reference guide, always by my side. It is a very useful resource – intelligent, flexible and practical.'
Ali Nawaz K Showkath, Change Management Specialist, Borouge, UAE

Praise for the previous editions of
Making Sense of Change Management

'There has long been a need for a readable, practical but theoretically under-pinned book on Change which recognized a multiplicity of perspectives. By combining the behavioural, humanistic, organizational and cognitive perspectives and by helping the reader make sense of what each perspective brings to understanding Change, this book should help students and practitioners. By linking in work on personality tests such as MBTI™ the book breaks new ground from a practitioner point of view not least because these tests are widely used in practice. I thoroughly recommend it.'
Professor Colin Carnall, Director, Executive Education, Cass Business School

'Change is a huge thing wherever you work. The key is to make change happen, and make it happen well – with everyone on side, and everyone happy. This book provides an extremely stimulating and accessible guide to doing just that. There are a few people at the Beeb who could do with this. I'll definitely be placing copies on a couple of desks at White City.'
Nicky Campbell, Presenter Radio Five Live and BBC1's *The Big Questions*

'This excellent, comprehensive, well-written and logically laid out book presents change management processes, concepts, models and frameworks in clear terms; managers on my post-graduate, courses have remarked that this book, has been of immense value to them when planning and implementing change in their organisations – a more fitting testimony one cannot ask for.'
Alec Bozas, Graduate School of Business & Leadership, University of KwaZulu-Natal

'In today's rapidly changing world, where emerging markets are becoming the hot centres of action, no company's change agenda can be a blueprint for another. It is in this context that Making Sense of Change Management, a deeply analytical and thoughtful book on change management, delights. Rather than applying a rather over-simplified 'silver bullet' to every problem, the authors attempt to give the flavours and the perspectives, leading to informed choices one has to make. That, to me, is truly valuable.'
Rajeev Suri, India-based entrepreneur, CEO and former Head of Global Marketing, Infosys

'This impressive book on change is an essential read for any professional manager who is serious about getting to grips with the important issues of making change happen.'
Dr Jeff Watkins, former MSc Course Director, Management Research Centre, University of Bristol

'I commend it highly. It has a good coverage of relevant theoretical work while at the same time giving plenty of practical examples. It is written in an accessible style that engages the reader and it is full of useful ideas without being overly prescriptive or formulaic.'
Philip Sadler, author of a number of acclaimed business titles and former chief executive of Ashridge Business School

'This provides a clear and thorough tour of different models of change.'
Richard Jolly, Adjunct Professor of Organizational Behaviour, London Business School

'I really enjoyed this book. I like the straightforward approach, the inclusion of the author's opinion and the insight provided by the case studies. This book will be very useful for those business managers in my organization who need to prepare themselves for tackling major organizational change.'
Andy Houghton, HR Director, Utilities Company and former Head of Organization Development, Retail Direct, Royal Bank of Scotland Group

'If you're interested in successfully managing and leading change, then read this book! It not only covers change from both the individual and organizational perspective, but also increases the number of options available to you.'
Judi Billing, former Director of IDeA Leadership Academy, Improvement and Development Agency

'This book is a great resource for managers thrown into the midst of change, who need to gain understanding of what happens when you try to make significant changes in a business, and how best to manage people through it. The authors have tackled a complex topic in a lively and engaging way, leading readers through the maze of theory available and offering just the right amount of practical advice.'
Andy Newall, Group HR Director, Imperial Tobacco

MAKING SENSE OF CHANGE MANAGEMENT

Additional online resources, including case studies and activities, can be accessed at **www.koganpage.com/product/making-sense-of-change-management-9780749472580**

MAKING SENSE OF CHANGE MANAGEMENT

A complete guide to the models, tools
and techniques of organizational change

4th edition

Esther Cameron and Mike Green

KoganPage

LONDON PHILADELPHIA NEW DELHI

Publisher's note

Every possible effort has been made to ensure that the information contained in this book is accurate at the time of going to press, and the publishers and authors cannot accept responsibility for any errors or omissions, however caused. No responsibility for loss or damage occasioned to any person acting, or refraining from action, as a result of the material in this publication can be accepted by the editor, the publisher or either of the authors.

First published in Great Britain and the United States in 2004 by Kogan Page Limited
Second edition 2009
Third edition 2012
Fourth edition 2015

2nd Floor, 45 Gee Street
London EC1V 3RS
United Kingdom
www.koganpage.com

1518 Walnut Street, Suite 1100
Philadelphia PA 19102
USA

4737/23 Ansari Road
Daryaganj
New Delhi 110002
India

ISBN   978 0 7494 7258 0
E-ISBN   978 0 7494 7259 7

British Library Cataloguing-in-Publication Data

A CIP record for this book is available from the British Library.

Library of Congress Cataloging-in-Publication Data
Cameron, Esther.
    Making sense of change management : a complete guide to the models, tools and techniques of organizational change / Esther Cameron, Mike Green. – Fourth edition.
        pages cm
    ISBN 978-0-7494-7258-0 (paperback) – ISBN 978-0-7494-7259-7 (ebk)   1. Organizational change–Management.   2. Teams in the workplace–Management.   3. Reengineering (Management)   4. Information technology–Management.   I. Green, Mike, 1959-   II. Title.
    HD58.8.C317 2015
    658.4'06–dc23
                                                                                            2014047414

Typeset by Graphicraft Limited, Hong Kong
Print production managed by Jellyfish
Printed and bound in Great Britain by CPI Group (UK) Ltd, Croydon CR0 4YY

Contents

Acknowledgements

We want to start by acknowledging the many people in organizations with whom we have worked over the years. You are all in here in some shape or form! We have worked with many generous, courageous and inspiring managers of change who we thank for the privilege of working alongside them to make real change happen. Without these experiences the book would be a dry catalogue of theory, devoid of life and character.

Then of course there are our colleagues who challenge and support us every day as we reflect on our work and make decisions about what to do next. Particular thanks go from Mike to Andy Holder, Mhairi Cameron, Philip Darley and Tim Hockridge, who probably do not know how much they are appreciated, and to Mike's MBA and Executive Education Programme Members at Henley Business School for a never-ending supply of ideas and challenges. Esther wants to specially acknowledge Nick Mayhew for his encouragement, wisdom and sensitive feedback, particularly in relation to Chapter 11, and Anne-Marie Saunders and Alex Clark for their humour, friendship and generosity in sharing their expertise; so many of their insights are embedded in this book. Also, thanks go to Esther's learning set who really boosted the leadership chapter in particular. Thanks too to Bill Critchley for his ideas on linking metaphor and change, which form the bedrock of the organizational change chapter.

Really special thanks go to Ailsa Cameron for her wonderful pictures, which soften the pages so beautifully.

who will ultimately cause the change to be a success or a failure. Without looking at the implications of change on individuals we can never really hope to manage large-scale change effectively.

In addition, one of the themes of organizational life over recent years has been the ascendancy of the team. Much of today's work is organized through teams and requires team collaboration and teamworking for it to succeed. Very little has been written about the role of teams in organizational change, and we have attempted to offer some fresh ideas mixed with some familiar ones.

A thread running through the book is the crucial role of leadership. If management is all about delivering on current needs, then leadership is all about inventing the future. There is a specific chapter on leadership, but you will find the importance of effective leadership arising throughout.

In some respects the chapters on individual, team and organizational change, together with the chapter on leadership of change, are freestanding and self-contained. However, we have also included application chapters where we have chosen a number of types of change, some of which, no doubt, will be familiar to you. These chapters aim to provide guidelines, case studies and learning points for those facing specific organizational challenges. Here the individual, team and organizational aspects of the changes are integrated into a coherent whole.

We have made a major revision to the culture change chapter and replaced the IT-based process change chapter with a new chapter on the effectiveness of project-led change.

WHY EXPLORE DIFFERENT APPROACHES TO CHANGE?

Managers in today's organizations face some bewildering challenges. Paul Evans (2000) says that 21st-century leadership of change issues is not simple; he sees modern leadership as a balancing act. He draws our attention to the need for leaders to accept the challenge of navigating between opposites. Leaders have to balance a track record of success with the ability to admit mistakes and meet failure well. They also have to balance short-term and long-term goals, be both visionary and pragmatic, pay attention to global and local issues and encourage individual accountability at the same time as enabling team work.

It is useful to note that while some pundits encourage leaders to lead rather than manage, Paul Evans is emphasizing the need for leaders to pay attention to both management and leadership. See the box for a list of paradoxes that managers at Lego are asked to deal with.

THE 11 PARADOXES OF LEADERSHIP THAT HANG ON THE WALL OF EVERY LEGO MANAGER

- *To be able to build a close relationship with one's staff, and to keep a suitable distance.*
- *To be able to lead, and to hold oneself in the background.*
- *To trust one's staff, and to keep an eye on what is happening.*
- *To be tolerant, and to know how you want things to function.*
- *To keep the goals of one's department in mind, and at the same time to be loyal to the whole firm.*
- *To do a good job of planning your own time, and to be flexible with your schedule.*
- *To freely express your view, and to be diplomatic.*
- *To be a visionary, and to keep one's feet on the ground.*
- *To try to win consensus, and to be able to cut through.*
- *To be dynamic, and to be reflective.*
- *To be sure of yourself, and to be humble.*

Source: Evans (2000)

We believe that anyone interested in the successful management of change needs to develop the ability to handle such paradoxes. Throughout this book we offer a range of ideas and views, some of which are contradictory. We would urge you to try to create a space within yourself for considering a variety of perspectives. Allow your own ideas and insights to emerge, rather than looking for ideas that you agree with, and discarding those you do not care for. It is highly probable that there is some merit in everything you read in this book!

With so many choices and so many dynamic tensions in leadership, how does a manager learn to navigate his or her way through the maze? We have developed a straightforward model of leadership that acts as a strong reminder to managers that they need to balance three key dimensions; see Figure 0.1.

Figure 0.1 Three dimensions of leadership
Source: developed by Mike Green, Andy Holder and Mhairi Cameron

Managers usually learn to focus on outcomes and tangible results very early on in their careers. This book is a reminder that although outcomes are extremely important, the leader must also pay attention to underlying emotions, and to the world of power and influence, in order to sustain change and achieve continued success in the long term. Leaders of change need to balance their efforts across all three dimensions of an organizational change:

- outcomes: developing and delivering clear outcomes;

- interests: mobilizing influence, authority and power;

- emotions: enabling people and culture to adapt.

Leaders are at the centre of all three. They shape, direct and juggle them. One dimension may seem central at any time: for example, developing a strategy. However, leadership is about ensuring that the other dimensions are also kept in view. The three balls must always be juggled successfully.

In our experience, if you as leader or manager of change are unaware of what is happening (or not happening) in each of the three dimensions, then you will have 'taken your eye off the ball'. Your chances of progressing in an effective way are diminished.

The early chapters of this book give the reader some underpinning theory and examples to illustrate how people initiate change and react to change at an individual level, when in teams, or when viewed as part of a whole organization. This theory will help managers to understand what is going on, how to deal with it and how to lead it with the help of others. The later chapters take real change situations and give specific tips and guidelines on how to tackle these successfully from a leadership point of view.

OVERVIEW OF STRUCTURE

We have structured the book principally in three parts.

Part One, 'The underpinning theory', comprises five chapters and aims to set out a wide range of ideas and approaches to managing change. Chapter 1 draws together the key theories of how individuals go through change. Chapter 2 compares different types of team, and examines the process of team development and also the way in which different types of team contribute to the organizational change process. Chapter 3 looks at a wide range of approaches to organizational change, using organizational metaphor to show how these are interconnected and related. Chapter 4 examines leadership of change, the role of visionary leadership, the roles that leaders play in the change process and the competencies that a leader needs to become a successful leader of change. Chapter 5 looks at the critical role and nature of the agent of change, both from a competency perspective and also from the use of the self as an instrument for change.

These chapters enable the reader to develop a broader understanding of the theoretical aspects of individual, team and organizational change, and to learn more about a variety of perspectives on how best to be a leader of change. This lays firm foundations for anyone wanting to learn about new approaches to managing change with a view to becoming more skilled in this area.

Part Two, 'The applications', focuses on specific change scenarios with a view to giving guidelines, hints and tips to those involved in these different types of change process. These chapters are illustrated with case studies and make reference to the models and methods discussed in Part

Table 0.1 Where to read about individual, team, organizational change and leading change

Type of change	Introduction	Chapter 1 Individual	Chapter 2 Team	Chapter 3 Organizational	Chapter 4 Leading change	Chapter 5 Change agent	Introduction to Part Two	Chapter 6 Restructuring	Chapter 7 M&A	Chapter 8 Culture	Chapter 9 Project- and programme-led	Introduction Part Three	Chapter 10 Complex change	Chapter 11 Uncertainty
Individual		xxx		x	x			xx	x	x	x			x
Team			xxx	x	x			xx	x	x	x			x
Organizational	x	x	x	xxx	x		x	xx	xx	xx	xx		xx	xx
Leading change	x	x	x	x	xxx	xx		xx	x	x	x			xx

One. Chapter 6 looks at organizational restructuring, why it goes wrong, and how to get it right. Chapter 7 tackles mergers and acquisitions by categorizing the different types of activity and examining the learning points resulting from research into this area. Chapter 8 examines cultural change by looking at culture through a number of perspectives and asking the question as to how you might facilitate cultural change, and Chapter 9 attempts to shed some light on the impact that programme- and project-led approaches to change are having, and what could be improved to increase the chances of sustainable success.

One of the clear things that has emerged for us in helping others lead and manage change is the tension between overly planning and controlling change on the one hand, and the fact that change is often not simple enough to plan or control on the other. In Part Three, Chapter 10 looks at the whole area of complexity science and how it can inform your approach when managing complex change. Chapter 11 looks at leading change in times of uncertainty.

Please do not read this book from beginning to end in one sitting. It is too much to take in. We recommend that if you prefer a purely pragmatic approach you should start by reading Part Two. You will find concrete examples and helpful guidelines. After that, you might like to go back into the theory in Part One to understand the choices available to you as a leader of change.

Likewise, if you are more interested in understanding the theoretical underpinning of change, then read Part One first. You will find a range of approaches together with their associated theories of change. After that, you might like to read Part Two to find out how the theory can be applied in real situations.

MESSAGE TO READERS

We wish you well in all your endeavours to initiate, adapt to and survive change. We hope the book provides you with some useful ideas and insights, and we look forward to hearing about your models, approaches and experiences, and to your thoughts on the glaring gaps in this book. We are sure we have left lots of important things out!

Do e-mail us with your comments and ideas, or visit us at:

Esther:
Website: www.integralchange.co.uk
E-mail: esther@integralchange.co.uk

Mike:
Website: www.transitionalspace.co.uk
E-mail: mike@transitionalspace.co.uk

Part One

The underpinning theory

All appears to change when we change.
Henri Amiel

Individual change is at the heart of everything that is achieved in organizations. Once individuals have the motivation to do something different, the whole world can begin to change. The conspiracy laws in the UK recognize this capacity for big change to start small. In some legal cases, the merest nod or a wink between two people seems to be considered adequate evidence to indicate a conspiratorial act. In some respects this type of law indicates the incredible power that individuals have within them to challenge existing power strongholds and alter the way things are done.

However, individuals are to some extent governed by the norms of the groups they belong to, and groups are bound together in a whole system of groups of people that interconnect in various habitual ways. So the story is not always that simple. Individuals, teams and organizations all play a part in the process of change, and leaders have a particularly onerous responsibility: that is, making all this happen.

We divided this book into three parts so that readers could have the option either to start their journey through this book by first reading about the theory of change, or to begin by reading about the practical applications. We understand that people have different preferences. However, we do think that a thorough grounding in the theory is useful to help each person to untangle and articulate his or her own assumptions about how organizations work and how change occurs. Do you, for instance, think that organizations can be changed by those in leadership positions to reach a predetermined end state, or do you think that people in organizations need to be collectively aware of the need for change before they can begin to adapt? Assumptions can be dangerous things when not explored, as they can restrict your thinking and narrow down your options.

Part One comprises five chapters. These have been chosen to represent five useful perspectives on change: individual change, team change, organizational change, leading change and the role of the change agent. Chapter 1 draws together the four key approaches to understanding individual change. These are the behavioural, cognitive, psychodynamic and humanistic psychology approaches. This chapter also looks at the connection between personality and change, and how to enable change in others when you are acting in a managerial role.

Chapter 2 identifies the main elements of team and group theory that we believe are useful to understand when managing change. This chapter compares different types of team, looks at the area of team effectiveness, and examines the process of team development. The composition of the team and the effect this has on team performance are also examined, as well as the way in which different types of team contribute to the organizational change process.

Chapter 3 looks at a wide range of approaches to organizational change, using organizational metaphor to show how these are interconnected and related. Familiar and unfamiliar models of the change process are described and categorized by metaphor to enable the underpinning assumptions to be examined, and we give our views on how useful these various models are to leaders of change.

Chapter 4 examines the leadership of change. We start by looking at the variety of leadership roles that arise from using different assumptions about how organizations work. The need for visionary leadership, the characteristics of successful leaders and some thoughts on the need for a different sort of leadership in the 21st century are all aired. The chapter also examines how communities of leaders can work together to make change happen, and what styles and skills are required of a leader, including the need for emotional competencies. The phases of a change process are looked at in order to illuminate the need for different leadership actions and attention during the different phases of change, and the importance of self-knowledge and self-awareness is highlighted.

Chapter 5 looks at the role of the change agent, highlighting areas of competence needed and exploring the unique role that the agent of change plays in the change process, particularly what is going on inside for them; how they can use that to great effect; and how they might need help in the change process itself.

1

Individual change

INTRODUCTION

This chapter draws together the key theories of how individuals go through change, using various models to explore this phenomenon. The aims of this chapter are to give managers and others experiencing or implementing change an understanding of the change process and how it impacts individuals, and strategies to use when helping people through change to ensure results are achieved.

This chapter covers the following topics, each of which takes a different perspective on individual change:

- Learning and the process of change – in what ways can models of learning help us understand individual change?

- The behavioural approach to change – how can we change people's behaviour?

- The cognitive approach to change – how change can be made attractive to people and how people can achieve the results that they want.

- The psychodynamic approach to change – what's actually going on for people.

- The humanistic psychology approach to change – how can people maximize the benefits of change?

- Personality and change – how do we differ in our responses to change?

- Managing change in self and others – if we can understand people's internal experience and we know what changes need to happen, what is the best way to effect change?

As the box points out, a key point for managers of change is to understand the distinction between the changes being managed in the external world and the concurrent psychological transitions that are experienced internally by people (including managers themselves).

FOOD FOR THOUGHT

It was the ancient Greek philosopher, Heraclitus, who maintained that you never step into the same river twice. Of course most people interpret that statement as indicating that the river – that is, the external world – never stays the same, is always changing: constant flux, in Heraclitus's words again. However, there is another way of interpreting what he said. Perhaps the 'you' who steps into the river today is not the same 'you' who will step into the river tomorrow. This interpretation – which might open up a whole can of existential and philosophical worms – is much more to do with the inner world of experience than with the external world of facts and figures.

Immediately, therefore, we have two ways of looking at and responding to change: the changes that happen in the outside world and those changes that take place in the internal world. Often though, it is the internal reaction to external change that proves the most fruitful area of discovery, and it is often in this area that we find the reasons external changes succeed or fail.

To demonstrate this we will draw on four approaches to change. These are the behavioural, the cognitive, the psychodynamic and the humanistic psychological approaches, as shown in Figure 1.1.

We will also look at Edgar Schein's analysis of the need to reduce anxiety about the change by creating psychological safety. This is further illuminated by discussion of the various psychodynamics that come into play when individuals are faced with change, loss and renewal.

Finally, we will explore tools and techniques that can be used to make the transition somewhat smoother and somewhat quicker. This will

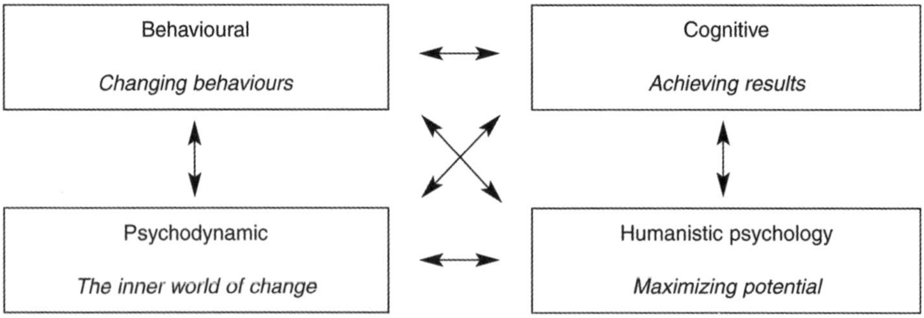

Figure 1.1 Four approaches to individual change

include a summary of how the Myers-Briggs Type Indicator™, which is used to develop personal and interpersonal awareness, can illuminate the managerial challenges at each stage of the individual change process. But first we will begin our exploration by looking at how individuals learn.

LEARNING AND THE PROCESS OF CHANGE

Buchanan and Huczynski (1985) define learning as 'the process of acquiring knowledge through experience which leads to a change in behaviour'. Learning is not just an acquisition of knowledge, but the application of it through doing something different in the world.

Many of the change scenarios that you find yourself in require you to learn something new, or to adjust to a new way of operating, or to unlearn something. Obviously this is not always the case – a company takes over your company but retains the brand name, the management team and it is 'business as usual' – but often in the smallest of changes you need to learn something new: your new boss's likes and dislikes, for example.

A useful way of beginning to understand what happens when we go through change is to take a look at what happens when we first start to learn something new. Let us take an example of driving your new car for the first time. For many people the joy of a new car is tempered by the nervousness of driving it for the first time. Getting into the driving seat of your old car is an automatic response, as is doing the normal checks, turning the key and driving off. However, with a new car all the buttons and control panels might be in different positions. One can go through the process of locating them either through trial and error, or perhaps religiously reading through the driver's manual first. But that is only the

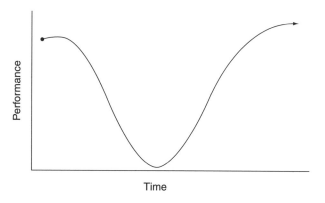

Figure 1.2   The learning dip

beginning, because you know that when you are actually driving any manner of things might occur that will require an instantaneous response: sounding the horn, flashing your lights, putting the hazard lights on or activating the windscreen wipers.

All these things you would have done automatically but now you need to think about them. Thinking not only requires time, it also requires a 'psychological space' which it is not easy to create when driving along at your normal speed. Added to this is the nervousness you may have about it being a brand new car and therefore needing that little bit more attention so as to avoid any scrapes to the bodywork.

As you go through this process, an external assessment of your performance would no doubt confirm a reduction in your efficiency and effectiveness for a period of time. And if one were to map your internal state your confidence levels would most likely dip as well. Obviously this anxiety falls off over time (see Figure 1.2). This is based on your capacity to assimilate new information, the frequency and regularity with which you have changed cars, and how often you drive.

Conscious and unconscious competence and incompetence

Another way of looking at what happens when you learn something new is to view it from a Gestalt perspective. The Gestalt psychologists suggested that people have a worldview that entails some things being in the foreground and others being in the background of their consciousness.

To illustrate this, the room where I am writing this looks out on to a gravel path which leads into a cottage garden sparkling with the sun shining on the frost-covered shrubs. Before I chose to look up, the garden was tucked back into the recesses of my consciousness. (I doubt whether it was even in yours.) By focusing attention on it I brought it into the foreground of my consciousness. Likewise all the colours in the garden are of equal note, until someone mentions white and I immediately start to notice the snowdrops, the white narcissi and the white pansies. They have come into my foreground.

Now in those examples it does not really matter what is fully conscious or not. However, in the example of driving a new car for the first time, something else is happening. Assuming that I am an experienced driver, many of the aspects of driving, for me, are unconscious. All of these aspects I hopefully carry out competently. So perhaps I can drive for many miles on a motorway, safe in the knowledge that a lot of the activities I am performing I am actually doing unconsciously. We might say I am unconsciously competent. However, as soon as I am in the new situation of an unfamiliar car I realize that many of the things I took for granted I cannot now do as well as before. I have become conscious of my incompetence. Through some trial and error and some practice and some experience I manage – quite consciously – to become competent again. But it has required focus and attention. All these tasks have been in the forefront of my world and my consciousness. It will only be after a further period of time that they recede to the background and I become unconsciously competent again (Figure 1.3).

Of course there is another cycle: not the one of starting at unconscious competence, but one of starting at unconscious incompetence! This is

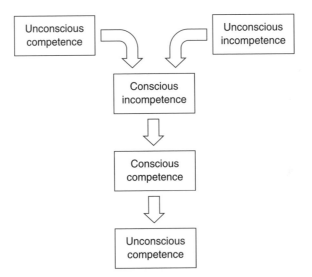

Figure 1.3   Unconscious competence

where you do not know what you do not know, and the only way of realizing is by making a mistake (and reflecting upon it), or when someone
kind enough and brave enough tells you. From self-reflection or from
others' feedback your unconscious incompetence becomes conscious, and
you are able to begin the cycle of learning.

Kolb's learning cycle

David Kolb (1984) developed a model of experiential learning, which
unpacked how learning occurs, and what stages a typical individual goes
through in order to learn. It shows that we learn through a process of
doing and thinking (see Figure 1.4). The labels of activist, reflector, theorist and pragmatist are drawn from the work of Honey and Mumford
(1992).

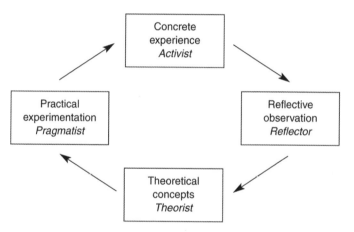

Figure 1.4   Kolb's learning cycle

Following on from the earlier definition of learning as 'the process of
acquiring knowledge through experience which leads to a change in
behaviour', Kolb saw this as a cycle through which the individual has a
concrete experience. The individual does something, reflects upon his or
her specific experience, makes some sense of the experience by drawing
some general conclusions, and plans to do things differently in the future.
Kolb would argue that true learning could not take place without someone going through all stages of the cycle.

In addition, research by Kolb suggested that different individuals have
different sets of preferences or styles in the way they learn. Some of us are
quite activist in our approach to learning. We want to experience what it

is that we need to learn. We want to dive into the swimming pool and see what happens (immerse ourselves in the task). Some of us would like to think about it first! We like to reflect, perhaps on others' experience, before we take action. The theorists might like to see how the act of swimming relates to other forms of sporting activity, or investigate how other mammals take the plunge. The pragmatists amongst us have a desire to relate what is happening to their own circumstances. They are interested in how the act of swimming will help them to achieve their goals.

Not only do we all have a learning preference but also the theory suggests that we can get stuck within our preference.

FOOD FOR THOUGHT

If you were writing a book on change and wanted to maximize the learning for all of your readers perhaps you would need to:

- encourage experimentation (activist);
- ensure there were ample ways of engendering reflection through questioning (reflector);
- ensure the various models were well researched (theorist);
- illustrate your ideas with case studies and show the relevance of what you are saying by giving useful tools, techniques and applications (pragmatist).

So activists may go from one experience to the next, not thinking to review how the last one went or planning what they would do differently. The reflector may spend inordinate amounts of time conducting project and performance reviews, but not necessarily embedding any learning into the next project. Theorists can spend a lot of time making connections and seeing the bigger picture by putting the current situation into a wider context, but they may not actually get around to doing anything. Pragmatists may be so intent on ensuring that it is relevant to their job that they can easily dismiss something that does not at first appear that useful.

STOP AND THINK!

Q 1.1 A new piece of software arrives in the office or in your home. How do you go about learning about it?

- Do you install it and start trying it out? (Activist)

- Do you watch as others show you how to use it? (Reflector)

- Do you learn about the background to it and the similarities with other programmes? (Theorist)

- Do you not bother experimenting until you find a clear purpose for it? (Pragmatist)

THE BEHAVIOURAL APPROACH TO CHANGE

The behavioural approach to change, as the name implies, very much focuses on how one individual can change another individual's behaviour using reward and punishment, to achieve intended results. If the intended results are not being achieved, an analysis of the individual's behaviour will lead to an understanding of what is contributing to success and what is contributing to non-achievement. To elicit the preferred behaviour the individual must be encouraged to behave that way, and discouraged from behaving any other way. This approach has its advantages and disadvantages.

For example, an organization is undergoing a planned programme of culture change, moving from being an inwardly-focused bureaucratic organization to a flatter and more responsive customer-oriented organization. Customer-facing and back office staff will all need to change the way they behave towards customers and towards each other to achieve

this change. A behavioural approach to change will focus on changing the behaviour of staff and managers. The objective will be behaviour change, and there will not necessarily be any attention given to improving processes, improving relationships or increasing involvement in goal setting. There will be no interest taken in how individuals specifically experience that change.

This whole field is underpinned by the work of a number of practitioners. The names of Pavlov and Skinner are perhaps the most famous. Ivan Pavlov noticed while researching the digestive system of dogs that when his dogs were connected to his experimental apparatus and offered food they began to salivate. He also observed that, over time, the dogs started to salivate when the researcher opened the door to bring in the food. The dogs had learnt that there was a link between the door opening and being fed. This is now referred to as classical conditioning.

CLASSICAL CONDITIONING

Unconditioned stimulus (food) leads to an unconditioned response (salivation).

If neutral stimulus (door opening) and unconditioned stimulus (food) are associated, neutral stimulus (now a conditioned stimulus) leads to unconditioned response (now a conditioned response).

Pavlov (1928)

Further experimental research led others to realize that cats could learn how to escape from a box through positive effects (rewards) and negative effects (punishments). Skinner (1953) extended this research into operant conditioning, looking at the effects of behaviours, not just at the behaviours themselves. His experiments with rats led him to observe that they soon learnt that an accidental operation of a lever led to there being food provided. The reward of the food then led to the rats repeating the behaviour.

Using the notion of rewards and punishments, additions and subtractions of positive and negative stimuli, four possible situations arise when you want to encourage a specific behaviour, as demonstrated in Table 1.1.

STOP AND THINK!

Q 1.2 What rewards and what punishments operate in your organization?

How effective are they in bringing about change?

Table 1.1 Rewards and punishments

Actions	Positive	Negative
Addition	**Positive reinforcement** Desired behaviour is deliberately associated with a reward, so that the behaviour is displayed more frequently.	**Negative addition** A punishment is deliberately associated with undesired behaviour, reducing the frequency with which the behaviour is displayed.
Subtraction	**Positive subtraction** An unpleasant stimulus previously associated with the desired behaviour is removed, increasing the frequency with which that desired behaviour is displayed.	**Negative subtraction** A pleasant stimulus previously associated with undesired behaviour is removed, which decreases the frequency of such behaviour.

So in what ways may behaviourism help us with individuals going through change? In any project of planned behaviour change a number of steps will be required:

- **Step 1:** The *identification* of the behaviours that impact performance.

- **Step 2:** The *measurement* of those behaviours. How much are these behaviours currently in use?

- **Step 3:** A *functional analysis* of the behaviours – that is, the identification of the component parts that make up each behaviour.

- **Step 4:** The generation of a *strategy of intervention* – what rewards and punishments should be linked to the behaviours that impact performance.

- **Step 5:** An *evaluation* of the effectiveness of the intervention strategy.

Reinforcement strategies

When generating reward strategies at Step 4 above, the following possibilities should be borne in mind.

Financial reinforcement

Traditionally financial reinforcement is the most explicit of the reinforcement mechanisms used in organizations today, particularly in sales-oriented cultures. The use of bonus payments, prizes and other tangible rewards is common. To be effective the financial reinforcement needs to be clearly, closely and visibly linked to the behaviours and performance that the organization requires.

A reward to an outbound call centre employee for a specific number of appointments made on behalf of the sales force would be an example of a reinforcement closely linked to a specified behaviour. A more sophisticated system might link the reward to not only the number of appointments but also the quality of the subsequent meeting and the quality of the customer interaction.

An organization-wide performance bonus unrelated to an individual's contribution to that performance would be an example of a poorly linked reinforcement.

Non-financial reinforcement

Feedback

Non-financial reinforcement tends to take the form of feedback given to an individual about performance on specific tasks. The more specific the feedback is, the more impactful the reinforcement can be. This feedback can take both positive and negative forms. This might well depend on the organizational culture and the managerial style of the boss. This feedback perhaps could take the form of a coaching conversation, where specific effective behaviours are encouraged, and specific ineffective behaviours are discouraged and alternatives generated.

Social reinforcement

Social reinforcement takes the form of interpersonal actions: that is, communications of either a positive or negative nature. Praise, compliments, general recognition, perhaps greater (or lesser) attention can all act as a positive reinforcement for particular behaviours and outcomes. Similarly social reinforcement could also take the form of 'naming and shaming' for ineffective performance.

Social reinforcement is not only useful for performance issues, but can be extremely useful when an organizational culture change is under way. Group approval or disapproval can be a determining factor in defining what behaviours are acceptable or unacceptable within the culture.

New starters in an organization often spend quite some time working out which behaviours attract which reactions from bosses and colleagues.

Motivation and behaviour

The pure behaviourist view of the world, prevalent in industry up to the 1960s, led to difficulties with motivating people to exhibit the 'right' behaviours. This in turn led researchers to investigate what management styles worked and did not work.

In 1960 Douglas McGregor published his book *The Human Side of Enterprise*. In it he described his Theory X and Theory Y, which looked at underlying management assumptions about an organization's workforce, as demonstrated in Table 1.2.

Theory X was built on the assumption that workers are not inherently motivated to work, seeing it as a necessary evil and therefore needing close supervision. Theory Y stated that human beings generally have a need and a desire to work and, given the right environment, are more than willing to contribute to the organization's success. McGregor's research appeared to show that those managers who exhibited Theory Y beliefs were more successful in eliciting good performance from their people.

Frederick Herzberg also investigated what motivated workers to give their best performance. He was an American clinical psychologist who suggested that workers have two sets of drives or motivators: a desire to avoid pain or deprivation (hygiene factors) and a desire to learn and

Table 1.2   Theory X and Theory Y

Theory X assumptions	Theory Y assumptions
People dislike work	People regard work as natural and normal
They need controlling and direction	They respond to more than just control or coercion, for example recognition and encouragement
They require security	
They are motivated by threats of punishment	They commit to the organization's objectives in line with the rewards offered
They avoid taking responsibility	They seek some inner fulfilment from work
They lack ambition	Given the right environment people willingly accept responsibility and accountability
They do not use their imagination	People can be creative and innovative

Source: McGregor (1960)

Table 1.3 Herzberg's motivating factors

Hygiene factors	Motivators
Pay	Achievement
Company policy	Recognition
Quality of supervision/management	Responsibility
Working relations	Advancement
Working conditions	Learning
Status	The type and nature of the work
Security	

Source: adapted from Herzberg (1968)

develop (motivators) (see Table 1.3). His work throughout the 1950s and 1960s suggested that many organizations provided the former but not the latter.

An important insight of his was that the hygiene factors did not motivate workers, but that their withdrawal would demotivate the workforce. Although later research has not fully replicated his findings, Herzberg's seminal, 'One more time: How do you motivate employees?' (1968) has generated more reprints than any other *Harvard Business Review* article.

STOP AND THINK!

Q 1.3 What are the underlying assumptions built into the behaviourist philosophy, and how do they compare to McGregor's theories?

Q 1.4 In a change programme based on the behaviourist approach, what added insights would Herzberg's ideas bring?

Q 1.5 If one of your team members is not good at giving presentations, how would you address this using behaviourist ideas?

Summary of the behavioural approach

If you were to approach change from a behavioural perspective you are more likely to be acting on the assumption of McGregor's Theory X: the only way to motivate and align workers to the change effort is through a combination of rewards and punishments. You would spend time and effort ensuring that the right reward strategy and performance management system was in place and was clearly linked to an individual's behaviours. Herzberg's ideas suggest that there is something more at play than reward and punishment when it comes to motivating people. That is not to say that the provision of Herzberg's motivators cannot be used as some sort of reward for correct behaviour.

THE COGNITIVE APPROACH TO CHANGE

Cognitive psychology developed out of a frustration with the behaviourist approach. The behaviourists focused solely on observable behaviour. Cognitive psychologists were much more interested in learning about developing the capacity for language and a person's capacity for problem solving. They were interested in things that happen within a person's brain. These are the internal processes which behavioural psychology did not focus on.

Cognitive theory is founded on the premise that our emotions and our problems are a result of the way we think. Individuals react in the way that they do because of the way they appraise the situation they are in. By changing their thought processes, individuals can change the way they respond to situations.

> _People control their own destinies by believing in and acting on the values and beliefs that they hold._
>
> R Quackenbush, Central Michigan University

Much groundbreaking work has been done by Albert Ellis on rational-emotive therapy (Ellis and Grieger, 1977) and Aaron Beck on cognitive therapy (1970). Ellis emphasized:

[T]he importance of 1) people's conditioning themselves to feel disturbed (rather than being conditioned by parental and other external sources); 2) their biological as well as cultural tendencies to think 'crookedly' and to needlessly upset themselves; 3) their uniquely human tendencies to invent and create disturbing beliefs, as well as their tendencies to upset themselves about their disturbances; 4) their unusual capacity to change their cognitive, emotive and behavioural processes so that they can: a) choose to react differently from the way they usually do; b) refuse to upset themselves about almost anything that may occur, and c) train themselves so that they can semi-automatically remain minimally disturbed for the rest of their lives.

(Ellis, in Henrik, 1980)

> *If you keep doing what you're doing you'll keep getting what you get.*
>
> Anon

Beck developed cognitive therapy based on 'the underlying theoretical rationale that an individual's affect (moods, emotions) and behaviour are largely determined by the way in which he construes the world; that is, how a person thinks determines how he feels and reacts' (A John Rush, in Henrik, 1980).

Belief system theory emerged principally from the work of Rokeach through the 1960s and 1970s. He suggested that an individual's self-concept and set of deeply held values were both central to that person's beliefs and were his or her primary determinant. Thus individuals' values influence their beliefs, which in turn influence their attitudes. Individuals' attitudes influence their feelings and their behaviour – 'an enduring belief that a specific mode of conduct or end-state of existence is personally or socially preferable to alternative modes of conduct or end-states of existence' (Rokeach, 1973: 5).

Out of these approaches has grown a way of looking at change within individuals in a very purposeful way. Essentially individuals need to look at the way they limit themselves through adhering to old ways of thinking, and replace that with new ways of being.

This approach is focused on the results that you want to achieve, although crucial to their achievement is ensuring that there is alignment throughout the cause and effect chain. The cognitive approach does not refer to the external stimuli and the responses to the stimuli. It is more concerned with what individuals plan to achieve and how they go about this.

Achieving results

Key questions in achieving results in an organizational context, as shown in Figure 1.5, are:

- Self-concept and values: what are my core values and how do they dovetail with those of my organization?

- Beliefs and attitudes: what are my limiting beliefs and attitudes and with what do I replace them?

- Feelings: what is my most effective state of being to accomplish my goals and how do I access it?

- Behaviour: what specifically do I need to be doing to achieve my goals and what is my first step?

- Results: what specific outcomes do I want and what might get in the way?

Self-concept & values ⇨ Beliefs ⇨ Attitudes ⇨ Feelings ⇨ Behaviour ⇨ Results

Figure 1.5   Achieving results

Setting goals

The cognitive approach advocates the use of goals. The assumption is that the clearer the goal, the greater the likelihood of achievement. Consider the following case study. Graduates at Yale University in the United States were surveyed over a period of 20 years. Of those surveyed, 3 per cent were worth more than the other 97 per cent put together. There were no correlations with parental wealth, gender or ethnicity. The only difference between the 3 per cent and the 97 per cent was that the former had clearly articulated and written goals, and the latter grouping did not. (This is perhaps just an apocryphal story, as the details of this case study are much-quoted on many 'positive thinking' websites but we have been unable to trace the research back to where it should have originated at Yale.)

However, research undertaken by one of the authors (Green, 2001) into what makes for an outstanding sales person suggests that in the two key areas of business focus and personal motivation, goal setting looms large. The outstanding sales people had clearer and more challenging business targets that they set themselves. These were coupled with very clear personal goals as to what the sales person wanted to achieve personally with the rewards achieved by business success.

This is further backed up by research conducted by Richard Bandler and John Grinder (1979), creators of neuro-linguistic programming, who found that the more successful psychotherapists were those who were able to get their clients to define exactly what wellness looked like. This in turn led to the idea of a 'well-formed outcome' that enabled significantly better results to be achieved by those who set clear goals as opposed to those with vague goals. The goals themselves were also more ambitious.

Making sense of our results

The cognitive approach suggests we pay attention to the way in which we talk to ourselves about results. For example, after a particularly good performance one person might say things such as, 'I knew I could do it, I'll be able to do that again.' Another person might say something like, 'That was lucky, I doubt whether I'll be able to repeat that.' Likewise, after a poor or ineffective performance our first person might say something like, 'I could do that a lot better next time', while the second person might say, 'I thought as much, I knew that it would turn out like this.'

Once we have identified our usual way of talking to ourselves we can look at how these internal conversations with ourselves limit us, then consider changing the script.

FOOD FOR THOUGHT

Reflect upon a time when you did not achieve one of your results:

- What did you say to yourself?
- What was your limiting belief?
- What is the opposite belief?
- What would it be like to hold the new belief?
- How might your behaviour change as a result?
- What results would you achieve as a consequence?

Techniques for change

The cognitive approach has generated numerous techniques for changing the beliefs of people and thereby improving their performance. These include the following.

Positive listings

Simply list all the positive qualities you have, such as good feelings, good experiences, good results, areas of skills, knowledge and expertise. By accepting that these are all part of you, the individual, you can reinforce all these positive thoughts, feelings and perceptions, which then lead to enhanced beliefs.

Affirmations

An affirmation is a positive statement describing the way that you want to be. It is important that the statement is:

- Personal: '**I** am always enthusiastic when it comes to work!' It is you who this is about, and it is as specific as you can make it.

- Present tense: '**I am always** enthusiastic when it comes to work!' It is not in the future, it is right now.

- Positive: 'I am always **enthusiastic** when it comes to work!' It describes a positive attribute, not the absence of a negative attribute.

- Potent: 'I am always **enthusiastic** when it comes to **work**!' Use words that mean something to you.

Try writing your own affirmation. Put it on a card and read it out 10 times a day. As you do so, remember to imagine what you would feel, what you would see, what you would hear if it were true.

Visualizations

Visualizations are very similar to affirmations but focus on a positive, present mental image. Effective visualizations require you to enter a relaxed state where you imagine a specific example of the way you want to be. You imagine what you and others would see, what would be heard and what would be felt. Using all your senses you imagine yourself achieving the specific goal. You need to practise this on a regular basis.

Reframing

Reframing is a technique for reducing feelings and thoughts that impact negatively on performance. You get daunted when going in to see the senior management team? Currently you see them looming large, full of colour, vitality and menacing presence? Imagine them in the boardroom, but this time see them all in grey. Maybe shrink them in size, as you would a piece of clip art in a document that you are word-processing. Turn down their volume so they sound quite quiet. Run through this several times and see what effect it has on your anxiety.

Pattern breaking

Pattern breaking is a technique of physically or symbolically taking attention away from a negative state and focusing it on a positive. Take the previous example of going into the boardroom to meet the senior management team (or it could be you as the senior manager going out to meet the staff and feeling a little awkward). You find you have slipped into being a bit nervous, and catch yourself. Put your hand in the shape of a fist to your mouth and give a deep cough, or at an appropriate moment clap your hands firmly together and say, 'Right, what I was thinking was...' Once you've done the distraction, you can say to yourself, 'That wasn't me. This is me right now.'

Detachment

This is a similar technique with the same aim. Imagine a time when you did not like who you were. Perhaps you were in the grip of a strong negative emotion. See yourself in that state, then imagine yourself stepping outside or away from your body, leaving all that negativity behind and becoming quite calm and detached and more rational. When you next catch yourself being in one of those moods, try stepping outside of yourself.

Anchoring and resource states

These are two techniques where you use a remembered positive experience from the past which has all the components of success. For example, remember a time in the past where you gave an excellent presentation. What did you see? What did you hear? What did you feel? Really enter into that experience, then pinch yourself and repeat a word that comes to mind. Rerun the experience and pinch yourself and say the word. Now try it the other way, pinch yourself and say the word – and the experience should return. Before your next presentation, as you go into the room reconnect to the positive experience by pinching yourself and saying the word. Does it work? If it does not, simply try something else.

Rational analysis

Rational analysis is a cognitive technique *par excellence*. It is based on the notion that our beliefs are not necessarily rational: 'I could never do that' or, 'I'm always going to be like that'. Rational analysis suggests you write down all the reasons that are incorrect. You need to be specific and not generalize (for example, 'I'm always doing that' – *always?*). You need to set measurable criteria, objectively based, and you need to use your powers of logic. By continuously proving that this is an irrational belief you will eventually come to disbelieve it.

STOP AND THINK!

Q 1.6   What might the main benefits be of a cognitive approach?

Q 1.7   What do you see as some of the limitations of this approach?

Summary of the cognitive approach

The cognitive approach builds on the behaviourist approach by putting behaviour into the context of beliefs, and focusing more firmly on outcomes. Many cognitive techniques are used in the field of management today, particularly in the coaching arena. This approach involves focusing on building a positive mental attitude and some stretching goals, backed up by a detailed look at what limiting beliefs produce behaviour that becomes self-defeating.

A drawback of the cognitive approach is the lack of recognition of the inner emotional world of the individual, and the positive and negative impact that this can have when attempting to manage change. Some obstacles to change need to be worked through, and cannot be made 'ok' by reframing or positive talk.

THE PSYCHODYNAMIC APPROACH TO CHANGE

The idea that humans go through a psychological process during change became evident due to research published by Elizabeth Kübler-Ross (1969). The word 'psychodynamic' is based on the idea that when facing change in the external world, an individual can experience a variety of internal psychological states. As with the behavioural and cognitive approaches to change, research into the psychodynamic approach began not in the arena of organizations, but for Kübler-Ross in the area of terminally ill patients. Later research showed that individuals going through changes within organizations can have very similar experiences, though perhaps less dramatic and less traumatic.

The Kübler-Ross model

Kübler-Ross published her seminal work, *On Death and Dying* in 1969. This described her work with terminally ill patients and the different psychological stages that they went through in coming to terms with their condition. Clearly this research was considered to have major implications for people experiencing other types of profound change.

Kübler-Ross realized that patients – given the necessary conditions – would typically go through five stages as they came to terms with their prognosis. The stages were denial, anger, bargaining, depression and finally acceptance.

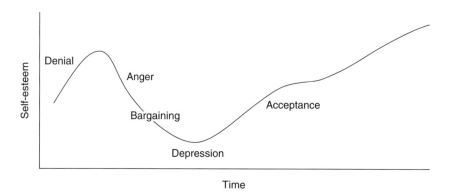

Figure 1.6   The process of change and adjustment
Source: based on Kübler-Ross (1969)

Denial

People faced with such potentially catastrophic change would often not be able to accept the information. They would deny it to themselves. That is, they would not actually take it in, but would become emotionally numb and have a sense of disbelief. Some would argue that this is the body's way of allowing people to prepare themselves for what is to follow. On a more trivial scale, some of us have experienced the numbness and disbelief when our favourite sports team is defeated. There is little that we can do but in a sense 'shut down'. We do not want to accept the news and expose ourselves to the heartache that that would bring.

Anger

When people allow themselves to acknowledge what is happening they enter the second stage, typically that of anger. They begin to ask themselves questions like, 'Why me?', 'How could such a thing happen to someone like me? If only it had been someone else', 'Surely it's the doctors who are to blame – perhaps they've misdiagnosed' (back into denial). 'Why didn't they catch it in time?'

Anger and frustration can be focused externally, but for some of us it is ourselves we blame. Why did we not see it coming, give up smoking? 'It's always me who gets into trouble.'

In some ways we can see this process as a continuation of our not wanting to accept the change and of wanting to do something, anything, other than fully believe it. Anger is yet another way of displacing our real feelings about the situation.

Bargaining

When they have exhausted themselves by attacking others (or themselves) people may still want to wrest back some control of the situation or of their fate. Kübler-Ross saw bargaining as a stage that people would enter now.

For those who themselves are dying, and also for those facing the death of a loved one, this stage can be typified by a conversation with themselves. Or if they are religious, this may be a conversation with God, which asks for an extension of time. 'If I promise to be good from now on, if I accept some remorse for any ills I have committed, if I could just be allowed to live to see my daughter's wedding, I'll take back all the nasty things I said about that person if you'll only let them live.'

Once again we can see this stage as a deflection of the true gravity of the situation. This is bargaining, perhaps verging on panic. The person is desperately looking around for something, anything, to remedy the situation. 'If only I could get it fixed or sorted everything would be all right.'

Depression

When it becomes clear that no amount of bargaining is going to provide an escape from the situation, perhaps the true momentousness of it kicks in. How might we react? Kübler-Ross saw her patients enter a depression at this stage. By depression we mean mourning or grieving for loss, because in this situation we will be losing all that we have ever had and all those we have ever known. We shall be losing our future, we shall be losing our very selves. We are at a stage where we are ready to give up on everything. We are grieving for the loss that we are about to endure.

For some, this depression can take the form of apathy or a sense of pointlessness. For others it can take the form of sadness, and for some a mixture of intense emotions and disassociated states.

Acceptance

Kubler-Ross saw many people move out of their depression and enter a fifth stage of acceptance. Perhaps we might add the word 'quiet' to acceptance, because this is not necessarily a happy stage, but it is a stage where people can in some ways come to terms with the reality of their situation and the inevitability of what is happening to them. People have a sense of being fully in touch with their feelings about the situation, their hopes and fears, their anxieties. They are prepared.

Further clinical and management researchers have added to Kubler-Ross's five stages, in particular Adams *et al* (1976) as follows and as illustrated in Figure 1.7:

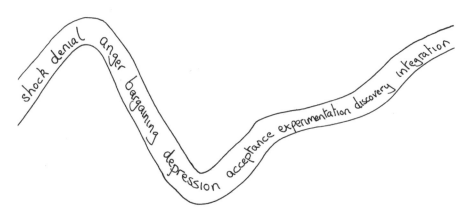

Figure 1.7   Adams, Hayes and Hopson's (1976) change curve

- **shock and/or surprise:** really a subset of denial but characterized by a sense of disbelief;

- **denial:** total non-acceptance of the change and maybe 'proving' to oneself that it is not happening and hoping that it will go away;

- **anger:** experiencing anger and frustration but really in an unaware sort of way, that is, taking no responsibility for your emotions;

- **bargaining:** the attempt to avoid the inevitable;

- **depression:** hitting the lows and responding (or being unresponsive) with apathy or sadness;

- **acceptance:** the reality of the situation is accepted;

- **experimentation:** after having been very inward-looking with acceptance, the idea arrives that perhaps there are things 'out there': 'Perhaps some of these changes might be worth at least thinking about. Perhaps I might just ask to see the job description of that new job';

- **discovery:** as you enter this new world that has changed there may be the discovery that things are not as bad as you imagined. Perhaps the company was telling the truth when it said there would be new opportunities and a better way of working.

The authors have noted that there can be a preliminary stage around the initial stage of shock – one of **relief:** 'At least I now know what's happening, I had my suspicions, I wasn't just being paranoid.'

Virginia Satir model

Virginia Satir, a family therapist, developed her model (Satir *et al*, 1991) after observing individuals and families experience a wide range of changes. Her model not only has a number of stages but also highlights two key events that disturb or move an individual's experience along: the foreign element and the transforming idea; see Figure 1.8.

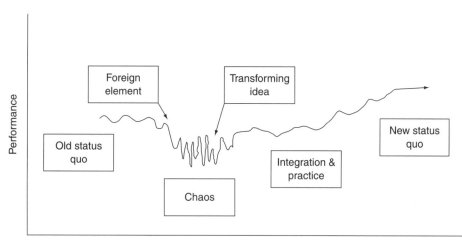

Figure 1.8 Satir's model

She describes the initial state as one of maintaining the status quo. We have all experienced periods within our lives – at home or at work – where day-to-day events continue today as they have done in previous days, and no doubt will be the same tomorrow. It may be that the organization you are working in is in a mature industry with well-established working practices which need little or no alteration. This is a state in which if you carry on doing what you are doing, you will continue to get what you are getting. The situation is one of relative equilibrium where all parts of the system are in relative harmony. That is not to say, of course, that there is no dissatisfaction. It is just that no one is effecting change.

This changes when something new enters the system. Satir calls it a 'foreign element' in the sense that a factor previously not present is introduced. As with the examples from the two previous models, it might be the onset of an illness or, in the world of work, a new chief executive with ideas about restructuring. Whatever the nature of this foreign element, it has an effect.

A period of chaos ensues. Typically this is internal chaos. The world itself may continue to function but the individual's own perceived world might be turned upside down, or inside out. He or she may be in a state of disbelief – denial or emotional numbness – at first, not knowing what to think or feel or how to act. Individuals may resist the notion that things are going to be different. Indeed they may actually try to redouble their efforts to ensure that the status quo continues as long as possible, even to the extent of sabotaging the new ideas that are forthcoming. Their support networks, which before had seemed so solid, might now not be trusted to help and support the individual. They may not know who to trust or where to go for help.

During this period of chaos, we see elements of anger and disorganization permeating the individual's world. Feelings of dread, panic and despair are followed by periods of apathy and a sense of pointlessness. At moments like this it may well seem like St John of the Cross's *Dark Night of the Soul* (2003) when all hope has vanished.

But it is often when things have reached their very worst that from somewhere – usually from within the very depths of the person – the germ of an idea or an insight occurs. In the Kübler-Ross model, the individual is coming to terms with the reality of the situation and experiencing acknowledgement and acceptance. He or she has seen the light, or at least a glimmer of hope. An immense amount of work may still need to be done, but the individual has generated this transforming idea, which spreads some light on to the situation, and perhaps shows him or her a way out of the predicament.

Once this transforming idea has taken root, the individual can begin the journey of integration. Thus this period of integration requires the new world order to be assimilated into the individual's own world.

Imagine a restructuring has taken place at your place of work. You have gone through many a sleepless night worrying what job you may end up in, or whether you will have a role at the end of the change. The jobs on offer do not appeal at all to you at first ('Why didn't they ask me for my views when they formulated the new roles?', 'If they think I'm applying for that they have another think coming!'). However, as the chief executive's thinking is made clearer through better communications, you grudgingly accept that perhaps he did have a point in addressing the complacency within the firm. Then perhaps one day you wake up and feel that maybe you might just have a look at that job description for the job in Operations. You have never worked in that area before and you have heard a few good things about the woman in charge.

You begin to accept the idea of a new role and 'try it on for size'. Perhaps at first you are just playing along, but soon it becomes less experimentation and more of an exploration. As time moves on the restructure is bedded into the organization, roles and responsibilities clarified, new objectives and ways of working specified and results achieved. A new status quo is born. The scars are still there perhaps but they are not hurting so much.

Gerald Weinberg (1997), in his masterly book on change, with a title that might not appeal to everyone (_Quality Software Management, Volume 4: Anticipating change_) draws heavily on the Satir model and maps on to it the critical points that can undermine or support the change process (see Figure 1.9). Weinberg shows that if the change is not planned well enough, or if the receivers of change consciously or unconsciously decide to resist, the change effort will falter.

Summary of the psychodynamic approach

The psychodynamic approach is useful for managers who want to understand the reactions of their staff during a change process and deal with them. These models allow managers to gain an understanding of why people react the way they do. It identifies what is going on in the inner world of their staff when they encounter change.

As with all models, the ones we have described simplify what can be quite a complex process. Individuals do not necessarily know that they are going through different phases. What they may experience is a range of different emotions (or lack of emotion), which may cluster together

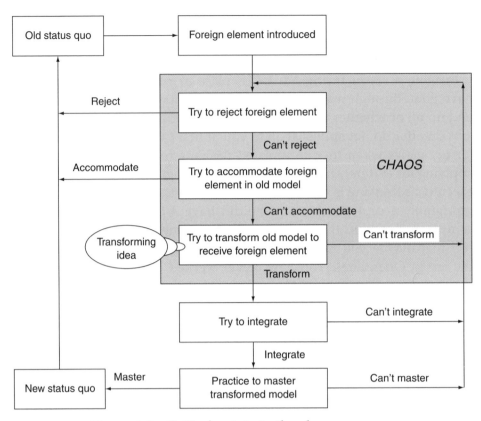

Figure 1.9 Critical points in the change process
Source: Weinberg (1997)

into different groupings which could be labelled one thing or another. Any observer, at the time, might see manifestations of these different emotions played out in the individual's behaviour.

Research suggests that these different phases may well overlap, with the predominant emotion of one stage gradually diminishing over time as a predominant emotion of the next stage takes hold. For example, the deep sense of loss and associated despondency, while subsiding over time, might well swell up again and engulf the individual with grief, either for no apparent reason, or because of a particular anniversary, contact with a particular individual or an external event reported on the news.

Individuals will go through a process which, either in hindsight or from an observer's point of view, will have a number of different phases which themselves are delineated in time and by different characteristics. However, the stages themselves will not necessarily have clear beginnings or endings, and characteristics from one stage may appear in other stages.

Satir's model incorporates the idea of a defining event – the transforming idea – that can be seen to change, or be the beginning of the change for, an individual. It may well be an insight, or waking up one morning and sensing that a cloud has been lifted. From that point on there is a qualitative difference in the person undergoing change. He or she can see the light at the end of the tunnel, or have a sense that there is a future direction.

Key learnings here are that everyone to some extent goes through the highs and lows of the transitions curve, although perhaps in different times and in different ways. It is not only perfectly natural and normal but actually an essential part of being human.

STOP AND THINK!

Q 1.8   Think of a current or recent change in your organization.

- Can you map the progress of the change on to Satir's or Weinberg's model?

- At what points did the change falter?

- At what points did it accelerate?

- What factors contributed in each case?

THE HUMANISTIC PSYCHOLOGY APPROACH TO CHANGE

The humanistic psychological approach to change combines some of the insights from the previous three approaches while at the same time developing its own. It emerged as a movement in the United States during the 1950s and 1960s. The American Association of Humanistic Psychology describes it as 'concerned with topics having little place in existing theories and systems: eg love, creativity, self, growth... self-actualization, higher values, being, becoming, responsibility, meaning... transcendental experience, peak experience, courage and related concepts'.

In this section we look at how the humanistic approach differs from the behavioural and cognitive approaches, list some of the key assumptions of this approach, and look at three important models within humanistic psychology.

Table 1.4 charts some of the similarities and differences between the psychoanalytic, behavioural, cognitive and humanistic approaches. Although taken from a book more concerned with counselling and psychotherapy, it illustrates where humanistic psychology stands in relation to the other approaches.

Table 1.4 The psychoanalytic, behavioural, cognitive and humanistic approaches

Theme	Psychoanalytic	Behavioural	Cognitive	Humanistic
Psychodynamic approach – looking for what is behind surface behaviour	Yes	No	Yes	Yes
Action approach – looking at actual conduct of person, trying new things	No	Yes	Yes	Yes
Acknowledgement of importance of sense-making, resistance, etc	Yes	No	No	Yes
Use of imagery, creativity	No	Yes	Yes	Yes
Use in groups as well as individual	Yes	No	No	Yes
Emphasis on whole person	No	No	No	Yes
Emphasis on gratification, joy, individuation	No	No	No	Yes
Adoption of medical model of mental illness	Yes	Yes	Yes	No
Felt experience of the practitioner important as a tool for change	Yes	No	No	Yes
Mechanistic approach to client	No	Yes	Yes	No
Open to new paradigm research methods	No	No	Yes	Yes

Source: adapted from Rowan (1983).
Note: Although the humanistic and psychoanalytic approaches are both psychodynamic, we have differentiated between them to focus on the maximizing potential aspect of the humanistic school.

Humanistic psychology has a number of key areas of focus:

- the importance of subjective awareness as experienced by the individual;

- the importance of taking responsibility for one's situations – or at least the assumption that whatever the situation there will be an element of choice in how you think, how you feel and how you act;

- the significance of the person as a whole entity (a holistic approach) in the sense that as humans we are not just what we think or what we feel, we are not just our behaviours. We exist within a social and cultural context.

In juxtaposition with Freud's view of the aim of therapy as moving the individual from a state of neurotic anxiety to ordinary unhappiness, humanistic psychology has 'unlimited aims... our prime aim is to enable the person to get in touch with their real self' (Rowan, 1983).

Maslow and the hierarchy of needs

Maslow did not follow the path of earlier psychologists by looking for signs of ill health and disease. He researched what makes men and women creative, compassionate, spontaneous and able to live their lives to the full. He therefore studied the lives of men and women who had exhibited these traits during their lives, and in so doing came to his theory of motivation, calling it a hierarchy of needs (see Figure 1.10).

Maslow believed that human beings have an inbuilt desire to grow and develop and move towards something he called self-actualization. However, in order to develop self-actualization an individual has to overcome or satisfy a number of other needs first.

Figure 1.10 Maslow's hierarchy of needs
Source: Maslow (1970)

41

One of Maslow's insights was that until the lower level needs were met an individual would not progress or be interested in the needs higher up the pyramid. He saw the first four levels of needs as 'deficiency' needs. By that he meant that it was the absence of satisfaction that led to the individual being motivated to achieve something.

Physiological needs are requirements such as food, water, shelter and sexual release. Clearly when they are lacking the individual will experience physiological symptoms such as hunger, thirst, discomfort and frustration.

Safety needs are those that are concerned with the level of threat and desire for a sense of security. Although safety needs for some might be concerned with actual physical safety, Maslow saw that for many in the western world the need was based more on the idea of psychological safety. We might experience this level of need when faced with redundancy.

Love and belonging needs are more interpersonal. This involves the need for affection and affiliation on an emotionally intimate scale. It is important here to note that Maslow introduces a sense of reciprocity into the equation. A sense of belonging can rarely be achieved unless an individual gives as well as receives. People have to invest something of themselves in the situation or with the person or group. Even though it is higher in the hierarchy than physical or safety needs, the desire for love and belonging is similar in that it motivates people when they feel its absence.

Self-esteem needs are met in two ways. They are met through the satisfaction individuals get when they achieve competence or mastery in doing something. They are also met through receiving recognition for their achievement.

Maslow postulated one final need – the need for self-actualization. He described it as 'the desire to become more and more what one is, to become everything that one is capable of becoming'. He observed that people continued to search for something else once all their other needs were being satisfied. Individuals try to become the person they believe or feel that they are capable of becoming. It is a difficult concept to put into words. Perhaps it is a longing for something to emerge from the depths of your being.

> *Before his death, Rabbi Zusya said, 'In the coming world, they will not ask me, "Why were you not Moses?" They will ask me, "Why were you not Zusya?"'*
>
> Martin Buber, 1961, *Tales of the Hasidim*

Self-actualization can take many forms, depending on the individual. These variations may include the quest for knowledge, understanding, peace, self-fulfilment, meaning in life, or beauty... but the need for beauty is neither higher nor lower than the other needs at the top of the pyramid. Self-actualization needs aren't hierarchically ordered.

(Griffin, 1991)

Rogers and the path to personal growth

Carl Rogers was one of the founders of the humanistic movement. He wrote extensively on the stages through which people travel on their journey towards 'becoming a person'. Rogers' work was predominately based on his observations in the field of psychotherapy. However, he was increasingly interested in how people learn, how they exercise power and how they behave within organizations.

Rogers is an important researcher and writer for consultants, as his 'client-centred approach' to growth and development provides clues and cues as to how we as change agents might bring about growth and development with individuals within organizations. Rogers (1967) high-lighted three crucial conditions for this to occur:

1 **Genuineness and congruence:** to be aware of your own feelings, to be real, to be authentic. Rogers' research showed that the more genuine and congruent the change agent is in the relationship, the greater the probability of change in the personality of the client.

2 **Unconditional positive regard:** a genuine willingness to allow the client's process to continue, and an acceptance of whatever feelings are going on inside the client. Whatever feeling the client is experiencing, be it anger, fear, hatred, then that is all right. It is saying that underneath all this the person is all right.

3 **Empathic understanding:** in Rogers' words, 'it is only as I understand the feelings and thoughts which seem so horrible to you, or so weak, or so sentimental, or so bizarre – it is only as I see them as you see them, and accept them and you, that you feel really free to explore all the hidden roots and frightening crannies of your inner and often buried experience.'

Rogers continues: 'in trying to grasp and conceptualize the process of change... I gradually developed this concept of a process, discriminating seven stages in it'. The following are the consistently recurring qualities at each stage as described by Rogers:

- One:
    - an unwillingness to communicate about self, only externals;
    - no desire for change;
    - feelings neither recognized nor owned;
    - problems neither recognized nor perceived.

- Two:
    - expressions begin to flow;
    - feelings may be shown but not owned;
    - problems perceived but seen as external;
    - no sense of personal responsibility;
    - experience more in terms of the past not the present.

- Three:
    - a little talk about the self, but only as an object;
    - expression of feelings, but in the past;
    - non-acceptance of feelings; seen as bad, shameful, abnormal;
    - recognition of contradictions;
    - personal choice seen as ineffective.

- Four:
    - more intense past feelings;
    - occasional expression of current feelings;
    - distrust and fear of direct expression of feelings;
    - a little acceptance of feelings;
    - possible current experiencing;
    - some discovery of personal constructs;
    - some feelings of self-responsibility in problems;
    - close relationships seen as dangerous;
    - some small risk taking.

- Five:
    - feelings freely expressed in the present;
    - surprise and fright at emerging feelings;
    - increasing ownership of feelings;
    - increasing self-responsibility;
    - clear facing up to contradictions and incongruence.

- Six:
    - previously stuck feelings experienced in the here and now;
    - the self seen as less of an object, more of a feeling;
    - some physiological loosening;
    - some psychological loosening – that is, new ways of seeing the world and the self;
    - incongruence between experience and awareness reduced.

- Seven:
    - new feelings experienced and accepted in the present;
    - basic trust in the process;
    - self becomes confidently felt in the process;
    - personal constructs reformulated but much less rigid;
    - strong feelings of choice and self-responsibility.

There are a number of key concepts that emerge from Rogers' work which are important when managing change within organizations at an individual level:

- The creation of a facilitating environment, through authenticity, positive regard and empathic understanding, enables growth and development to occur.

- Given this facilitating environment and the correct stance of the change agent, clients will be able to surface and work through any negative feelings they may have about the change.

- Given this facilitating environment and the correct stance of the change agent, there will be a movement from rigidity to more fluidity in the client's approach to thinking and feeling. This allows more creativity and risk taking to occur.

- Given this facilitating environment and the correct stance of the change agent, clients will move towards accepting a greater degree of self-responsibility for their situation, enabling them to have more options from which to choose.

The role and the stance of the change agent will be discussed in Chapter 5; many of the attributes of Rogers' approach would be a welcome addition to the change agent's 'kit bag'.

Gestalt approach to individual and organizational change

Gestalt therapy originated with Fritz Perls, who was interested in the here and now. Perls believed that a person's difficulties today arise because of the way he or she is acting today, here and now. In Perls' words:

> [The] goal... must be to give him the means with which he can solve his present problems and any that may arise tomorrow or next year. The tool is self-support, and this he achieves by dealing with himself and his problems with all the means presently at his command, right now. If he can be truly aware at every instant of himself and his actions on whatever level – fantasy, verbal or physical – he can see how he is producing his difficulties, he can see what his present difficulties are, and he can help himself to solve them in the present, in the here and now.
>
> (Perls, 1976)

A consultant using a Gestalt approach has the primary aim of showing clients that they interrupt themselves in achieving what they want. Gestalt is experiential, not just based on talking, and there is an emphasis on doing, acting and feeling. Gestaltists use a cycle of experience to map how individuals and groups enact their desires, but more often than not how they block themselves from completing the cycle as shown in Figure 1.11.

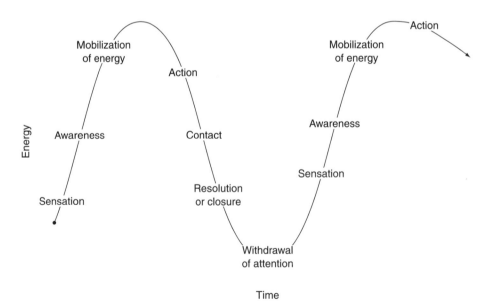

Figure 1.11   The Gestalt cycle

A favourite saying of Fritz Perls was to 'get out of your mind and come to your senses'. Gestalt always begins with what one is experiencing in the here and now. Experiencing has as its basis what one is sensing. 'Sensing determines the nature of awareness' (Perls _et al_, 1951).

What we sense outside of ourselves or within leads to awareness. Awareness comes when we alight or focus upon what we are experiencing. Nevis (1998) describes it as 'the spontaneous sensing of what arises or becomes figural, and it involves direct, immediate experience'. He gives a comprehensive list of the many things that we can be aware of at any one moment, including the following:

- **what we sense:** sights, sounds, textures, tastes, smells, kinaesthetic stimulations and so on;

- **what we verbalize and visualize:** thinking, planning, remembering, imagining and so on;

- **what we feel:** happiness, sadness, fearfulness, wonder, anger, pride, empathy, indifference, compassion, anxiety and so on;

- **what we value:** inclinations, judgements, conclusions, prejudices and so on;

- **how we interact:** participation patterns, communication styles, energy levels, norms and so on.

Although your awareness can only ever be in the present, this awareness can include memory of the past, anticipation of the future, inner experience and awareness of others and the environment.

Mobilization of energy occurs as awareness is focused on a specific facet. Imagine you have to give a piece of negative feedback to a colleague. As you focus on this challenge by bringing it into the foreground, you might start to feel butterflies in your stomach, or sweaty palms. This is like using a searchlight to illuminate a specific thing and bring it into full awareness. In Nevis's terminology, this brings about an 'energized concern'.

This energy then needs to be released, typically by doing something, by taking action, by making contact in and with the outside world. You give the feedback.

Closure might come when the colleague thanks you for the feedback and compliments you on the clarity and level of insight. Or perhaps you have an argument and agree to disagree. You will then experience a reduction in your energy, and will complete the cycle by having come to a resolution, with the object of attention fading into the background once more. The issue of the colleague's performance becomes less important.

For real change to have occurred (either internally or out in the world) the full Gestalt cycle will need to have been experienced.

Nevis shows how the Gestalt cycle maps on to stages in managerial decision making:

- **Awareness.** Data generation, Seeking information, Sharing information, Reviewing past performance, Environmental scanning.

- **Energy/action.** Attempts to mobilize energy and interest in ideas or proposals, Supporting ideas presented by others, Identifying and experiencing differences and conflicts of competing interests or views, Supporting own position, Seeking maximum participation.

- **Contact.** Joining in a common objective, Common recognition of problem definition, Indications of understanding, not necessarily agreement, Choosing a course of possible future action.

- **Resolution/closure.** Testing, checking for common understanding, Reviewing what's occurred, Acknowledgement of what's been accomplished and what remains to be done, Identifying the meaning of the discussion, Generalizing from what's been learned, Beginning to develop implementation and action plans.

- **Withdrawal.** Pausing to let things 'sink in', Reducing energy and interest in the issue, Turning to other tasks or problems, Ending the meeting.

STOP AND THINK!

Q 1.9   Use the Gestalt curve to describe how a manager moves from a concern about the team's performance to launching and executing a change initiative.

Summary of the humanistic psychology approach

For the manager, the world of humanistic psychology opens up some interesting possibilities and challenges. For years we have been told that the world of organizations is one that is ruled by the rational mind. Recent studies such as Daniel Goleman's (1998) on emotional intelligence and management competence (see Chapter 4) suggest that what makes for more effective managers is their degree of emotional self-awareness and ability to engage with others on an emotional level. Humanistic psychology would not only agree, but would go one step further in stating that without being fully present emotionally in the situation you cannot be fully effective, and you will not be able to maximize your learning, or anyone else's learning.

PERSONALITY AND CHANGE

We have looked at different approaches to change, and suggested that individuals do not always experience these changes in a consistent or uniform way. However, we have not asked whether people are different, and if so, whether their difference affects the way they experience change.

We have found in working with individuals and teams through change that it is useful to identify and openly discuss people's personality types. This information helps people to understand their responses to change. It also helps people to see why other people are different from them, and to be aware of how that may lead to either harmony or conflict.

The most effective tool for identifying personality type is the Myers-Briggs Type Indicator™ (MBTI™). This is a personality inventory developed by Katharine Briggs and her daughter Isabel Myers. The MBTI™ is based on the work of the Swiss analytical psychologist Carl Jung. The MBTI™ identifies eight different personality 'preferences' that we all use at different times – but each individual will have a preference for one particular combination over the others. These eight preferences can be paired as set out below.

Where individuals draw their energy

Extroversion is a preference for drawing energy from the external world, tasks and things, whereas **Introversion** is a preference for drawing energy from the internal world of one's thoughts and feelings.

What individuals pay attention to and how they receive data and information

Sensing is concerned with the five senses and what is and has been whereas **Intuition** is concerned with possibilities and patterns and what might be.

MANAGING CHANGE IN SELF AND OTHERS

We now look at some of the factors that arise when you as a manager are required to manage change within your organization. We will:

- discuss individual and group propensity for change;

- introduce the work of Edgar Schein and his suggestions for managing change;

- describe some of the ways that change can be thwarted;

- identify how managers or change agents can help others to change.

RESPONSES TO CHANGE

Those who let it happen.
Those who make it happen.
Those who wonder what happened.

Anon

Propensity for change

We have isolated five factors, shown in Figure 1.12, that have an influence on an individual's response to change. As a manager of change you will need to pay attention to these five areas if you wish to achieve positive responses to change:

- The nature of the change varies. Changes can be externally imposed or internally generated. They can be evolutionary or revolutionary in nature. They can be routine or one-off. They can be mundane or transformative. They can be about expansion or contraction. Different types of change can provoke different attitudes and different behaviours.

- The consequences of the change are significant. For whose benefit are the changes seen to be (employees, customers, the community, the shareholders, the board)? Who will be the winners and who will be the losers?

- The organizational history matters too. This means the track record of how the organization has handled change in the past (or how the

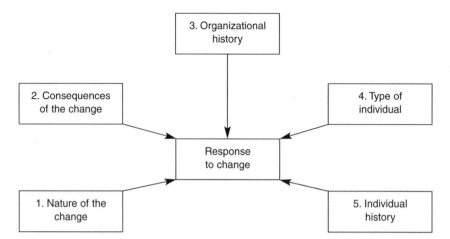

Figure 1.12   Five factors in responding to change

acquiring organization is perceived), what the prevailing culture is, what the capacity of the organization is in terms of management expertise and resources to manage change effectively, and what the future, beyond the change, is seen to hold.

- The personality type of the individual is a major determining factor in how she or he responds to change. The Myers-Briggs type of the individual (reviewed earlier) can give us an indication of how an individual will respond to change. People's motivating forces are also important – for example, are they motivated by power, status, money or affiliation and inclusion?

- The history of an individual can also give us clues as to how he or she might respond. By history we mean previous exposure and responses to change, levels of knowledge, skills and experience the individual has, areas of stability in his or her life and stage in his or her career. For example an individual who has previously experienced redundancy might re-experience the original trauma and upheaval regardless of how well the current one is handled. Or he or she may have acquired sufficient resilience and determination from the previous experience to be able to take this one in his or her stride.

Schein's model of transformative change

Edgar Schein has been a leading researcher and practitioner in the fields of individual, organizational and cultural change over the last 20 years.

His seminal works have included *Process Consultation* (1988) and *Organizational Culture and Leadership* (1992).

Schein elaborated on Lewin's (1952) model by drawing on other disciplines such as clinical psychology and group dynamics. This model influenced much OD and coaching work throughout the 1990s. (See Chapter 3 for Lewin's original model.)

SCHEIN'S ELABORATION OF LEWIN'S MODEL

Stage One
Unfreezing: Creating the motivation to change:

- Disconfirmation.
- Creation of survival anxiety or guilt.
- Creation of psychological safety to overcome learning anxiety.

Stage Two
Learning new concepts and new meanings for old concepts:

- Imitation of and identification with role models.
- Scanning for solutions and trial-and-error learning.

Stage Three
Refreezing: Internalizing new concepts and meanings:

- Incorporation into self-concept and identity.
- Incorporation into ongoing relationships.

Schein sees change as occurring in three stages:

1 unfreezing: creating the motivation to change;

2 learning new concepts and new meanings from old concepts;

3 internalizing new concepts and meanings.

During the initial unfreezing stage people need to unlearn certain things before they can focus fully on new learning.

Schein says that there are two forces at play within every individual undergoing change. The first force is learning anxiety. This is the anxiety associated with learning something new. Will I fail? Will I be exposed? The second, competing force is survival anxiety. This concerns the pressure to change. What if I don't change? Will I get left behind?

These anxieties can take many forms. Schein lists four of the associated fears:

1 Fear of temporary incompetence: the conscious appreciation of one's lack of competence to deal with the new situation.

2 Fear of punishment for incompetence: the apprehension that you will somehow lose out or be punished when this incompetence is discovered or assessed.

3 Fear of loss of personal identity: the inner turmoil when your habitual ways of thinking and feeling are no longer required, or when your sense of self is defined by a role or position that is no longer recognized by the organization.

4 Fear of loss of group membership: in the same way that your identity can be defined by your role, for some it can be profoundly affected by the network of affiliations you have in the workplace. In the same way that the stable equilibrium of a team or group membership can foster states of health, instability caused by shifting team roles or the disintegration of a particular group can have an extremely disturbing effect.

What gets in the way of change: resistance to change

Leaders and managers of change sometimes cannot understand why individuals and groups of individuals do not wholeheartedly embrace changes that are being introduced. They often label this 'resistance to change'.

Schein suggests that there are two principles for transformative change to work: first, survival anxiety must be greater than learning anxiety, and second, learning anxiety must be reduced rather than increasing survival anxiety. Used in connection with Lewin's force field (see Chapter 3), we see that survival anxiety is a driving force and learning anxiety is a restraining force. Rather than attempting to increase the individual or group's sense of survival anxiety, Schein suggests reducing the individual's learning anxiety. Remember also that the restraining forces may well have some validity.

How do you reduce learning anxiety? You do it by increasing the learner's sense of psychological safety through a number of interventions. Schein lists a few:

- a compelling vision of the future;

- formal training;

- involvement of the learner;

- informal training of relevant family groups/teams;

- practice fields, coaches, feedback;

- positive role models;

- support groups;

- consistent systems and structures;

- imitation and identification versus scanning and trial and error.

STOP AND THINK!

Q 1.11 Think of a recent skill that you had to learn in order to keep up with external changes. This could be installing a new piece of software, or learning about how a new organization works.

- What were your survival anxieties?
- What were your learning anxieties?
- What helped you to change?

How managers and change agents help others to change

We have listed in Table 1.6 some of the interventions that an organization and its management could carry out to facilitate the change process. We have categorized them into the four approaches described earlier in this chapter.

From the behavioural perspective a manager must ensure that reward policies and performance management are aligned with the changes taking place. For example if the change is intended to improve the quality of output, then the company should not reward quantity of output. Kerr (1995) lists several traps that organizations fall into:

We hope for:	But reward:
Teamwork and collaboration	The best team members
Innovative thinking and risk taking	Proven methods and no mistakes
Development of people skills	Technical achievements
Employee involvement and empowerment	Tight control over operations
High achievement	Another year's effort

Managers and staff need to know in detail what they are expected to do and how they are expected to perform. Behaviour needs to be defined, especially when many organizations today are promoting 'the company way'.

From the cognitive perspective a manager needs to employ strategies that link organizational goals, individual goals and motivation. This will create both alignment and motivation. An additional strategy is to provide ongoing coaching through the change process to reframe obstacles and resistances.

The psychodynamic perspective suggests adapting one's managerial approach and style to the emotional state of the change implementers.

Table 1.6 Representative interventions to facilitate the change process

Behavioural	Cognitive
Performance management	Management by objectives
Reward policies	Business planning and
Values translated into behaviours	performance frameworks
Management competencies	Results-based coaching
Skills training	Beliefs, attitudes and
Management style	cultural interventions
Performance coaching	Visioning
360 degree feedback	
Understanding change dynamics	Living the values
Counselling people	Developing the learning
through change	organization
Surfacing hidden issues	Addressing the hierarchy of needs
Addressing emotions	Addressing emotions
Treating employees and	Fostering communication and
managers as adults	consultation
Psychodynamic	**Humanistic**

2

Team change

INTRODUCTION

This chapter will look at teams, team development and change from a number of perspectives and will be asking a number of pertinent questions:

- What is a group and when is it a team?

- Why do you need teams?

- What types of organizational teams are there?

- How do you improve team effectiveness?

- What does team change look like?

- What are the leadership issues in team change?

- How do individuals affect team dynamics?

- How well do teams initiate and adapt to organizational change?

The chapter aims to enhance understanding of the nature of teams and how they develop, identify how teams perform in change situations, and develop strategies for managing teams through change and change through teams.

We open with a discussion around what constitutes a group and what constitutes a team. We will also look at the phenomena of different types of teams: for example, virtual teams, self-organizing teams and project teams.

Models of team functioning, change and development will be explored. We look at the various components of teamworking, and at how teams develop and how different types of people combine to make a really effective (or not) team.

We take as our basic model Tuckman's (1965) model of team development to illustrate how teams change over time. This is the forming, storming, norming and performing model. But we will add to it by differentiating between the task aspects of team development and the people aspects of team development.

Finally we look at the way in which teams can impact or react to organizational change.

WHAT IS A GROUP AND WHEN IS IT A TEAM?

There has been much academic discussion as to what constitutes a team and what constitutes a group. In much of the literature the two terms are used indistinguishably. Yet there are crucial differences, and anyone working in an organization instinctively knows when he or she is in a team and when he or she is in a group. We will attempt to clarify the essential similarities and differences. This is important when looking at change because teams and groups experience change in different ways.

Schein and Bennis (1965) suggest that a group is 'any number of people who interact with each other, are psychologically aware of each other, and who perceive themselves to be a group'. Morgan *et al* (1986) suggest that 'a team is a distinguishable set of two or more individuals who interact interdependently and adaptively to achieve specified, shared, and valued objectives'. Sundstrom *et al* (1990) define the work team as 'A small group of individuals who share responsibility for outcomes for their organizations.'

Cohen and Bailey (1997) define a team as 'a collection of individuals who are interdependent in their tasks, who share responsibility for outcomes, who see themselves and who are seen by others as an intact social entity embedded in one or more larger social systems (for example, business unit or the corporation), and who manage their relationships across organizational boundaries'. Our own list of differentiators appears in Table 2.1.

Table 2.1 Differences between groups and teams

Group	Team or work group
Indeterminate size	Restricted in size
Common interests	Common overarching objectives
Sense of being part of something or seen as being part of something	Interaction between members to accomplish individual and group goals
Interdependent as much as individuals might wish to be	Interdependency between members to accomplish individual and group goals
May have no responsibilities other than a sense of belonging to the group	Shared responsibilities
May have no accountabilities other than 'contractual' ones	Individual accountabilities
A group does not necessarily have any work to do or goals to accomplish	The team works together, physically or virtually

A group is a collection of individuals who draw a boundary around themselves. Or perhaps we from the outside might draw a boundary around them and thus define them as a group. A team on the other hand, with its common purpose, is generally tighter and clearer about what it is and what its *raison d'être* is. Its members know exactly who is involved and what their goal is. Of course it turns out that we are speaking hypothetically here, as any one of us has seen teams within organizations that appear to have no sense at all of what they are really about!

Let us illustrate the difference between a team and a group by using an example. We might look into an organization and see the Finance Department. The Finance Controller heads up a Finance Management Team that leads, manages and coordinates the activities within this area. The team members work together on common goals, meet regularly and have clearly defined roles and responsibilities (usually).

Perhaps the senior management team has decreed that all the high-potential managers in the organization shall be members of the Strategic Management Group. So the finance controller, who is on the high-potential list, gets together with others at his or her level to form a collection of individuals who contribute to the overall strategic direction of the organization. Apart from gatherings every six months, this group rarely meets or communicates. It is a grouping, which might be bounded but does not have any ongoing goals or objectives that require members to work together.

STOP AND THINK!

Q 2.1 Within your working life, what teams are you a member of and to which groups do you belong?

Q 2.2 Within your personal life, what teams are you a member of and to which groups do you belong?

Q 2.3 In what ways was it easier to answer in your personal life, and in what ways more difficult?

WHY WE NEED TEAMS

Why do we need teams and teamworking? Casey (1993), from Ashridge Management College, researched this question by asking a simple question of each team he worked with: 'Why should you work together as a team?' The simplest answer is, 'Because of the work we need to

accomplish.' Teamwork may be needed because there is a high volume of interconnected pieces of work, or because the work is too complex to be understood and worked on by one person.

What about managers? Do they need to operate as teams, or can they operate effectively as groups? The Ashridge-based writers say that a management team does not necessarily have to be fully integrated as a team all of the time. Nor should it be reduced to a mere collection of individuals going about their own individual functional tasks.

Casey believes that there is a clear link between the level of uncertainty of the task being handled and the level of teamwork needed. The greater the uncertainty, the greater the need for teamwork. The majority of management teams deal with both uncertain and certain tasks, so need to be flexible about the levels of teamworking required. Decisions about health and safety, HR policy, reporting processes and recruitment are relatively certain, so can be handled fairly quickly without a need for much sharing of points of view. There is usually a right answer to these issues, whereas decisions about strategy, structure and culture are less certain. There is no right answer, and each course of action involves taking a risk. This means more teamworking, more sharing of points of view, and a real understanding of what is being agreed and what the implications are for the team.

THE TYPES OF ORGANIZATIONAL TEAMS

Robert Keidal (1984) identified a parallel between sports teams and organizational teams. He uses baseball, American football and basketball teams to show the differences.

A baseball team is like a sales organization. Team members are relatively independent of one another, and while all members are required to be on the field together, they virtually never interact together all at the same time.

Football is quite different. There are really three subteams within the total team: offence, defence and the special team. When the subteam is on the field, every player is involved in every play, which is not the case in baseball. But the teamwork is centred in the subteam, not the total team.

Basketball is a different breed. Here the team is small, with all players in only one team. Every player is involved in all aspects of the game, offence and defence, and all must pass, run, shoot. When a substitute comes in, all must play with the new person.

Many different types of team exist within organizations. Let us look at a range of types of team found in today's organizations (see Table 2.2).

Work team

Work teams or work groups are typically the type of team that most people within organizations will think of when we talk about teams. They are usually part of the normal hierarchical structure of an organization. This means that one person manages a group of individuals, and that person is responsible for delivering a particular product or service either to the customer or to another part of the organization.

These teams tend to be relatively stable in terms of team objectives, processes and personnel. Their agenda is normally focused on maintenance

Table 2.2 Types of team

Team	Group	Work	Parallel	Project
Continuity	Variable	Stable	Stable or one-off project	Focused on project achievement
Lifespan	Variable	Unlimited	Variable	Time limited
Organizational links	Can be part of the formal and/or informal organization	Part of management structure	Outside of normal management structure	Separate management structure
Led by	Dependent on nature and purpose of group	One manager or supervisor	Normally coordinated or facilitated	Project manager
Location	Variable	Co-located	Converge for meetings	Co-located, dispersed, virtual
Purpose	Variable	Business as usual	Maintenance function or part of change infrastructure	Change or development
Authority	Dependent on nature and purpose of group	Through the line	Depends	Via project manager and project sponsor
Focus	Communication	Task	Communication	Task

and management of what is. This is a combination of existing processes and operational strategy. Any change agenda they have is usually on top of their existing agenda of meeting the current operating plan.

Self-managed team

A sub-set of the work team is the self-managed team. The self-managed team has the attributes of the work team but without a direct manager or

Table 2.2 *continued*

Team	Matrix	Virtual	Network	Management	Change
Continuity	Stable as a structure but fluid by project	Potential fluid	Potential fluid	Stable	Fluid
Lifespan	Unlimited	Variable	Variable	Unlimited	Variable
Organizational links	Part of management structure Dual accountability	Can be part of the management structure	More distributed across the organization	Part of management structure	Variable
Led by	Project manager and functional head	One manager or supervisor	Potentially distributed leadership or coordination	One manager	Sponsor or change manager
Location	Co-located, dispersed, virtual	Dispersed	Dispersed	Often co-located	Co-located, dispersed, virtual
Purpose	Project achievement	BAU or Project	Change or development	Business as usual Change and development	Change and development
Authority	Dual accountability	Through the line or project manager	Depends	Through the line	Via project manager and project sponsor
Focus	Task	Task	Communication	Task and communication	Task and communication

supervisor. This affects the way decisions are made and the way in which individual and team performance is managed. Generally this is through collective or distributed leadership.

Self-managed work teams are more prevalent in manufacturing industries than in the service arena. Once again there is an emphasis on delivery of service or product rather than delivering change.

Parallel team

Parallel teams are different from work teams because they are not part of the traditional management hierarchy. They are run in tandem or parallel to this structure. Examples of parallel teams are:

- teams brought together to deliver quality improvement (for example, quality circles, continuous improvement groups);

- teams that have some problem-solving or decision-making input, other than the normal line management processes (for example, creativity and innovation groups);

- teams formed to involve and engage employees (for example, staff councils, diagonal slice groups);

- teams set up for a specific purpose such as a task force looking at an office move.

These teams have variable longevity, and are used for purposes that tend to be other than the normal 'business as usual' management. They are often of a consultative nature, carrying limited authority. Although not necessarily responsible or accountable for delivering changes, they often feed into a change management process.

Project team

Project teams are teams that are formed for the specific purpose of completing a project. They therefore are time limited, and we would expect to find clarity of objectives. The project might be focused on an external client or it might be an internal one-off, or cross-cutting project with an internal client group.

Depending on the scale of the project the team might comprise individuals on a full- or part-time basis. Typically there is a project manager, selected for his or her specialist or managerial skills, and a project sponsor. Individuals report to the project manager for the duration of the project (although if they work part-time on the project they might also be reporting to a line manager). The project manager reports to the project sponsor, who typically is a senior manager.

We know the project team has been successful when it delivers the specific project on time, to quality and within budget. Brown and Eisenhardt (1995) noted that cross-functional teams, which are teams comprised of individuals from a range of organizational functions, were found to enhance project success.

Project teams are very much associated with implementing change. However, although change may be their very *raison d'être* it does not necessarily mean that their members' ability to handle change is any different from the rest of us. Indeed built into their structure are potential dysfunctionalities:

- The importance of task achievement often reigns supreme, at the expense of investing time in meeting individual and team maintenance needs.

- The fact that individuals have increased uncertainty concerning their future can impact on motivation and performance.

- The dynamic at play between the project team and the organizational area into which the change will take place can be problematic.

Matrix team

Matrix teams generally occur in organizations that are run along project lines. The organization typically has to deliver a number of projects to achieve its objectives. Each project has a project manager, but the project team members are drawn from functional areas of the organization. Often projects are clustered together to form programmes, or indeed whole divisions or business units (for example, aerospace, defence or oil industry projects). Thus the team members have accountability both to the project manager and to their functional head. The balance of power between the projects and the functions varies from organization to organization, and the success of such structures often depends on the degree to which the project teams are enabled by the structure and the degree to which they are disabled.

Virtual team

Increasing globalization and developments in the use of new technologies mean that teams are not necessarily co-located any more. This has been true for many years for sales teams. Virtual teams either never meet or they meet only rarely. Townsend *et al* (1998) defined virtual teams as 'groups of geographically and/or organizationally dispersed co-workers that are assembled using a combination of telecommunications and information technologies to accomplish an organizational task'. An advantage of virtual teams is that an organization can use the most appropriately skilled people for the task, wherever they are located. In larger companies the probability that the necessary and desired expertise for any sophisticated or complex task is in the same place geographically is low.

Disadvantages spring from the distance between team members. Virtual teams cross time zones, countries, continents and cultures. All these things create their own set of challenges. Current research suggests that synchronous working (face-to-face or remote) is more effective in meeting more complex challenges. Team leadership for virtual teams also creates its own issues, with both day-to-day management tasks and developmental interventions being somewhat harder from a distance.

When it comes to change, virtual teams are somewhat paradoxical. Team members can perhaps be more responsive, balancing autonomy and interdependence, and more focused on their part of the team objective. However, change creates an increased need for communication, clear goals, defined roles and responsibilities, and support and recognition processes. These things are more difficult to manage in the virtual world.

Erich Barthel (Building relationships and working in teams across cultures) and Inger Buus (Leading in a virtual environment) write about this in more detail in *Leadership and Personal Development* (2011).

Networked team

National, international and global organizations can use networked teams in an attempt to add a greater cohesion, which would not otherwise be there. Additionally they may wish to capture learning in one part and spread it across the whole organization.

We might have grouped virtual and networked teams under the same category. However, we could think of the networked team as being similar to a parallel team, in the sense that its primary purpose is not business as usual, but part of an attempt by the organization to increase sustainability and build capacity through increasing the reservoir of knowledge across the whole organization.

Networked teams are an important anchor for organizations in times of change. They can be seen as part of the glue that gives a sense of cohesion to people within the organization.

Management team

> Management teams coordinate and provide direction to the sub-units under their jurisdiction, laterally integrating interdependent sub-units across key business processes.
>
> (Mohrman et al, 1995)

The management team is ultimately responsible for the overall performance of the business unit. In itself it may not deliver any product, service or project, but clearly its function is to enable that delivery. Management teams are pivotal in translating the organization's overarching goals into specific objectives for the various sub-units to do their share of the organization task.

Management teams are similar to work teams in terms of delivery of current operational plan, but are much more likely to be in a position of designing and delivering change as well. We expect a more senior management team to spend less time on 'business as usual' matters and more time on the change agenda.

The senior management team in any organization is the team most likely to be held responsible for the organization's ultimate success or failure. It is in a pivotal position within the organization. On the one hand it is at the top of the organization, and therefore team members have a collective leadership responsibility; on the other, it is accountable to the non-executive board and shareholders in limited companies, or to politicians in local and central government, or to trustees in not-for-profit organizations. Along with the change team (see below) the management team has a particular role to play within most change scenarios, for it is its members who initiate and manage the implementation of change.

Change team

Change teams are often formed within organizations when a planned or unplanned change of significant proportions is necessary. We have separated out this type of team because of its special significance. Sometimes the senior management team is called the change team, responsible for directing and sponsoring the changes. Sometimes the change team is a special project team set up to implement change. At other times the change team is a parallel team, set up to tap into the organization and be a conduit for feedback as to how the changes are being received.

Obviously different organizations have different terminologies, so what in one organization is called a project team delivering a change will be a change team delivering a project in another organization.

More and more organizations also realize that the management of change is more likely to succeed if attention is given to the people side of change. Hence a parallel team drawn from representatives of the whole workforce can be a useful adjunct in terms of assessing and responding to the impact of the changes on people.

We see the change team as an important starting point in the change process. Research by one of the authors (Green, 2007a) and Prosci (2003, 2007) suggests the criticality of a credible effective dedicated change management team.

STOP AND THINK!

Q 2.4   Of the teams of which you are a member, which are more suitable to lead change and which more suitable to implement change? Justify your answer.

HOW TO IMPROVE TEAM EFFECTIVENESS

Rollin and Christine Glaser (1992) have identified five elements that contribute to the level of a team's effectiveness or ineffectiveness over time. They are:

1   team mission, planning and goal setting;

2   team roles;

3   team operating processes;

4   team interpersonal relationships; and

5   inter-team relations.

If you can assess where a team is in terms of its ability to address these five elements, you will discover what it needs to do to develop into a fully functioning team.

Team mission planning and goal setting

A number of studies have found that the most effective teams have a strong sense of their purpose, organize their work around that purpose, and plan and set goals in line with that purpose. Larson and LaFasto (1989) report: 'in every case, without exception, when an effectively functioning team was identified, it was described by the respondent as having a clear understanding of its objective'.

Clarity of objectives together with a common understanding and agreement of these was seen to be key. In addition Locke and Latham (1984) report that the very act of goal setting was a prime motivator for the team; the more your team sets clear goals the more likely it is to succeed. They also reported a 16 per cent average improvement in effectiveness for teams that use goal setting as an integral part of team activities.

Clear goals are even more important when teams are involved in change, partly because unless they know where they are going they are unlikely to get there, and partly because a strong sense of purpose can mitigate some of the more harmful effects of change. The downside occurs when a team rigidly adheres to its purpose when in fact the world has moved on and other objectives are more appropriate.

Team roles

The best way for a team to achieve its goals is for the team to be structured logically around those goals. Individual team members need to have clear roles and accountabilities. They need to have a clear understanding not only of what their individual role is, but also what the roles and accountabilities of other team members are.

When change happens – within, to or by the team – clarity about roles has two useful functions. It provides a clear sense of purpose and it provides a supportive framework for task accomplishment. However, during change the situation becomes more fluid. Too much rigidity results in tasks falling down the gaps between roles, or overlaps going unnoticed. It might result in team members being less innovative or proactive or courageous.

Team operating processes

A team needs to have certain enabling processes in place for people to carry out their work together. Certain things are needed to allow the task to be achieved in a way that is as efficient and as effective as possible. Glaser and Glaser (1992) comment: 'both participation in all of the processes of the work group and the development of a collaborative approach are at the heart of effective group work. Because of the tradition of autocratic leadership, neither participation nor collaboration are natural or automatic processes. Both require some learning and practice.'

Typical areas that a team need actively to address by discussing and agreeing include:

- frequency, timing and agenda of meetings;

- problem-solving and decision-making methodologies;

- ground rules;

- procedures for dealing with conflict when it occurs;

- reward mechanisms for individuals contributing to team goals;

- type and style of review process.

In the turbulence created by change, all these areas will come under additional stress and strain, hence the need for processes to have been discussed and agreed at an earlier stage. During times of change when typically pressures and priorities can push people into silo mentality and away from the team, the team operating processes can act like a lubricant, enabling healthy team functioning to continue.

Team interpersonal relationships

The team members must actively communicate among themselves. To achieve clear understanding of goals and roles, the team needs to work together to agree and clarify them. Operating processes must also be discussed and agreed.

To achieve this level of communication, the interpersonal relationships within the team need to be in a relatively healthy state. Glaser and Glaser (1992) found that the literature on team effectiveness 'prescribes open communication that is assertive and task focused, as well as creating opportunities for giving and receiving feedback aimed at the development of a high trust climate'.

In times of change, individual stress levels rise and there is a tendency to focus more on the task than the people processes. High levels of trust within a team are the bedrock for coping with conflict.

Inter-team relations

Teams cannot work in isolation with any real hope of achieving their organizational objectives. The nature of organizations today – complex,

sophisticated and with increasingly loose and permeable boundaries – creates situations where a team's goals can rarely be achieved without input from and output to others.

However smart a team has been in addressing the previous four categories, the authors have found in consulting with numerous organizations that attention needs to be paid to inter-team relations now more than ever before. This is because of the rise of strategic partnerships and global organizations. Teams need to connect more. It is also because the environment is changing faster and is more complex, so keeping in touch with information outside of your own team is a basic survival strategy.

STOP AND THINK!

Q 2.5 Using the five elements above, what is your current team effectiveness?

Q 2.6 What needs to change, and how would you go about it?

WHAT TEAM CHANGE LOOKS LIKE

All teams go through a change process when they are first formed, and when significant events occur such as a new member arriving, a key member leaving, a change of scope, increased pressure from outside, or a change in organizational climate.

Tuckman (1965) is one of the most widely quoted of researchers into the linear model of team development. His work is regularly used in team building within organizations. Most people will have heard of it as the 'forming, storming, norming, performing' model of team development. His basic premise is that any team will undergo distinct stages of development as it works or struggles towards effective team functioning. Although we will describe Tuckman's model in some detail, we have selected a range of models to illustrate the team development process, as shown in Table 2.4.

Table 2.3 Effective and ineffective teams

Element	Team mission, planning and goal setting	Team roles	Team operating processes	Team interpersonal relationships	Inter-team relations
Outcome					
Team more effective, adaptive and change oriented	Clarity of goals and clear direction lead to greater task accomplishment and increased motivation.	Clear roles and responsibilities increase individual accountability and allow others to work at their tasks.	Problem solving and decision making are smoother and faster. Processes enable task accomplishment without undue conflict.	Open data flow and high levels of team working leading to task accomplishment in a supportive environment.	Working across boundaries ensures that organizational goals are more likely to be achieved.
Team less effective, less adaptive and change oriented	Lack of purpose and unclear goals result in dissipation of energy and effort.	Unclear roles and responsibilities lead to increased conflict and reduced accountability.	Unclear operating processes increase time and effort needed to progress task achievement.	Dysfunctional team working causes tensions, conflict, stress and insufficient focus on task accomplishment.	Teams working in isolation or against other teams reduce the likelihood of organizational goal achievement.

Table 2.4 Key attributes in the stages of team development

Tuckman (1965)	**Forming** Attempt at establishing primary purpose, structure, roles, leader, task and process relationships, and boundaries of the team	**Storming** Dealing with arising conflicts surrounding key questions from forming stage	**Norming** Settling down of team dynamic and stepping into team norms and agreed ways of working	**Performing** Team is now ready and enabled to focus primarily on its task while attending to individual and team maintenance needs
Modlin and Faris (1956)	**Structuralism** Attempt to recreate previous power within new team structures	**Unrest** Attempt to resolve power and interpersonal issues	**Change** Roles emerge based on task and people needs Sense of team emerges	**Integration** Team purpose and structure emerge and accepted, action towards team goals
Whittaker (1970)	**Preaffiliation** Sense of unease, unsure of team engagement, which is superficial	**Power and control** Focus on who has power and authority within the team Attempt to define roles	**Intimacy** Team begins to commit to task and engage with one another	**Differentiation** Ability to be clear about individual roles and interactions become workmanlike
Scott Peck (1990)	**Pseudocommunity** Members try to fake teamliness	**Chaos** Attempt to establish pecking order and team norms	**Emptiness** Giving up of expectations, assumptions and hope of achieving anything	**Community** Acceptance of each other and focus on the task
Schutz (1982)	**In or out** Members decide whether they are part of the team or not	**Top or bottom** Focus on who has power and authority within the team		**Near or far** Finding levels of commitment and engagement within their roles
Hill and Gruner (1973)	**Orientation** Structure sought	**Exploration** Exploration around team roles and relations		**Production** Clarity of team roles and team cohesion
Bion (1961)	**Dependency** Team members invest the leaders with all the power and authority	**Fight or flight** Team members challenge the leaders or other members Team members withdraw		**Pairing** Team members form pairings in an attempt to resolve their anxieties

Tuckman's model of team change

Forming

Forming is the first stage. This involves the team asking a set of fundamental questions:

- What is our primary purpose?
- How do we structure ourselves as a team to achieve our purpose?
- What roles do we each have?
- Who is the leader?
- How will we work together?
- How will we relate together?
- What are the boundaries of the team?

(Bion's insights – see below – refer to observed phenomena and do not imply a sequence.)

If we were to take a logical rational view of the team we could imagine that this could all be accomplished relatively easily and relatively painlessly. And sometimes, on short projects with less than five team members, it is. However, human beings are not completely logical rational creatures, and sometimes this process is difficult. We all have emotions, personalities, unique characteristics and personal motivations.

As we saw when we were exploring individual change, human beings react to change in different ways. And the formation of a new team is about individuals adjusting to change in their own individual ways.

Initially the questions may be answered in rather a superficial fashion. The primary task of the team might be that which was written down in a memo from the departmental head, along with the structure they first thought of. The leader might typically have been appointed beforehand and 'imposed' upon the team. Individuals' roles are agreed to in an initial and individual cursory meeting with the team leader.

The team may agree to relate via a set of ground rules using words that nobody could possibly object to, but nobody knows what they really mean in practice: 'be honest', 'team before self', 'have fun', and so on.

Storming

Tuckman's next stage is storming. This is a description of the dynamic that occurs when a team of individuals come together to work on a common task, and have passed through the phase of being nice to one another and not voicing their individual concerns. This dynamic occurs as the team strives or struggles to answer fully the questions postulated in the forming stage.

Statements articulated (or left unsaid) in some fashion or form might include ones such as:

- I don't think we should be aiming for that.

- This structure hasn't taken account of this.

- There are rather a lot of grey areas in our individual accountabilities.

- Why was he appointed as team leader when he hasn't done this before?

- I don't know whether I can work productively with these people.

- How can we achieve our goals without the support from others in the organization?

An alternative word to storming is 'testing'. Individuals and the team as a whole are testing out the assumptions that had been made when the team was originally formed. Obviously different teams will experience this stage with different degrees of intensity, but important points to note here are:

- it is a natural part of the process;

- it is a healthy part of the process;

- it is an important part of the process.

The storming phase – if successfully traversed – will achieve clarity on all the fundamental questions of the first phase, and enable common understanding of purpose and roles to be achieved. In turn it allows the authority of the team leader to be seen and acknowledged, and it allows everyone to take up his or her rightful place within the team. It also gives team members a sense of the way things will happen within the team. It becomes a template for future ways of acting, problem solving, decision making and relating.

Norming

The third stage of team development occurs when the team finally settles down into working towards achievement of its task without too much attention needed on the fundamental questions. As further challenges develop, or as individuals grow further into their roles, then further scrutiny of the fundamental questions may happen. They may be discussed, but if they instead remain hidden beneath the surface this can result in loss of attention on the primary task.

Tuckman suggests in his review of the research that this settling process can be relatively straightforward and sequential. The team moves through the storming phase into a way of working that establishes team norms. It can also be more sporadic and turbulent, with the team needing further storming before team norms are established. Indeed some readers might have experienced teams that permanently move back and forth between the norming and storming stages – a clear signal that some team issues are not being surfaced and dealt with.

Performing

The final stage of team development is performing. The team has successfully traversed the three previous stages and therefore has clarity about its purpose, its structure and its roles. It has engaged in a rigorous process of working out how it should work and relate together, and is comfortable with the team norms it has established. Not only has the team worked these things through, but it has embodied them as a way of working. It has developed a capacity to change and develop, and has learnt how to learn.

The team can quite fruitfully get on with the task in hand and attend to individual and team needs at the same time.

Adjourning

A fifth stage was later added that acknowledged that teams do not last for ever. This stage represents the period when the team's task has been completed and team members disperse. Some practitioners call this stage _mourning_, highlighting the emotional component. Others call it _transforming_ as team members develop other ways of working.

THE LEADERSHIP ISSUES IN TEAM CHANGE

FOOD FOR THOUGHT

Ralph Stacey, in his book *Strategic Management and Organisational Dynamics* (1993), describes what happens when a group is brought together to study the experience of being in a group, without any further task and without an appointed leader. Known as a Group Relations Conference and run by the Tavistock Institute in London, this process involves a consultant who forms part of the group to offer views on the group process but otherwise takes no conscious part in the activity. This:

always provokes high levels of anxiety in the participants... which... find expression in all manner of strange behaviours. Group discussions take on a manic form with asinine comments and hysterical laughter... the participants attack the visiting consultant... becoming incredibly rude....

Members try to replace the non-functioning consultant... but they rarely seem to be successful in this endeavour. They begin to pick on an individual, usually some highly individualistic or minority member of the group, and then treat this person as some kind of scapegoat. They all become very concerned with remaining part of the group, greatly fearing exclusion. They show strong tendencies to conform to rapidly established group norms and suppress their individual differences, perhaps they are afraid of becoming the scapegoat... the one thing they hardly do at all is to examine the behaviour they are indulging in, the task they have actually been given.

The situation described in the box offers a way of exploring some of the unconscious group processes that are at work just below the surface. These are not always visible in more conventional team situations. The work of Bion (1961) and Scott Peck (1990) is useful to illuminate some of the phenomena that can be observed and experienced in groups, and highlight the challenges for leaders.

Moving through dependency

In any team formation the first thing people look for is someone to tell them what to do. This is a perfectly natural phenomenon, given that many people will want to get on with the task and many people will believe someone else knows what the task is and how it should be done.

In any unfamiliar situation or environment people can become dependent. Jon Stokes (in Obholzer and Roberts, 1994) describes what Bion observed in his experience with groups and called basic group assumptions:

> a group dominated by basic assumption of dependency behaves as if its primary task is solely to provide for the satisfaction of the needs and wishes of its members. The leader is expected to look after, protect and sustain the members of the group, to make them feel good, and not to face them with the demands of the group's real purpose.

The job of the leader, and indeed the group, is not only to establish leadership credibility and accountability but to establish its limits. This will imbue the rest of the team with sufficient power for them to accomplish their tasks. The leader can do this by modelling the taking of individual responsibility and empowering others to do the same, and by ensuring that people are oriented in the right direction and have a common understanding of team purpose and objectives.

Moving through conflict

Bion's second assumption is labelled 'fight or flight'. Bion (1961) says:

> There is a danger or 'enemy', which should either be attacked or fled from ... members look to the leader to devise some appropriate action... for instance, instead of considering how best to organize its work, a team may spend most of the time worrying about rumours of organizational change. This provides a sense of togetherness, whilst also serving to avoid facing the difficulties of the work itself. Alternatively, such a group may spend its time protesting angrily, without actually planning any specific action to deal with the perceived threat.

The threat might not necessarily be coming from outside, but instead might be an externalization – or projection – from the team. The real threat is from within, and the potential for conflict is between the leader and the rest of the team, and between team members themselves. Issues about power and authority and where people sit in the 'pecking order' may surface at this stage.

The leadership task here is to surface any of these dynamics and work them through, either by the building of trust and the frank, open and honest exchange of views, or by seeking clarity and gaining agreement on roles and responsibilities.

Moving towards creativity

The third assumption that Bion explored was that of pairing. This is:

> based on the collective and unconscious belief that, whatever the actual problems and needs of the group, a future event will solve them. The group behaves as if pairing or coupling between two members within the group, or perhaps between the leaders of the group and some external person, will bring about salvation... the group is in fact not interested in working practically towards this future, but only sustaining a vague sense of hope as a way out of its current difficulties... members are inevitably left with a sense of disappointment and failure, which is quickly superseded by a hope that the next meeting will be better.

Once again there is a preoccupation. This time it is about creating something new, but in a fantasized or unreal way, as a defence against doing anything practical or actually performing. The antidote of course is for the leader to encourage the team members to continue in their endeavours and to take personal responsibility for moving things on. Collaborative working requires greater openness of communication and data flow.

Moving through cohesion and cosiness

Turquet (1974) has added a fourth assumption, labelled 'oneness'. This is where the team seems to believe it has come together almost for a higher purpose, or with a higher force, so the members can lose themselves in a sense of complete unity.

There are parallels to the stage of performing but somehow, once again, the team has fallen into an unconscious detraction from the primary task in hand. Attainment of a sense of oneness, cohesiveness or indeed cosiness is not the purpose the team set out to achieve. Good and close teamworking is often essential and can be individually satisfying, but it is not the purpose. Too much focus on team cohesion can lead to abdication from the task, and is only a stage on the way to full teamworking. The goal is interdependent working co-existing with collaborative problem solving. This requires the leader to set the scene and the pace, and team members to act with maturity.

See Chapter 4 for more ideas on leading change.

STOP AND THINK!

Q 2.7 Imagine that you are one of a team of five GPs working at a local practice. You want to initiate some changes in the way the team approaches non-traditional medical methods such as counselling, homeopathy and osteopathy. The GPs meet monthly for one hour to discuss finances and review medical updates. They do not really know each other well or work together on patient care. There is no real team leader, although the Practice Manager takes the lead when the group discusses administration.

Using one of the models of team development described above, explain how you could lead the team towards a new way of working together. What obstacles to progress do you predict, and how might you deal with them?

HOW INDIVIDUALS AFFECT TEAM DYNAMICS

Here we use the Myers-Briggs Type Indicator™ to see how individual personalities might influence and be influenced by the team. We also use Meredith Belbin's (1981) research into team types to indicate what types of individuals best make up an effective team.

MBTI™ and teams

The Myers-Briggs Type Indicator™ suggests that if you are a particular type you have particular preferences and are different from other people of different types (see Table 1.5 for MBTI™ types). This means that when it comes to change, people with different preferences react differently to change, both when they initiate it and when they are on the receiving end of it. This is also true when you are a member of a team. Different people will bring their individual preferences to the table and behave in differing ways.

'If it ain't broke, don't fix it'

'Let's think ahead'

'Let's just do it'   'Let's change it'

When undergoing team change, individual team members will typically react in one of four ways (see the four illustrations):

- Some will want to ascertain the difference between what should be preserved and what could be changed. There will be things they want to keep.

- Some will think long and hard about the changes that will emerge internally from their visions of the future. They will be intent on thinking about the changes differently.

- Some will be keen to move things on by getting things to run more effectively and efficiently. They will be most interested in doing things now.

- Some will be particularly inventive and want to try something different or novel. They will be all for changing things.

The use of MBTI™, or any other personality-profiling instrument, can have specific benefits when teams are experiencing or managing change. It can identify where individuals and the team itself might have strengths to be capitalized on, and where it might have weaknesses that need to be supported.

Behaviours exhibited by team members will run 'true to type', so knowing your preferences and those of the rest of the team will help aid understanding. It is also true that different team tasks might be suitable for different types – either because they are best matched or because it provides a development opportunity. Surfacing differences helps individuals see things from the other person's perspective, and adds to the effective use of diversity within the team.

Researching in the health care industry, McCaulley (1975) made the point that similarity and difference within teams can have both advantages and disadvantages:

- The more similar the team members are, the sooner they will reach common understanding.

- The more disparate the team members, the longer it takes for understanding to occur.

- The more similar the team members, the quicker the decision will be made, but the greater the possibility of error through exclusion of some possibilities.

- The more disparate the team members, the longer the decision-making process will be, but the more views and opinions will be taken into account.

McCaulley also recognized that teams valuing different types can ultimately experience less conflict.

A particular case worth mentioning is the management team. Management teams both in the United States and the United Kingdom are skewed from the natural distribution of Myers-Briggs types within the whole population. Typically they are composed of fewer people of the feeling types and fewer people of the perceiving types. This means that management teams, when making decisions about change, are more likely to put emphasis on the business case for change, and less likely to think or worry about the effect on people. You can see the result of this in most change programmes in most organizations. They are also more likely to want to close things down, having made a decision, rather than keep their options open – thus excluding the possibility of enhancing and improving on the changes or responding to feedback.

There are some simple reminders of the advantages and disadvantages of the preferences for teams making decisions about managing change within organizations listed in Table 2.5.

Table 2.5   Complementarity and conflict in teams

Extroversion	Where individuals draw their energy from	Introversion
Needed to raise energy, show enthusiasm, make contacts and take action. But they can appear superficial, intrusive and overwhelming.		Needed for thinking things through and depth of understanding. But can appear withdrawn, cold and aloof.
Sensing	**What an individual pays attention to or how he/she receives data and information**	**Intuition**
Needed to base ideas firmly in reality and be practical and pragmatic. Can appear rather mundane and pessimistic.		Needed to prepare for the future and generate innovative solutions. Can appear to have head in the clouds, impractical and implausible.
Thinking	**How an individual makes decisions**	**Feeling**
Needed to balance benefits against the costs and make tough decisions. Can appear rather critical and insensitive.		Needed to be in touch with emotional intelligence, to negotiate and to reconcile. Can appear irrational and too emotional.
Judging	**What sort of lifestyle an individual enjoys**	**Perceiving**
Needed for his/her organization and ability to complete things and see them through. Can appear overly rigid and immovable.		Needed for his/her flexibility, adaptability and information gathering. Can appear rather unorganized and somewhat irresponsible.

Belbin's team types

What people characteristics need to be present for a team to function effectively? Belbin (1981) has been researching this question for a number of years. The purpose of his research was to see whether high and low performing teams had certain characteristics. He looked at team members and found that in the higher performing teams, members played a role or number of roles. Any teams without members playing one of these roles would be more likely to perform at a lower level of effectiveness. (Of course different situations require certain different emphases.) He identified the roles shown in Table 2.6, with their contributions and allowable weaknesses.

STOP AND THINK!

Q 2.8   What team role(s) are you likely to use?

Q 2.9   What are the advantages and disadvantages of each of the eight roles?

Belbin concluded that if teams were formed with individuals' preferences and working styles in mind, they would have a better chance of team cohesion and work-related goal achievement. Teams need to contain a good spread of Belbin team types.

Different teams might need different combinations of roles. Marketing and design teams probably need more Plants, while project implementation teams need Implementers and Completer Finishers. Likewise, the lack of a particular team type can be an issue. A management team without a Co-ordinator or Shaper would have problems. An implementation team without a Complete Finisher might also struggle.

HOW WELL TEAMS INITIATE AND ADAPT TO ORGANIZATIONAL CHANGE

Throughout the last decades of the 20th century many organizations repeated the mantra, 'people are our greatest assets', and many would then apologize profusely when they were forced into downsizing or 'rightsizing' the workforce. Similarly, many organizations have sung the praises of teams and how essential they are within the modern organization. Many organizations have sets of competences or stated values that

Table 2.6   Belbin team-role summary sheet

Team-Role Descriptions

Team Role	Contribution	Allowable Weakness
Plant	Creative, imaginative, unorthodox. Solves difficult problems.	Ignores incidentals. Too pre-occupied to communicate effectively.
Resource Investigator	Extrovert, enthusiastic, communicative. Explores opportunities. Develops contacts.	Over-optimistic. Loses interest once initial enthusiasm has passed.
Co-ordinator	Mature, confident, a good chairperson. Clarifies goals, promotes decision-making, delegates well.	Can be seen as manipulative. Offloads personal work.
Shaper	Challenging, dynamic, thrives on pressure. The drive and courage to overcome obstacles.	Prone to provocation. Offends people's feelings.
Monitor Evaluator	Sober, strategic and discerning. Sees all options. Judges accurately.	Lacks drive and ability to inspire others.
Teamworker	Co-operative, mild, perceptive and diplomatic. Listens, builds, averts friction.	Indecisive in crunch situations.
Implementer	Disciplined, reliable, conservative and efficient. Turns ideas into practical actions.	Somewhat inflexible. Slow to respond to new possibilities.
Completer Finisher	Painstaking, conscientious, anxious. Searches out errors and omissions. Delivers on time.	Inclined to worry unduly. Reluctant to delegate.
Specialist	Single-minded, self-starting, dedicated. Provides knowledge and skills in rare supply.	Contributes on only a narrow front. Dwells on technicalities.

implicitly and explicitly pronounce that their employees need to work in the spirit of teamwork and partnership.

It was therefore interesting for the authors to discover that there was a real lack of any authoritative research on the interplay between organizational change and teamworking. We have seen the effect that change has on individuals and groups of individuals, but what has not been studied is the effect of change on teams. And as a consequence there is very little research on strategies for managing and leading teams through organizational change.

Whelan-Berry and Gordon (2000), in their research into effective organizational change, conducted a multi-level analysis of the organizational change process. To quote them:

> They found no change process models at the group or team level of analysis in the organization studies and change literature. Literature exists which explores different aspects of team or group development, team or group effectiveness, implementation of specific interventions, and organizational and individual aspects of the change, but not a group/team change process model … the lack of change process models for the team or group level change process in the context of organizational change leaves a major portion of the organizational change process unclear.

They continue:

> The primary focus of existing organizational change models is what to do as opposed to explaining or predicting the change process. Most of the models implicitly, and a few explicitly, acknowledge the inherent (sub) processes of group level and individual level change, but do not include the details of these processes in the model. The question is how does the change process vary when considered across levels of analysis? For example, how does a vision get 'translated,' that is, take on meaning, in each location or department? In addition, what happens at the point of implementation? We must 'double click' at the point of implementation in the organizational level change process; that is, we must look at the group and individual levels and their respective change processes to understand the translation and implementation of the organizational-level change vision and desired change outcomes to group and subsequently to individual meanings, frameworks, and behaviours.

Table 2.7 examines each type of team previously identified and looks at the way in which this type of team can impact or react to organizational change. We also look at the pros and cons of each team type when involved in an organizational change process.

Table 2.7 Teams going through change

Team type	Group	Work	Parallel	Project	Matrix
Propensity to initiate change	Dependent on nature and composition of group	Limited	Limited in terms of organizational impact	Potentially high depending on integration into organization	Fair given propensity to address change
Propensity to adapt to change	Dependent on purpose and composition of group	Dependent on team members and team culture	Dependent on purpose and team members	Theoretically high. Good for limited changes in scope but not total	Dependent on degree of enabling or disabling structure
Advantages during change	Difficult to get alignment	Good at implementation once it is clear	Good for pilot schemes	Good focus for specific implementation goals	Flexible, so good for initiating ideas
Disadvantages during change	Useful for coming up with out-of-the-box ideas	Does not like change too often	Can become alienated through failure, or through boasting about success	Not good for tackling complex topics such as values or leadership	Leadership sometimes not clear, so discussion can go on for ever
Advice for leaders	Good for initiating ideas and spreading the word	Need to involve the leaders or shapers of these teams early – especially if you need their commitment rather than compliance	Useful for starting things up and proving an idea. Do not let members become too isolated. Encourage them to link in with the outside world	Good for short-range tasks such as appointing consultants or researching techniques. Not good for the complex stuff. Do not be tempted to give complex issues like 'improve communication' to a project team	Good for initiating ideas and spreading the word

Table 2.7 *continued*

Team type	Virtual	Network	Management	Change
Propensity to initiate change	Limited unless project-specific	Potentially large depending on nature and composition of group	Theoretically and practically high. Typically should be the team that initiates change	*Raison d'être*
Propensity to adapt to change	Dependent on purpose and team members	Dependent on purpose and team members	Theoretically and practically high. Sometimes will have difficulty adapting to others' change	Theoretically and practically high
Advantages during change	Brings disparate groups together if tightly focused	Wide reaching, so good for sharing sense of purpose and sense of urgency	Powerful, so makes an impact	Has increased energy and sense of purpose because it was set up to make change happen
Disadvantages during change	Lack of cohesion means purpose may be misunderstood and important issues are not raised	Not good for monitoring implementation because of lack of process and regularity	Often resistant to changing through lack of time or lack of teamwork, so role-modelling of desired changes can be weak. Focus on events after the launch often poor due to packed agenda and belief that it will all happen smoothly	Not impactful if it lacks influence (presence of powerful people)
Advice for leaders	Involve the key virtual teams early especially the leaders and shapers, but do not expect them to implement anything complicated	Good for initiating ideas and spreading the word	Do something surprising yourself if you want your management team to change the way it works. Insist on role-modelling. Keep your eye on the ball because there *will* be problems	Recruit powerful people. Work on alignment. Ensure resources

Team development processes are disturbed in times of change. An external event can shift a performing team back into the storming stage. Only teams that are quite remote from the changes can simply incorporate a new scope or a new set of values and remain relatively untouched.

SUMMARY AND CONCLUSIONS

- Groups and teams are different, with different characteristics and different reasons for existing.

- Teams are important in organizational life for accomplishing large or complex tasks.

- Teamwork is important for management teams when they work on risky issues that require them to share views and align.

- There are many different types of organizational team, each with significant benefits and downsides.

- Teams can become more effective by addressing five elements:
    - team mission, planning and goal setting;
    - team roles;
    - team operating processes;
    - team interpersonal relationships;
    - inter-team relations.

- Teams develop over time. Tuckman's forming, storming, norming and performing model is useful for understanding this process.

- The team development process involves different leadership challenges at each stage.

- Bion's work highlights four possible pitfalls that need to be worked through:
    - dependency;
    - fight or flight;
    - pairing; and
    - oneness.

- The composition of a team is an important factor in determining how it can be successful. Belbin says that well-rounded teams are best. Deficiencies in a certain type can cause problems.

- The Myers-Briggs profile allows mutual understanding of team members' preferences for initiating or adapting to change.

- Belbin's team types offer a way of analysing a team's fitness for purpose and encouraging team members to do something about any significant gaps.

- Leaders need to be aware of the types of team available during a change process, and how to manage these most effectively.

Below is a summary checklist of the key questions you need to be asking and answering before, during and after the change process:

- Where are the teams affected by the change process?

- What types of team are they and how might they respond to change?

- What do they need to be supported through the change process?

- How can we best use them throughout the change process?

- What additional types of team do we need for designing and implementing the changes?

- As all teams go through the transition, what resources shall we offer to ensure they achieve their objectives of managing business as usual and the changes?

- How do we ensure that teams that are dispersing, forming, integrating or realigning stay on task?

- What organizational process do we have for ensuring teams are clear about their:
    - mission, planning and goal setting;
    - roles and responsibilities
    - operating processes;
    - interpersonal relationships;
    - inter-team relations?

4   cultures;

5   political systems;

6   psychic prisons;

7   flux and transformation; and

8   instruments of domination.

We have selected four of Morgan's organizational metaphors to explore the range of assumptions that exists about how organizational change works. These are the four that we see in use most often by managers, writers and consultants, and that appear to us to provide the most useful insights into the process of organizational change. These are:

- organizations as machines;

- organizations as political systems;

- organizations as organisms;

- organizations as flux and transformation.

Descriptions of these different organizational metaphors appear below. See also Table 3.1, which sets out how change might be approached using the four different metaphors. In reality most organizations use combinations of approaches to tackle organizational change, but it is useful to pull the metaphors apart to see the difference in the activities resulting from different ways of thinking.

MACHINE METAPHOR?

The new organizational structure represents an injection of fresh skills into the Marketing Function.

Fred Smart will now head up the implementation of the Marketing Plan, which details specific investment in marketing skills training and IT systems. We intend to fill the identified skills gaps and to upgrade our customer databases and market intelligence databank. A focus on following correct marketing procedures will ensure consistent delivery of well-targeted brochures and advertising campaigns.

MD, Engineering Company

Table 3.1 Four different approaches to the change process

Metaphor	How change is tackled	Who is responsible	Guiding principles
Machine	Senior managers define targets and timescale. Consultants advise on techniques. Change programme is rolled out from the top down. Training is given to bridge behaviour gap.	Senior management	Change must be driven. Resistance can be managed. Targets set at the start of the process define the direction.
Political system	A powerful group of individuals builds a new coalition with new guiding principles. There are debates, manoeuvrings and negotiations which eventually leads to the new coalition either winning or losing. Change then ensues as new people are in power with new views and new ways of allocating scarce resources. Those around them position themselves to be winners rather than losers.	Those with power	There will be winners and losers. Change requires new coalitions and new negotiations.
Organisms	There is first a research phase where data is gathered on the relevant issue (customer feedback, employee survey etc). Next the data is presented to those responsible for making changes. There is discussion about what the data means, and then what needs to be done. A solution is collaboratively designed and moved towards, with maximum participation. Training and support are given to those who need to make significant changes.	Business improvement/ HR/OD managers	There must be participation and involvement, and an awareness of the need for change. The change is collaboratively designed as a response to changes in the environment. People need to be supported through change.

Table 3.1 *continued*

Metaphor	How change is tackled	Who is responsible	Guiding principles
Flux and transformation	The initial spark of change is an emerging topic. This is a topic that is starting to appear on everyone's agenda, or is being talked about over coffee. Someone with authority takes the initiative to create a discussion forum. The discussion is initially fairly unstructured, but well facilitated. Questions asked might be 'Why have you come?' 'What is the real issue?' 'How would we like things to be?' The discussion involves anyone who has the energy to be interested. A plan for how to handle the issue emerges from a series of discussions. More people are brought into the net.	Someone with authority to act	Change cannot be managed; it emerges. Conflict and tension give rise to change. Managers are part of the process. Their job is to highlight gaps and contradictions.

Gareth Morgan's metaphors used with permission of Sage Publications Inc.

Organizations as machines

The machine metaphor is a well-used one that is worth revisiting to examine its implications for organizational change. Gareth Morgan says, 'When we think of organizations as machines, we begin to see them as rational enterprises designed and structured to achieve predetermined ends.' This picture of an organization implies routine operations, well-defined structure and job roles, and efficient working inside and between the working parts of the machine (the functional areas). Procedures and standards are clearly defined, and are expected to be adhered to.

Many of the principles behind this mode of organizing are deeply ingrained in our assumptions about how organizations should work. This links closely into behaviourist views of change and learning (see description of behavioural approach to change in Chapter 1). The key beliefs are:

- each employee should have only one line manager;

- labour should be divided into specific roles;

- each individual should be managed by objectives;

- teams represent no more than the summation of individual efforts;

- management should control and there should be employee discipline.

This leads to the following assumptions about organizational change:

- the organization can be changed to an agreed end state by those in positions of authority;

- there will be resistance, and this needs to be managed;

- change can be executed well if it is well planned and well controlled.

What are the limitations of this metaphor? The mechanistic view leads managers to design and run the organization as if it were a machine. This approach works well in stable situations, but when the need for a significant change arises, this will be seen and experienced by employees as a major overhaul that is usually highly disruptive and therefore encounters resistance. Change when approached with these assumptions is therefore hard work. It will necessitate strong management action, inspirational vision, and control from the top down. (See the works of Frederick Taylor and Henri Fayol if you wish to examine further some of the original thinking behind this metaphor.)

Organizations as political systems

When we see organizations as political systems we are drawing clear parallels between how organizations are run and systems of political rule. We may refer to 'democracies', 'autocracy' or even 'anarchy' to describe what is going on in a particular organization. Here we are describing the style of power rule employed in that organization.

The political metaphor is useful because it recognizes the important role that power-play, competing interests and conflict have in organizational life. Gareth Morgan comments: 'Many people hold the belief that business and politics should be kept apart... But the person advocating the case of employee rights or industrial democracy is not introducing a political issue so much as arguing for a different approach to a situation that is already political.'

The key beliefs are:

- you can't stay out of organizational politics: you're already in it;

- building support for your approach is essential if you want to make anything happen;

- you need to know who is powerful, and who they are close to;

- there is an important political map that overrides the published organizational structure;

- coalitions between individuals are more important than work teams;

- the most important decisions in an organization concern the allocation of scarce resources, that is, who gets what, and these are reached through bargaining, negotiating and vying for position.

This leads to the following assumptions about organizational change:

- the change will not work unless it's supported by a powerful person;

- the wider the support for this change, the better;

- it is important to understand the political map, and to understand who will be winners and losers as a result of this change;

- positive strategies include creating new coalitions and renegotiating issues.

What are the limitations of this metaphor? The disadvantage of using this metaphor to the exclusion of others is that it can lead to the potentially unnecessary development of complex Machiavellian strategies, with an assumption that in any organizational endeavour, there are always winners and losers. This can turn organizational life into a political war zone. (See Pfeiffer's book, *Managing with Power: Politics and influence in organizations* (1992) to explore this metaphor further.)

Organizations as organisms

This metaphor of organizational life sees the organization as a living, adaptive system. Gareth Morgan says: 'The metaphor suggests that different environments favour different species of organizations based on different methods of organizing... congruence with the environment is the key to success.' For instance, in stable environments a more rigid bureaucratic organization would prosper. In more fluid, changing environments a looser, less structured type of organization would be more likely to survive.

This metaphor represents the organization as an 'open system'. Organizations are seen as sets of interrelated sub-systems designed to balance the requirements of the environment with internal needs of groups and individuals. This approach implies that when designing organizations, we should always do this with the environment in mind. Emphasis is placed on scanning the environment and developing a healthy adaptation to the outside world. Individual, group and organizational health and happiness are essential ingredients of this  metaphor. The assumption is that if the social needs of individuals and groups in the organization are met, and the organization is well designed to meet the needs of the environment, there is more likelihood of healthy adaptive functioning of the whole system (socio-technical systems).

The key beliefs are:

- there is no 'one best way' to design or manage an organization;

- the flow of information between different parts of the system and its environment is key to the organization's success;

- it is important to maximize the fit between individual, team and organizational needs.

This leads to the following assumptions about organizational change:

- changes are made only in response to changes in the external environment (rather than using an internal focus);

- individuals and groups need to be psychologically aware of the need for change in order to adapt;

- the response to a change in the environment can be designed and worked towards;

- participation and psychological support are necessary strategies for success.

What are the limitations of this metaphor? The idea of the organization as an adaptive system is flawed. The organization is not really just an adaptive unit, at the mercy of its environment. It can in reality shape the environment by collaborating with communities or with other organizations, or by initiating a new product or service that may change the environment in a significant way. In addition, the idealized view of coherence and flow between functions and departments is often unrealistic. Sometimes different parts of the organization run independently, and do so for good reason. For example the research department might run in a very different way to and entirely separately from the production department.

The other significant limitation of this view is noted by Morgan, and concerns the danger that this metaphor becomes an ideology. The resulting ideology says that individuals should be fully integrated with the organization. This means that work should be designed so that people can fulfil their personal needs through the organization. This can then become a philosophical bone of contention between 'believers' (often, but not always the HR Department) and 'non-believers' (often, but not always, the business directors). (See Burns and Stalker's book *The Management of Innovation* (1961) for the original thinking behind this metaphor.)

Organizations as flux and transformation

Viewing organizations as flux and transformation takes us into areas such as complexity, chaos and paradox. This view of organizational life sees the organization as part of the environment, rather than as distinct from it. So instead of viewing the organization as a separate system that adapts to the environment, this metaphor allows us to look at organizations as simply part of the ebb and flow of the whole environment, with a capacity to self-organize, change and self-renew in line with a desire to have a certain identity.

This metaphor is the only one that begins to shed some light on how change happens in a turbulent world. This view implies that managers can nudge and shape progress, but cannot ever be in control of change. Gareth Morgan says: 'In complex systems no one is ever in a position to control or design system operations in a comprehensive way. Form emerges. It cannot be imposed.'

The key beliefs are:

- order naturally emerges out of chaos;

- organizations have a natural capacity to self-renew;

- organizational life is not governed by the rules of cause and effect;

- key tensions are important in the emergence of new ways of doing things;

- the formal organizational structure (teams, hierarchies) only represents one of many dimensions of organizational life.

This leads to the following assumptions about organizational change:

- Change cannot be managed. It emerges.

- Managers are not outside the systems they manage. They are part of the whole environment.

- Tensions and conflicts are an important feature of emerging change.

- Managers act as enablers. They enable people to exchange views and focus on significant differences.

What are the limitations of this metaphor? This metaphor is disturbing for both managers and consultants. It does not lead to an action plan, or a process flow diagram, or an agenda to follow. Other metaphors of change appear to allow you to predict the process of change before it happens (although we believe that this is illusory!). With the flux and transformation metaphor, order emerges as you go along, and can only be made sense of during or after the event. This can lead to a sense of powerlessness that is disconcerting, but probably realistic! (See Chapter 10 on complex change for further reading on this metaphor.)

STOP AND THINK!

Q 3.1 Which view of organizational life is most prevalent in your organization?

What are the implications of this for the organization's ability to change?

Q 3.2 Which view are you most drawn to personally?

What are the implications for you as a leader of change?

Q 3.3   Which views are being espoused here? (See A, B, C and D.)

A: All staff memo from management team

The whole organization is encountering a range of difficult environmental issues, such as increased demand from our customers for faster delivery and higher quality, more legislation in key areas of our work, and rapidly developing competition in significant areas.

Please examine the attached information regarding the above (customer satisfaction data, benchmarking data vs competitors, details of new legislation) and start working in your teams on what this means for you, and how you might respond to these pressures.

The whole company will gather together in October of this year to begin to move forward with our ideas, and to strive for some alignment between different parts of the organization. We will present the management's vision and decide on some concrete first steps.

B: E-mail from CEO

A number of people have spoken to me recently about their discomfort with the way we are tackling our biggest account. This seems to be an important issue for a lot of people. If you are interested in tackling this one, please come to an open discussion session in the Atrium on Tuesday between 10.00 and 12.00 where we will start to explore this area of discomfort. Let Sarah know if you intend to come.

C: E-mail from one manager to another

John seems to be in cahoots with Sarah on this issue. If we want their support for our plans we need to reshape our agenda to include their need for extra resource in the operations team. I will have a one-to-one with Sarah to check out her viewpoint. Perhaps you can speak to John.

Our next step should be to talk this through with the key players on the Executive Board and negotiate the necessary investment.

D: Announcement from MD

As you may know, consultants have been working with us to design our new objective-setting process, which is now complete. This will be rolled out from 1 May 2011 starting with senior managers and cascading to team members.

The instructions for objective setting are very clear. Answers to frequently asked questions will appear on the company website next week.

This should all be working smoothly by end of May 2011.

MODELS OF AND APPROACHES TO ORGANIZATIONAL CHANGE

Now that we have set the backdrop to organizational behaviour and our assumptions about how things really work, let us now examine ways of looking at organizational change as represented by the range of models and approaches developed by the key authors in this field. Table 3.2 links Gareth Morgan's organizational metaphors with the models of and approaches to change discussed below.

Table 3.2   Models of change and their associated metaphors

Model or approach	Machine	Political system	Organism	Flux and transformation
Lewin, three-step model	✓		✓	
Bullock and Batten, planned change	✓			
Kotter, eight steps	✓	✓	✓	
Beckhard and Harris, change formula			✓	
Nadler and Tushman, congruence model		✓	✓	
William Bridges, managing the transition	✓		✓	✓
Carnall, change management model		✓	✓	
Senge, systemic model		✓	✓	✓
Stacey and Shaw, complex responsive processes		✓		✓

Lewin, three-step model: *organism, machine*

Kurt Lewin (1951) developed his ideas about organizational change from the perspective of the organism metaphor. His model of organizational change is well known and much quoted by managers today. Lewin is responsible for introducing force field analysis, which examines the driving and resisting forces in any change situation (see Figure 3.1). The underlying principle is that driving forces must outweigh resisting forces in any situation if change is to happen.

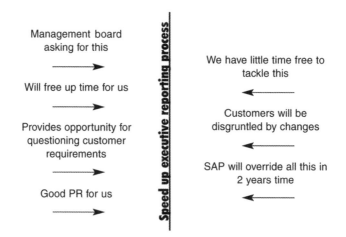

Figure 3.1   Lewin's force field analysis
Source: Lewin (1951)

Using the example illustrated in Figure 3.1, if the desire of a manager is to speed up the executive reporting process, then either the driving forces need to be augmented or the resisting forces decreased. Or even better, both of these must happen. This means, for example, ensuring that those responsible for making the changes to the executive reporting process are aware of how much time it will free up if they are successful, and what benefits this will have for them (augmenting driving force). It might also mean spending some time and effort managing customer expectations and supporting them in coping with the new process (reducing resisting force).

Lewin suggested a way of looking at the overall process of making changes. He proposed that organizational changes have three steps. The first step involves unfreezing the current state of affairs. This means defining the current state, surfacing the driving and resisting forces and picturing a desired end state. The second is about moving to a new state through participation and involvement. The third focuses on refreezing and stabilizing the new state of affairs by setting policy, rewarding success and establishing new standards. See Figure 3.2 for the key steps in this process.

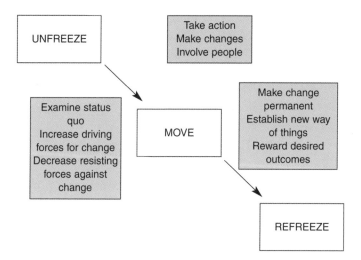

Figure 3.2 Lewin's three-step model
Source: Lewin (1951)

Lewin's three-step model uses the organism metaphor of organizations, which includes the notion of *homeostasis* (see box). This is the tendency of an organization to maintain its equilibrium in response to disrupting changes. This means that any organization has a natural tendency to adjust itself back to its original steady state. Lewin argued that a new state of equilibrium has to be intentionally moved towards, and then strongly established, so that a change will 'stick'.

Lewin's model was designed to enable a process consultant to take a group of people through the unfreeze, move and refreeze stages. For example, if a team of people began to see the need to radically alter their recruitment process, the consultant would work with the team to surface the issues, move to the desired new state and reinforce that new state.

HOMEOSTASIS IN ACTION

In the 1990s many organizations embarked on TQM (total quality management) initiatives that involved focusing on customer satisfaction (both internally and externally) and process improvement in all areas of the organization. An Economic Intelligence Unit report (Binney, 1992) indicated that two-thirds of these initiatives started well, but failed to keep the momentum going after 18 months. Focus groups were very active to start with, and suggestions from the front line came rolling in. After a while the focus groups stopped meeting and the suggestions dried up. Specific issues had been solved, but a new way of working had not emerged. Things reverted to the original state of affairs.

Our view

Lewin's ideas provide a useful tool for those considering organizational change. The force field analysis is an excellent way of enabling, for instance, a management team to discuss and agree on the driving and resisting forces that currently exist in any change situation. When this analysis is used in combination with a collaborative definition of the current state versus the desired end state, a team can quickly move to defining the next steps in the change process. These next steps are usually combinations of:

- communicating the gap between the current state and the end state to the key players in the change process;

- working to minimize the resisting forces;

- working to maximize or make the most of driving forces; and

- agreeing a change plan and a timeline for achieving the end state.

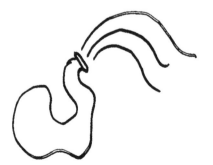

We have observed that this model is sometimes used by managers as a planning tool rather than as an organizational development process. The unfreeze becomes a planning session. The move translates to implementation. The refreeze is a post-implementation review. This approach ignores the fundamental assumption of the organism metaphor, which is that groups of people will change only if there is a 'felt need' to do so. The change process can then turn into an ill-thought-out plan that does not tackle resistance and fails to harness the energy of the key players. This is rather like the process of blowing up a balloon and forgetting to tie a knot in the end!

Bullock and Batten, planned change: _machine_

Bullock and Batten's (1985) phases of planned change draw on the disciplines of project management. There are many similar 'steps to changing your organization' models to choose from. We have chosen Bullock and Batten's:

- exploration;
- planning;
- action; and
- integration.

Exploration involves verifying the need for change, and acquiring any specific resources (such as expertise) necessary for the change to go ahead. Planning is an activity involving key decision makers and technical experts. A diagnosis is completed and actions are sequenced in a change plan. The plan is signed off by management before moving into the action phase. Actions are completed according to plan, with feedback mechanisms that allow some re-planning if things go off track. The final integration phase is started once the change plan has been fully actioned. Integration involves aligning the change with other areas in the organization, and formalizing them in some way via established mechanisms such as policies, rewards and company updates.

This particular approach implies the use of the machine metaphor of organizations. The model assumes that change can be defined and moved towards in a planned way. A project management approach simplifies the change process by isolating one part of the organizational machinery in order to make necessary changes, for example developing leadership skills in middle management, or reorganizing the sales team to give more engine power to key sales accounts.

Our view

This approach implies that the organizational change is a technical problem that can be solved with a definable technical solution. We have observed that this approach works well with isolated issues, but works less well when organizations are facing complex, unknowable change that may require those involved to discuss the current situation and possible futures at greater length before deciding on one approach.

For example, we worked with one organization recently which, on receiving a directive from the CEO to 'go global', immediately set up four tightly defined projects to address the issue of becoming a global organization. These were labelled 'global communication', 'global values', 'global leadership' and 'global balanced scorecard'. While on the surface this seems a sensible and structured approach, there was no upfront opportunity for people to build any awareness of current issues, or to talk and think more widely about what needed to change to support this directive. Predictably, the projects ran aground in the 'action' stage due to confusion about goals and dwindling motivation within the project teams.

Kotter, eight steps: *machine, political, organism*

Kotter's (1995) 'eight steps to transforming your organization' goes a little further than the basic machine metaphor. Kotter's eight-step model derives from analysis of his consulting practice with 100 different organizations going through change. His research highlighted eight key lessons, and he converted these into a useful eight-step model. The model addresses some of the power issues in making change happen, highlights the importance of a 'felt need' for change in the organization, and emphasizes the need to communicate the vision and keep communication levels extremely high throughout the process (see box).

KOTTER'S EIGHT-STEP MODEL

1 **Establish a sense of urgency.** *Discussing today's competitive realities, looking at potential future scenarios. Increasing the 'felt-need' for change.*

2 **Form a powerful guiding coalition.** *Assembling a powerful group of people who can work well together.*

3 **Create a vision.** *Building a vision to guide the change effort together with strategies for achieving this.*

4 **Communicate the vision.** *Kotter emphasizes the need to communicate at least 10 times the amount you expect to have to communicate. The vision and accompanying strategies and new behaviours need to*

be communicated in a variety of different ways. The guiding coalition should be the first to role model new behaviours.

5 **Empower others to act on the vision.** This step includes getting rid of obstacles to change such as unhelpful structures or systems. Allow people to experiment.

6 **Plan for and create short-term wins.** Look for and advertise short-term visible improvements. Plan these in and reward people publicly for improvements.

7 **Consolidate improvements and produce still more change.** Promote and reward those able to promote and work towards the vision. Energize the process of change with new projects, resources, change agents.

8 **Institutionalize new approaches.** Ensure that everyone understands that the new behaviours lead to corporate success.

Source: Kotter (1995)

Our view

This eight-step model is one that appeals to many managers with whom we have worked. However, what it appears to encourage is an early burst of energy, followed by delegation and distance. The eight steps do not really emphasize the need for managers to follow through with as much energy on Steps 7 and 8 as was necessary at the start. Kotter peaks early, using forceful concepts such as 'urgency', 'power' and 'vision'. Then after Step 5, words like 'plan', 'consolidate' and 'institutionalize' seem to imply a rather straightforward process that can be managed by others lower down the hierarchy. In our experience the change process is challenging, exciting and difficult all the way through.

When we work as change consultants, we use our own model of organizational change (see Figure 3.3), which is based on our experiences of change, but has close parallels with Kotter's eight steps. We prefer to model the change process as a continuous cycle rather than as a linear progression, and in our consultancy work we emphasize the importance of management attention through all phases of the process.

STOP AND THINK!

Q 3.4 Reflect on an organizational change in which you were involved. How much planning was done at the start? What contribution did this make to the success or otherwise of the change?

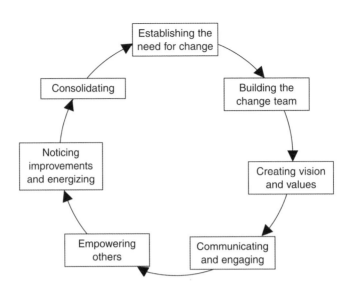

Figure 3.3   Cycle of change
Source: Cameron Change Consultancy Ltd

Beckhard and Harris, change formula: *organism*

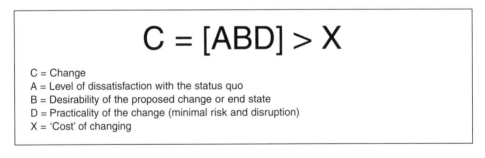

$$C = [ABD] > X$$

C = Change
A = Level of dissatisfaction with the status quo
B = Desirability of the proposed change or end state
D = Practicality of the change (minimal risk and disruption)
X = 'Cost' of changing

Figure 3.4   Beckhard's formula

Beckhard and Harris (1987) developed their change formula from some original work by Gleicher (1969). The change formula is a concise way of capturing the process of change and identifying the factors that need to be strongly in place for change to happen. Beckhard and Harris say:

> Factors A, B, and D must outweigh the perceived costs [X] for the change to occur. If any person or group whose commitment is needed is not sufficiently dissatisfied with the present state of affairs [A], eager to achieve the proposed end state [B] and convinced of the feasibility of the change [D], then the cost [X] of changing is too high, and that person will resist the change.

... resistance is normal and to be expected in any change effort. Resistance to change takes many forms; change managers need to analyze the type of resistance in order to work with it, reduce it, and secure the need for commitment from the resistant party.

The formula is sometimes written $(A \times B \times D) > X$. This adds something useful to the original formula. The multiplication implies that if any one factor is zero or near zero, the product will also be zero or near zero and the resistance to change will not be overcome. This means that if the vision is not clear, or dissatisfaction with the current state is not felt, or the plan is obscure, the likelihood of change is severely reduced. These factors (A, B, D) do not compensate for each other if one is low. All factors need to have weight.

This model comes from the organism metaphor of organizations, although it has been adopted by those working with a planned change approach to target management effort. Beckhard and Harris emphasized the need to design interventions that allow these three factors to surface in the organization.

Our view

This change formula is deceptively simple but extremely useful. It can be brought into play at any point in a change process to analyse how things are going. When the formula is shared with all parties involved in the change, it helps to illuminate what various parties need to do to make progress. This can highlight several of the following problem areas:

- staff are not experiencing dissatisfaction with the status quo;

- the proposed end state has not been clearly communicated to key people;

- the proposed end state is not desirable to the change implementers;

- the tasks being given to those implementing the change are too complicated or ill-defined.

We have noticed that depending on the metaphor in use, distinct differences in approach result from using this formula as a starting point. For instance, one public sector organization successfully used this formula to inform a highly consultative approach to organizational change. The vision was built and shared at a large-scale event involving hundreds of people. Dissatisfaction was captured using an employee survey that was fed back to everyone in the organization and discussed at team meetings. Teams were asked to work locally on using the employee feedback and commonly created vision to define their own first steps.

In contrast, a FTSE 100 company based in the UK used the formula as a basis for boosting its change management capability via a highly rated change management programme. Gaps in skills were defined and training workshops were run for the key managers in every significant project team around the company. Three areas of improvement were targeted:

1 **Vision:** project managers were encouraged to build and communicate clearer, more compelling project goals.

2 **Dissatisfaction:** this was translated into two elements – clear rationale and a felt sense of urgency. Project managers were encouraged to improve their ability to communicate a clear rationale for making changes. They were also advised to set clear deadlines and stick to them, and to visibly resource important initiatives, to increase the 'felt need' for change.

3 **Practical first steps:** project managers were advised to define their plans for change early in the process and to communicate these in a variety of ways, to improve the level of buy-in from implementers and stakeholders.

Nadler and Tushman, congruence model: *political, organism*

Nadler and Tushman's congruence model takes a different approach to looking at the factors influencing the success of the change process (Nadler and Tushman, 1997). This model aims to help us understand the dynamics of what happens in an organization when we try to change it.

This model is based on the belief that organizations can be viewed as sets of interacting sub-systems that scan and sense changes in the external environment. This model sits firmly in the open systems school of thought, which uses the organism metaphor to understand organizational behaviour. However, the political backdrop is not ignored; it appears as one of the sub-systems (informal organization – see below).

This model views the organization as a system that draws inputs from both internal and external sources (strategy, resources and environment) and transforms them into outputs (activities, behaviour and performance of the system at three levels: individual, group and total). The heart of the model is the opportunity it offers to analyse the transformation process in a way that does not give prescriptive answers, but instead stimulates

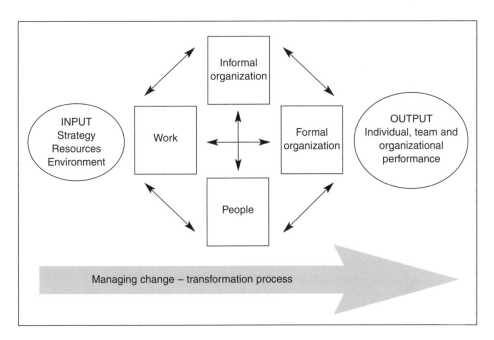

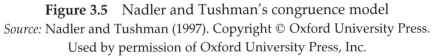

Figure 3.5 Nadler and Tushman's congruence model
Source: Nadler and Tushman (1997). Copyright © Oxford University Press.
Used by permission of Oxford University Press, Inc.

thoughts on what needs to happen in a specific organizational context. David Nadler writes: 'it's important to view the congruence model as a tool for organizing your thinking... rather than as a rigid template to dissect, classify and compartmentalize what you observe. It's a way of making sense out of a constantly changing kaleidoscope of information and impressions.'

The model draws on the sociotechnical view of organizations that looks at managerial, strategic, technical and social aspects of organizations, emphasizing the assumption that everything relies on everything else. This means that the different elements of the total system have to be aligned to achieve high performance as a whole system; so the higher the congruence the higher the performance.

In this model of the transformation process, the organization is composed of four components, or sub-systems, which are all dependent on each other. These are:

1   **The work.** This is the actual day-to-day activities carried out by individuals. Process design, pressures on the individual and available rewards must all be considered under this element.

2   **The people.** This is about the skills and characteristics of the people who work in an organization. What are their expectations, what are their backgrounds?

3   **The formal organization.** This refers to the structure, systems and policies in place. How are things formally organized?

4   **The informal organization.** This consists of all the unplanned, unwritten activities that emerge over time such as power, influence, values and norms.

This model proposes that effective management of change means attending to all four components, not just one or two components. Imagine

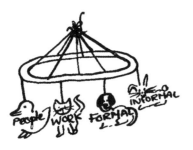

tugging only one part of a child's mobile. The whole mobile wobbles and oscillates for a bit, but eventually all the different components settle down to where they were originally. So it is with organizations. They easily revert to the original mode of operation unless you attend to all four components.

For example, if you change one component, such as the type of work done in an organization, you need to attend to the other three components too. The following questions pinpoint the other three components that may need to be aligned:

• How does the work now align with individual skills? (The people.)

• How does a change in the task line up with the way work is organized right now? (The formal organization.)

• What informal activities and areas of influence could be affected by this change in the task? (The informal organization.)

If alignment work is not done, organizational 'homeostasis' (see earlier in this chapter) will result in a return to the old equilibrium and change will fizzle out. The fizzling out results from forces that arise in the system as a direct result of lack of congruence. When a lack of congruence occurs, energy builds in the system in the form of resistance, control and power:

• Resistance comes from a fear of the unknown or a need for things to remain stable. A change imposed from the outside can be unsettling for individuals. It decreases their sense of independence. Resistance

Ending

Before you can begin something new, you have to end what used to be. You need to identify who is losing what, expect a reaction and acknowledge the losses openly. Repeat information about what is changing – it will take time to sink in. Mark the endings.

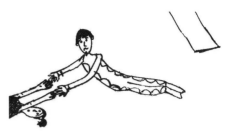

Neutral zone

In the neutral zone, people feel disoriented. Motivation falls and anxiety rises. Consensus may break down as attitudes become polarized. It can also be quite a creative time. The manager's job is to ensure that people recognize the neutral zone and treat it as part of the process. Temporary structures may be needed – possibly task forces and smaller teams. The manager needs to find a way of taking the pulse of the organization on a regular basis.

William Bridges suggested that we could learn from Moses and his time in the wilderness to really gain an understanding of how to manage people during the neutral zone.

MOSES AND THE NEUTRAL ZONE

- **Magnify the plagues.** *Increase the felt need for change.*
- **Mark the ending.** *Make sure people are not hanging on to too much of the past.*
- **Deal with the murmuring.** *Don't ignore people when they complain; it might be significant.*
- **Give people access to the decision makers.** *Two-way communication with the top is vital.*
- **Capitalize on the creative opportunity provided by the wilderness.** *The neutral zone provides a difference that allows for creative thinking and acting.*
- **Resist the urge to rush ahead.** *You can slow things down a little.*
- **Understand the neutral zone leadership is special.** *This is not a normal time. Normal rules do not apply.*

Source: Bridges and Mitchell (2002)

New beginning

Beginnings should be nurtured carefully. They cannot be planned and predicted, but they can be encouraged, supported and reinforced. Bridges suggests that people need four key elements to help them make a new beginning:

1   the *purpose* behind the change;

2   a *picture* of how this new organization will look and feel;

3   a step by step *plan* to get there;

4   a *part to play* in the outcome.

The beginning is reached when people feel they can make the emotional commitment to doing something in a new way. Bridges makes the point that the neutral zone is longer and the endings are more protracted for those further down the management hierarchy. This can lead to impatience from managers who have emotionally stepped into a new beginning, while their people appear to lag behind, seemingly stuck in an ending (see box).

IMPATIENT FOR ENDINGS?

As part of the management team, I knew about the merger very early, so by the time we announced it to the rest of the company, we were ready to fly with the task ahead.

What was surprising, and annoying, was the slow speed with which everyone else caught up. My direct reports were asking detailed questions about their job specifications and exactly how it was all going to work when we had fully merged. Of course I couldn't answer any of these questions. I was really irritated by this.

The CEO had to have a long, intensive heart-to-heart with the whole team explaining what was going on and how much we knew about the future state of the organization before we could really get moving.

Our view

This phased model is particularly useful when organizations are faced with inevitable changes such as closure of a site, redundancy, acquisition or merger. The endings and new beginnings are real tangible events in these situations, and the neutral zone important, though uncomfortable. It is more difficult to use the model for anticipatory change or home-grown change where the endings and beginning are more fluid and therefore harder to discern.

We use this model when working with organizations embarking on mergers, acquisitions and significant partnership agreements. In particular, the model encourages everyone involved to get a sense of where they are in the process of transition. The image of the trapeze artist is often appreciated as it creates the feeling of leaping into the unknown, and trusting in a future that cannot be grasped fully. This is a scary process.

The other important message Bridges communicates well is that those close to the changes (managers and team leaders) may experience difficulty when they have reached a new beginning and their people are still working on an ending. This is one of the great frustrations of this type of change process, and we counsel managers to:

- recognize what is happening;

- assertively tell staff what will happen while acknowledging their feelings;

- be prepared to answer questions about the future again and again and again;

- say you don't know, if you don't know;

- expect the neutral zone to last a while and give it a positive name such as 'setting our sights' or 'moving in' or 'getting to know you'.

Carnall, change management model: _political, organism_

Colin Carnall (1990) has produced a useful model that brings together a number of perspectives on change. He says that the effective management of change depends on the level of management skill in the following areas:

- managing transitions effectively;

- dealing with organizational cultures;

- managing organizational politics.

A manager who is skilled in _managing transitions_ is able to help people to learn as they change and create an atmosphere of openness and risk taking.

A manager who *deals with organizational cultures* examines the current organizational culture and starts to develop what Carnall calls 'a more adaptable culture'. This means, for example, developing better information flow, more openness and greater local autonomy.

A manager who is able to *manage organizational politics* can understand and recognize different factions and different agendas. He or she develops skills in utilizing and recognizing various political tactics such as building coalitions, using outside experts and controlling the agenda.

Carnall (see Figure 3.7) makes the point that 'only by synthesizing the management of transition, dealing with organizational cultures and handling organizational politics constructively, can we create the environment in which creativity, risk taking and the rebuilding of self-esteem and performance can be achieved'.

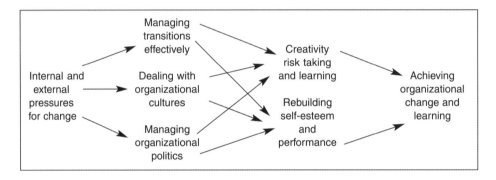

Figure 3.7 Carnall: managing transitions
Source: Carnall (1990). Printed with permission of Pearson Education Ltd.

Our view

Carnall's model obviously focuses on the role of the manager during a change process, rather than illuminating the process of change. It provides a useful checklist for management attention, and has strong parallels with William Bridges' ideas of endings, transitions and beginnings.

STOP AND THINK!

Q 3.5 Compare the Nadler and Tushman congruence model with William Bridges' ideas on managing transitions. How are these ideas the same? How are they different?

Senge *et al*: systemic model: *political, organism, flux and transformation*

 If you are interested in sustainable change, then the ideas and concepts in Senge *et al* (1999) will be of interest to you. This excellent book, *The Dance of Change*, seeks to help 'those who care deeply about building new types of organizations' to understand the challenges ahead.

Senge *et al* observe that many change initiatives fail to achieve hoped-for results. They reflect on why this might be so, commenting, 'To understand why sustaining significant change is so elusive, we need to think less like managers and more like biologists.' Senge *et al* talk about the myriad of 'balancing processes' or forces of homeostasis that act to preserve the status quo in any organization.

HOMEOSTASIS IN ACTION

We wanted to move to a matrix structure for managing projects. There was significant investment of time and effort in this initiative as we anticipated pay-off in terms of utilization of staff and ability to meet project deadlines. This approach would allow staff to be freed up when they were not fully utilized, so that they could work on a variety of projects.

Consultants worked with us to design the new structure. Job specs were rewritten. People understood their new roles. For a couple of months, it seemed to be working. But after four months, we discovered that the project managers were just carrying on working in the old way, as if they still owned the technical staff. They would even lie about utilization, just to stop other project managers from getting hold of their people.

I don't think we have moved on very much at all.

Business Unit Manager, Research Projects Department

Senge *et al* say:

> Most serious change initiatives eventually come up against issues embedded in our prevailing system of management. These include managers' commitment to change as long as it doesn't affect them; 'undiscussable' topics that feel risky to talk about; and the ingrained habit of attacking symptoms and ignoring deeper systemic causes of problems.

Their guidelines are:

- start small;

- grow steadily;

- don't plan the whole thing;

- expect challenges – it will not go smoothly!

Senge *et al* use the principles of environmental systems to illustrate how organizations operate and to enhance our understanding of what forces are at play. Senge says in his book, *The Fifth Discipline* (1993):

> Business and other human endeavours are also systems. They too are bound by invisible fabrics of interrelated actions, which often take years to fully play out their effects on each other. Since we are part of that lacework ourselves, it's doubly hard to see the whole patterns of change. Instead we tend to focus on snapshots of isolated parts of the systems, and wonder why our deepest problems never seem to get solved.

The approach taken by Senge *et al* is noticeably different from much of the other work on change, which focuses on the early stages such as creating a vision, planning, finding energy to move forward and deciding on first steps. They look at the longer-term issues of sustaining and renewing organizational change. They examine the challenges of first initiating, second sustaining and third redesigning and rethinking change. The book does not give formulaic solutions, or 'how to' approaches, but rather gives ideas and suggestions for dealing with the balancing forces of equilibrium in organizational systems (resistance).

What are the balancing forces that those involved in change need to look out for? Senge *et al* say that the key challenges of initiating change are the balancing forces that arise when any group of people starts to do things differently:

- 'We don't have time for this stuff!' People working on change initiatives will need extra time outside of the day-to-day to devote to change efforts, otherwise there will be push back.

- 'We have no help!' There will be new skills and mindsets to develop. People will need coaching and support to develop new capabilities.

- 'This stuff isn't relevant!' Unless people are convinced of the need for effort to be invested, it will not happen.

- 'They're not walking the talk!' People look for reinforcement of the new values or new behaviours from management. If this is not in place, there will be resistance to progress.

They go on to say that the challenges of sustaining change come to the fore when the pilot group (those who start the change) becomes successful and the change begins to touch the rest of the organization:

- 'This stuff is _____!' This challenge concerns the discomfort felt by individuals when they feel exposed or fearful about changes. This may be expressed in a number of different ways such as, 'This stuff is taking our eye off the ball' or, 'This stuff is more trouble than it's worth.'

- 'This stuff isn't working!' People outside the pilot group, and some of those within it, may be impatient for positive results. Traditional ways of measuring success do not always apply, and may end up giving a skewed view of progress.

- 'We have the right way!'/'They don't understand us!' The pilot group members become evangelists for the change, setting up a reaction from the 'outsiders'.

The challenges of redesigning and rethinking change appear when the change achieves some visible measure of success and starts to impact on ingrained organizational habits:

- 'Who's in charge of this stuff?' This challenge is about the conflicts that can arise between successful pilot groups, who start to want to do more, and those who see themselves as the governing body of the organization.

- 'We keep reinventing the wheel!' The challenge of spreading knowledge of new ideas and processes around the organization is a tough one. People who are distant from the changes may not receive good quality information about what is going on.

- 'Where are we going and what are we here for?' Senge says: 'engaging people around deep questions of purpose and strategy is fraught with challenges because it opens the door to a traditionally closed inner sanctum of top management'.

Our view

We like the ideas of Senge *et al* very much. They are thought-provoking and highly perceptive. If we can persuade clients to read their book, we will. However, in the current climate of time pressure and the need for fast results, these ideas are often a bitter pill for managers struggling to make change happen despite massive odds.

Whenever possible we encourage clients to be realistic in their quest for change, and to notice and protect areas where examples of the right sort of behaviours already exist. The messages we carry with us resulting from Senge *et al*'s thoughts are:

- consider running a pilot for any large-scale organizational change;

- keep your change process goals realistic, especially when it comes to timescales and securing resources;

- understand your role in staying close to change efforts beyond the kick-off;

- recognize and reward activities that are already going the right way;

- be as open as you can about the purpose and mission of your enterprise.

There are no standard 'one size fits all' answers in the book, but plenty of thought-provoking ideas and suggestions, and a thoroughly inspirational reframing of traditional ways of looking at change. However, those interested in rapid large-scale organizational change are unlikely to find any reassurance or support in Senge *et al*'s book. The advice is, start small.

STOP AND THINK!

Q 3.6 Reflect on an organizational change in which you were involved that failed to achieve hoped-for results. What were the balancing forces that acted against the change? Use Senge *et al*'s ideas to prompt your thinking.

Stacey and Shaw, complex responsive processes: *political, flux and transformation*

There is yet another school of thought represented by people such as Ralph Stacey (2001) and Patricia Shaw (2002). These writers use the metaphor of flux and transformation to view organizations. The implications of this mode of thinking for those interested in managing and enabling change are significant:

- Change, or a new order of things, will emerge naturally from clean communication, conflict and tension (not too much).

- As a manager, you are not outside of the system, controlling it, or planning to alter it: you are part of the whole environment.

In Patricia Shaw's book _Changing Conversations in Organizations_, rather than address the traditional question of 'How do we manage change?' she addresses the question: 'How do we participate in the ways things change over time?' This writing deals bravely with the paradox that 'our interaction, no matter how considered or passionate, is always evolving in ways that we cannot control or predict in the longer term, no matter how sophisticated our planning tools'.

Our view

This can be disturbing stuff, and a paradox that sets up some anxiety in managers and consultants who are disquieted by the suggestion that our intellectual strivings to collectively diagnose problems and design futures may be missing the point. Shaw says: 'I want to help us appreciate ourselves as fellow improvisers in ensemble work, constantly constructing the future and our part in it.' Stacey says of traditional views of organizations as systems: 'This is not to say that systems thinking has no use at all. It clearly does if one is trying to understand, and even more, trying to design interactions of a repetitive kind to achieve kinds of performance that are known in advance.'

Ralph Stacey and Patricia Shaw have both written about complexity and change. Managers, and particularly consultants, often find this difficult reading because on first viewing it appears to take away the rational powers we have traditionally endowed upon our managers, change agents and consultants. Patricia Shaw says of the traditional view of the process consultant:

> I would say that [the] ideal of the reflective practitioner [who can surface subconscious needs so that groups of people can consciously create a directed form of change] is the one that mostly continues to grip our imaginations and shape our aspirations to be effective and competent individual practitioners engaged in lifelong learning. Instead, I have been asking what happens when spontaneity, unpredictability and our capacity to be surprised by ourselves are not explained away but kept at the very heart [of our work].

In contrast, those working in hugely complex environments such as the health sector or government have told us that they find the ideas in this area to be a tremendous relief. The notion that change cannot be managed reflects their own experiences of trying to manage change; the overwhelming feeling they have of constantly trying to push heavy weights uphill.

But how can managers and consultants use these ideas in real situations? We have distilled some ground rules for those working with complex change processes, although the literature we have researched studiously avoids any type of prescription for action.

In complex change, the leader's role is to:

- decide what business the organization is in, and stretch people's thinking on how to get there;

- ensure that there is a high level of connectivity between different parts of the organization, encouraging feedback, optimizing information flow, enabling learning;

- focus people's attention on important differences: between current and desired performance, between styles of working, between past and present results.

(See Chapters 10 and 11 for more insights and tips in the areas of complex change and leading through uncertainty.)

SUMMARY AND CONCLUSIONS

- It is useful to understand our own assumptions about managing change, in order to challenge them and examine the possibilities offered by different assumptions. It is useful to compare our own assumptions with the assumptions of others with whom we work. This increased understanding can often reduce frustration.

- Gareth Morgan's work on organizational metaphors provides a useful way of looking at the range of assumptions that exist about how organizations work.

- The four most commonly used organizational metaphors are:
    - the machine metaphor;
    - the political metaphor;

- the organism metaphor;
- the flux and transformation metaphor.

- The machine metaphor is deeply ingrained in our ideas about how organizations run, so it tends to inform many of the well-known approaches to organizational change, particularly project management and planning-oriented approaches.

- Models of organizations as open, interconnected, interdependent sub-systems sit within the organism metaphor. This model is very prevalent in the human resource world, as it underpins much of the thinking that drove the creation of the HR function in organizations. The organism metaphor views change as a process of adapting to changes in the environment. The focus is on designing interventions to decrease resistance to change and increase the forces for change.

- The political map of organizational life is recognized by many of the key writers on organizational change as highly significant.

- The metaphor of flux and transformation appears to model the true complexity of how change really happens. If we use this lens to view organizational life it does not lead to neat formulae, or concise how-to approaches. There is less certainty to inform our actions. This can be on the one hand a great relief, and on the other quite frustrating.

- There are many approaches to managing and understanding change to choose from, none of which appears to tell the whole story, but most of which are convincing up to a point. See Table 3.3 for a summary of our conclusions for each model.

Table 3.3 Our conclusions about each model of change

Model	Conclusions
Lewin, three-step model	Lewin's ideas are valuable when analysing the change process at the start of an initiative. His force-field analysis and current state/end state discussions are extremely useful tools. However, the model loses its worth when it is confused with the mechanistic approach, and the three steps become 'plan, implement, review'.
Bullock and Batten, planned change	The planned change approach is good for tackling isolated, less complex issues. It is not good when used to over-simplify organizational changes, as it ignores resistance and overlooks interdependencies between business units or sub-systems.

Table 3.3 *continued*

Model	Conclusions
Kotter, eight steps	Kotter's eight steps are an excellent starting point for those interested in making large or small-scale organizational change. The model places most emphasis on getting the early steps right: building coalition and setting the vision rather than later steps of empowerment and consolidation. Change is seen as linear rather than cyclical, which implies that a pre-designed aim can be reached rather than iterated towards.
Beckhard and Harris, change formula	The change formula is simple but highly effective. It can be used at any point in the change process to analyse what is going on. It is useful for sharing with the whole team to illuminate barriers to change.
Nadler and Tushman, congruence model	The congruence model provides a memorable checklist for the change process, although we think the seven 'S' model gives a more rounded approach to the same problem of examining interdependent organizational sub-systems. Both are also useful for doing a post-change analysis of what went wrong! Both encourage a problem focus rather than enabling a vision-setting process.
William Bridges, managing the transition	Bridges' model of endings, neutral zone and beginnings is good for tackling inevitable changes such as redundancy, merger or acquisition. It is less good for understanding change grown from within, where endings and beginnings are less distinct.
Carnall, change management model	Carnall's model combines a number of key elements of organizational change together in a neat process. Useful checklist.
Senge, systemic model	Senge challenges the notion of top-down, large-scale organizational change. He provides a hefty dose of realism for those facing organizational change: start small, grow steadily, don't plan the whole thing. However, this advice is hard to follow in today's climate of fast pace, quick results and maximum effectiveness.
Stacey and Shaw, complex responsive processes	The complex responsive process school of thought is new, exciting and challenging; however it is not for the faint-hearted. There are no easy solutions (if any at all), the leader's role is hard to distinguish and the literature on the subject tends to be almost completely non-prescriptive.

- To be an effective manager or consultant we need to be able flexibly to select appropriate models and approaches for particular situations. See the illustrations of different approaches in Part Two.

STOP AND THINK!

Q 3.7   Which model of organizational change would help you to move forward with each of the following changes:

- Combining two well-respected universities to form one excellent seat of learning.

- Turning the Boston Philharmonic Orchestra into the Boston Improvisational Jazz Band.

- Evolving a group of mature MBA students into a networked organization of management consultants.

Q 3.8   A fast food organization introduced a set of values recently which were well communicated and enthusiastically welcomed. The senior management team publicly endorsed the values and said: 'This is where we want to be in 12 months' time so that we are ready for industry consolidation. You will all be measured on achieving these values in your day-to-day work.'

The values were put together by a consultancy, which put a great deal of effort into interviewing a broad range of people in the organization. People at all levels liked the look of the values, but the situation three months later is that activity and conversations on the values are diminishing. A lot of people are saying: 'We are doing this already.' There is still some enthusiasm, but people are now getting scared that they will fall short of the values somehow, and are starting to resent them.

What needs to happen now?

Q 3.9   If Stacey and Shaw have 'got it right' with their ideas about how change emerges naturally, does that make books such as this one redundant? Answers on a postcard!

4

Leading change

INTRODUCTION

In this chapter we look at the leader's role in the change process. The objectives of the chapter are to:

- enable leaders of change to explore the different roles they and their colleagues need to play in a change process;

- explore the range of skills and qualities that leaders need to ensure success;

- identify how leaders of change can adapt their style and focus to the different phases of the change process;

- emphasize the importance of self-knowledge and inner resources in any leadership role.

The chapter is divided into six sections:

1   visionary leadership;

2   roles that leaders play;

3 leadership styles, qualities and skills;

4 different leadership for different phases of change;

5 the importance of self-knowledge and inner resources; and

6 summary and conclusions.

It is important to first make the point that good leadership is well-rounded leadership. We believe that all four metaphors of organizations give rise to useful notions of leadership. Leaders go wrong when they become stuck in one metaphor, or in one way of doing things, and therefore appear one-dimensional in their range of styles and approaches.

To begin, we link leadership to the ideas presented in Chapter 3 on organizational change by looking at the type of leadership that follows from approaching organizational change using each of the four key metaphors (see Table 4.1):

1 the machine metaphor;

2 the political system metaphor;

3 the organism metaphor; and

4 the flux and transformation metaphor.

Table 4.1 illustrates that the use of each metaphor brings both advantages and disadvantages for those wishing to be successful leaders of change.

The machine metaphor draws attention to clear goals and the need for structure, but overuse of this metaphor results in micromanagement of

Table 4.1 Leadership linked to organizational metaphors

Metaphor	Nature of change	Leader's role	Type of leadership required	Typical pitfalls for the leader
Machine	The designed end state can be worked towards. Resistance must be managed. Change needs to be planned and controlled.	Chief designer and implementer of the changes.	Project management. Goal setting. Monitoring and controlling.	Micro-management by leader means activity focuses on measuring, rather than experimenting or taking risks.

Table 4.1 *continued*

Metaphor	Nature of change	Leader's role	Type of leadership required	Typical pitfalls for the leader
Political system	Changes must be supported by a powerful person. Change needs a powerful coalition behind it. Winners and losers are important.	Politician – powerful speaker and behind the scenes negotiator.	Visionary. Building a powerful coalition. Connecting agendas.	Change leaders are seen as Machiavellian manipulators. Leaders cannot be trusted, so people comply rather than commit. People do the minimum. Leaders begin to follow their own agenda (cover their backs), rather than some higher purpose.
Organism	Change is adaptive. Individuals and groups need to be psychologically aware of the 'felt need' for change. End state can be defined and worked towards.	Coach, counsellor and consultant, holding up the mirror.	Coaching and supporting.	The metaphor becomes an ideology. The change process becomes self-serving and achieves very little. There is a focus on reacting rather than initiating. Change happens, but too little too late.
Flux and transformation	Change cannot be managed, it emerges. Managers are part of the system, not outside the system. Conflict is useful. Managers enable good connections between people.	Facilitator of emergent change.	Getting the governing principles right. Enabling connectivity. Amplifying issues.	Leaders and others involved become confused and frustrated. There is chaos. The change effort becomes vague and directionless. There is no sense of progress to motivate future effort. Contradictions become sticking points.

outcomes and too little risk taking. The political system metaphor adds the harsh reality of organizational life, and reminds us of the necessity of involving influential people when change is desired, but overuse can be seen as manipulation. The organism metaphor highlights the need for people to be involved, and to feel the need for change, but runs the risk of moving too slowly and too late. Finally, the flux and transformation model is useful as a reminder that organizations and their people cannot be wholly controlled unless we rule by fear! Leaders must encourage discussion of conflicts and tensions to enable change to emerge, while avoiding the trap of being too vague and lacking direction.

We believe that successful change leadership is achieved by combining aspects of all four metaphors. This is evidenced by the models and approaches introduced in Chapter 3, Table 3.2, which combine different metaphors to some degree.

COMBINING THE METAPHORS: REFLECTIVE COACHING SESSION

Once I realized that my boss was using a completely different organizational metaphor from myself, I began to see how we were clashing in our discussions about how to run projects and how to improve processes.

I prefer the machine metaphor. I like things to be pretty clear. In my area we have a well-defined structure with clear roles and objectives set for each person. The team runs like a well-oiled machine, with me in the engine room pulling levers and thinking about plans and processes.

On the other hand, my boss prefers a more fluid style of working. Objectives are flexible and revised daily, and the hierarchy means very little to him. If someone shows initiative and promise, he will go directly to that person and have a quite intense conversation to convey the importance of a particular initiative. It used to drive me crazy. I couldn't keep control.

One day we had a chat about this using metaphor to discuss our differences. It was most illuminating, and we started to see the pros and cons of each approach. As a result I agreed to incorporate more flexibility in certain projects, and he agreed to stick with the plan rather than review and change other, more stable processes. We still clash from time to time, but it doesn't cause quite so much irritation!

Global Services Manager, Oil Company – on use of metaphor to enhance understanding of other people's viewpoints

Table 4.1 is also useful because it reveals a wide range of styles and skills required of leaders, depending on the metaphor in use:

- goal setting;
- monitoring and controlling;
- coaching and supporting;
- building vision;
- communicating vision;
- building coalitions;
- networking;
- negotiating;
- facilitating;
- dealing with conflict.

The difficulty with a list of skills this long is that is seems unattainable. In this chapter we try to help leaders to find a way through the various requirements of a leader to pinpoint the most important roles, skills, styles and areas of focus needed to make change happen.

VISIONARY LEADERSHIP

The first basic ingredient of leadership is a guiding vision. The leader has a clear idea of what he wants to do – professionally and personally – and the strength to persist in the face of setbacks, even failures. Unless you know where you are going, and why, you cannot possibly get there.

Warren Bennis (1994)

Visionary leadership has become something of a holy grail. It seems to be a rare commodity which is greatly sought after. Our recent research (see box) indicates that today's business leaders place considerable value on visionary leadership as a tool for organizational change. But is visionary leadership really the answer?

In our change leadership sessions with private sector senior and middle managers in the UK we ask people to name significant leaders of change. The top four names mentioned over the period 1997–2002 were:

1 Winston Churchill;

2 Margaret Thatcher;

3 Nelson Mandela;

4 Adolf Hitler.

The top five characteristics that emerged through a typical discussion of these significant leaders were:

1 clear vision;

2 determination;

3 great speaker, great presence;

4 tough when needed; and

5 able to stand alone.

Cameron Change Consultancy data, 2002

Here we explore the views of the supporters of visionary leadership, and those who make the case against it.

Bennis on the characteristics of visionary leaders

Warren Bennis identified three basic ingredients of leadership:

1   a guiding vision;

2   passion; and

3   integrity.

He also developed a useful comparison of the differences between management and leadership (see Table 4.2), which unpacks some of the different qualities of a visionary leader.

This comparison exercise separates management from leadership in a very clear way. This is useful for those wishing to take on more of a leadership role, although it is sometimes interpreted as slightly downplaying the important role of a good manager in organizational life. Most managers have to do both roles.

Table 4.2 Managers and leaders

A manager	A leader
Administers	Innovates
Is a copy	Is an original
Maintains	Develops
Focuses on systems and structure	Focuses on people
Relies on control	Inspires trust
Has a short-range view	Has a long-range perspective
Asks how and when	Asks why
Has his eye on the bottom line	Has his eye on the horizon
Imitates	Originates
Accepts the status quo	Challenges the status quo
Classic good soldier	His own person
Does things right	Does the right thing

Source: Bennis (1994)

Kotter on what leaders really do

Kotter (1996) echoes the ideas of Bennis. He says: 'we have raised a generation of very talented people to be managers, not leader/managers, and vision is not a component of effective management. The management equivalent to vision creation is planning.' He says that leaders are different from managers: 'They don't make plans; they don't solve problems; they don't even organize people. What leaders really do is prepare organizations for change and help them cope as they struggle through it.' He identifies three areas of focus for leaders and contrasts these with the typical focus of a manager:

1   setting direction versus planning and budgeting;

2   aligning people versus organizing and staffing; and

3   motivating people versus controlling and problem solving.

VISIONARY LEADERSHIP

We go to liberate, not to conquer.
We will not fly our flags in their country.
We are entering Iraq to free a people and the only flag which will be flown in that ancient land is their own.
Show respect for them.

There are some who are alive at this moment who will not be alive shortly.
Those who do not wish to go on that journey, we will not send.
As for the others, I expect you to rock their world.
Wipe them out if that is what they choose.
But if you are ferocious in battle remember to be magnanimous in victory.
Iraq is steeped in history.
It is the site of the Garden of Eden, of the Great Flood and the birthplace of Abraham.
Tread lightly there.

You will see things that no man could pay to see
– and you will have to go a long way to find a more decent, generous and upright people than the Iraqis.
You will be embarrassed by their hospitality even though they have nothing.

Don't treat them as refugees for they are in their own country.
Their children will be poor; in years to come they will know that the light of liberation in their lives was brought by you.

Extract from speech widely hailed in the UK press at the time as visionary. It was given by Lieutenant Colonel Tim Collins to around 800 men of the battle group of the 1st Battalion of the Royal Irish Regiment, at their Fort Blair Mayne camp in the Kuwaiti desert about 20 miles from the Iraqi border on Wednesday 19 March 2003. His intention was to prepare the men for the battle that lay ahead. Many of the men were young and the support from people back in the UK was patchy.

Since 2003 Tim Collins has had cause to reflect on his celebrated visionary call to action. He says he made assumptions about the motives at higher levels of the army and government, and is quoted as saying:

> What I had not realized is that there was no plan at the higher levels to replace anything, indeed a simplistic and unimaginative overreliance in some quarters on the power of destruction and crude military might... If freedom and a chance to live a dignified and stable life free from terror was the motive, then I can think of more than 170 families in Iraq last week who would have settled for what they had under Saddam.
>
> *The Observer*, 18 September 2005

I HAVE A DREAM

I have a dream that one day this nation will rise up and live out the true meaning of its creed: 'We hold these truths to be self-evident: that all men are created equal.' I have a dream that one day on the red hills of Georgia the sons of former slaves and the sons of former slave owners will be able to sit down together at the table of brotherhood.

I have a dream that one day even the state of Mississippi, a state sweltering with the heat of injustice, sweltering with the heat of oppression, will be trans-formed into an oasis of freedom and justice.

I have a dream that my four little children will one day live in a nation where they will not be judged by the color of their skin but by the content of their character.

I have a dream today.

I have a dream that one day, down in Alabama, with its vicious racists, with its governor having his lips dripping with the words of interposition and nullifi-cation; one day right there in Alabama, little black boys and black girls will be able to join hands with little white boys and white girls as sisters and brothers.

I have a dream today.

I have a dream that one day every valley shall be exalted, every hill and moun-tain shall be made low, the rough places will be made plain, and the crooked places will be made straight, and the glory of the Lord shall be revealed, and all flesh shall see it together. This is our hope. This is the faith that I go back to the South with. With this faith we will be able to hew out of the mountain of despair a stone of hope. With this faith we will be able to transform the jangling discords of our nation into a beautiful symphony of brotherhood. With this faith we will be able to work together, to pray together, to struggle together, to go to jail together, to stand up for freedom together, knowing that we will be free one day.

Extract from speech by Martin Luther King, Jr. He was a driving force in the non-violent push for racial equality in the 1950s and the 1960s. This speech was given on 28 August 1963, on the steps of the Lincoln Memorial. It mobilized supporters and acted as the catalyst for the 1964 Civil Rights Act.

Bass: proof that visionary leadership works!

Bass (in Bryman, 1992) developed the notion of transformation leader-ship, which many managers find meaningful and helpful. He distin-guished between transactional leadership and transformational leadership (see box), and identified through extensive research that charismatic and inspirational leadership were the components most likely to be associated with leadership success.

Gardner: the need for leaders to embody a story

Howard Gardner's (1996) influential research into the nature of successful leaders gave rise to some interesting lessons about visionary leadership. He chose 11 20th-century leaders who have really made a difference, and researched their lives and their work by reading their biographies and tracking down any speeches, letters, audiotapes and videotapes that were available.

He chose a mixture of different types of leader, combining business leaders, political leaders and those who influenced our thinking and behaviours without being in a position to lead directly. The list included, among others, Alfred Sloan, head of General Motors, Pope John XXIII, one of the most influential and popular popes of modern times, Martin Luther King, the advocate of African

Americans, and Margaret Mead, a cultural anthropologist who deeply influenced our ideas about childhood, family life and society. (There have been attempts made to discredit her research, but she is still supported by many as being highly innovative and influential.)

Gardner's findings indicated that those leaders who had really made a difference to the way others thought, felt and acted all appeared to have a central story or message. Stories not only provide background but also help the followers to picture the future. The story must connect with the audience's needs and be embodied in the leader him- or herself. Gardner makes the point that phonies are never in short supply, and the individual who does not embody or act out his or her messages will eventually be found out.

LEADERS' STORIES

Margaret Thatcher
'Britain has lost its way in defeatism and socialism. We must reclaim the leadership from "them" (socialists, union trouble makers and the "wets") and restore earlier grandeur.'

Margaret Mead
'As human beings we can make wise decisions about our own lives by studying options that many other cultures pursue.'

Mahatma Gandhi
'We in India are equal in status and worth to all other human beings. We should work cooperatively with our antagonists if possible, but be prepared to be confrontational if necessary.'

Leadership stories from Gardner (1996)

Heifetz and Laurie: vision is not the answer

Heifetz and Laurie (1997) say that vision is not the answer. They say that the senior executive needs to alter his or her approach to match the needs of 21st-century organizations. They say that what is needed is adaptive leadership. This is about challenging people, taking them out of their comfort zones, letting people feel external pressure and exposing conflict.

'Followers want comfort and stability, and solutions from their leaders. But that's babysitting. Real leaders ask hard questions and knock people out of their comfort zones. Then they manage the resulting distress.' They believe the call for vision and inspiration is counter-productive and encourages dependency from employees.

There is a difference between the type of leadership needed to solve a routine technical problem and the type of leadership needed to enable complex organizational change. Leaders of change should concentrate on scanning the environment, and drawing people's attention to the complex adaptive challenges that the organization needs to address, such as culture changes, or changes in core processes. This means not solving the problems for people, but giving the work back to them. It also means not protecting people from bad news and difficulty, but allowing them to feel the distress of things not working well. These ideas are quite a long way from the concept of transformational leadership mentioned above, which indicates that successful leaders are charismatic, visionary and inspirational.

Jean Lipman-Blumen: leaders need to make connections rather than build one vision

Jean Lipman-Blumen (2002) says that vision is no longer the answer. She encourages leaders to search for meaning and make connections, rather than build one vision. She notes that there is a growing sense that old forms of leadership are untenable in an increasingly global environment. She says that the sea change in the conditions of leadership imposed by the new global environment requires new ways of thinking and working that confront and deal constructively with both interdependence (overlapping visions, common problems) and diversity (distinctive character of individuals, groups and organizations).

Lipman-Blumen talks about connective leaders (see box) who perceive connections among diverse people, ideas and institutions even when the parties themselves do not. In the new 'connective era', she says that leaders will need to reach out and collaborate even with old adversaries. Mikhail Gorbachev is a good example of this in the political arena. Nelson Mandela is another.

Again, this approach is different from the suggestion that leaders need to develop and communicate clear vision in an inspiring way. Jean Lipman-Blumen encourages leaders to help others to make good connections, and to develop a sense of common purpose across boundaries, thus building commitment across a wide domain.

SIX IMPORTANT STRENGTHS FOR CONNECTIVE LEADERS

- **Ethical political savvy.** *A combination of political know-how with strong ethics. Adroit and transparent use of others and themselves to achieve goals.*
- **Authenticity and accountability.** *Authenticity is achieved by dedicating yourself to the purpose of the group. Accountability is achieved by being willing to have every choice scrutinized.*
- **A politics of commonalities.** *Searching for commonalities and common ground, and building communities.*
- **Thinking long term, acting short term.** *Coaching and encouraging successors, and building for a long-term future despite the current demands of the day to day.*
- **Leadership through expectation.** *Scrupulously avoiding micromanaging. Setting high expectations and trusting people.*
- **A quest for meaning.** *Calling supporters to change the world for the better.*

Source: Lipman-Blumen (2002)

Leadership for the 21st century: less vision, more connection?

The world is changing. Organizations are more dispersed and less hierarchical. More information is more freely available. People want more from their jobs than they used to. Does this change the role of the leader of change?

As we write this book, the world's economy is in turmoil, with a particular focus on the difficulties of the Eurozone. It seems that many of the old certainties are dissolving, and it's almost impossible for leaders to lead through offering a clear, authoritative vision. The increasingly globalized economy, access to immediate, 24-hour news and information and the rise of social media all work to create more independence of mind of individuals, increased inter-connectivity between interest groups and less reliance on traditional forms of leadership. Are people's needs for strong leadership starting to shift? Perhaps clear, visionary, authoritative leadership is no longer working.

When we look inside organizations, the territory is also changing. John Kotter (1996) draws our attention to changes in organizational structures, systems and cultures (see Table 4.3). What does this mean for leading change? We think this means a shift from expectations of one visionary leader to the need for increased connectivity and overlapping agendas between different groups.

STOP AND THINK!

Q 4.1 Name your top five contemporary leaders and say why you chose each one. Reflect on how important visionary leadership is to you.

Q 4.2 What are the most significant changes that have happened in the world since your childhood? Who was responsible for leading these? Did visionary leadership play a key role?

Q 4.3 Draw up a table identifying the pros and cons of:

- visionary leadership;
- adaptive leadership;
- connective leadership.

Q 4.4 Re-read Kotter's (1996) comparison of 20th- and 21st-century organizational structures, systems and cultures. Then fill in your own ideas about leadership of change.

ROLES THAT LEADERS PLAY

There are various views about the role a leader should play in the change process (see Table 4.1, page 133):

- The machine metaphor implies that the leader sits at the top of the organization, setting goals and driving them through to completion.

- The political system metaphor implies that the leader needs to become the figurehead of a powerful coalition which attracts followers by communicating a compelling and attractive vision, and through negotiation and bargaining.

- The organism metaphor says the leader's primary role is that of coach, counsellor and consultant.

Table 4.3 20th-century organizations and 21st-century organizations

	Structure	Systems	Culture	Leadership of change
20th-century organizations	• bureaucratic; • multilevelled; • organized with the expectation that senior management will manage; • characterized by policies and procedures that create many complicated internal interdependencies.	• depend on fewer performance information systems; • distribute performance information to executives only; • offer management training and support systems to senior people only.	• inwardly focused; • centralized; • slow to make decisions; • political; • risk averse.	*Our thoughts:* • directive; • visionary; • charismatic; • participative at top levels only.
21st-century organizations	• non-bureaucratic, with fewer rules and employees; • limited to fewer levels; • organized with the expectation that management will lead, lower-level employees will manage; • characterized by policies and procedures that produce the minimal internal interdependence needed to serve customers.	• depend on many performance information systems, providing data on customers especially; • distribute performance information widely; • offer management training and support systems to many people.	• externally oriented; • empowering; • quick to make decisions; • open and candid; • more risk tolerant.	*Our thoughts:* • scanning and interpreting environmental changes; • encouraging connectedness; • giving meaning and purpose.

Source: adapted from Kotter (1996)

- The flux and transformation metaphor says the leader is a facilitator of emergent change.

How does the leader of a change process ensure that all the necessary roles are carried out? Should the leader try to perform all these roles personally, or select a specific role for him- or herself and distribute supporting roles among his or her colleagues?

Senge: dispersed leadership

Senge (Senge *et al*, 1999) has some fairly challenging ideas about this. He says that successful leadership of change does not have to come from the top of an organization. It comes from within the organization. He remarks that senior executives do not have as much power to change things as they would like to think.

He asks why we are struggling so much with changing our organizations, and he attacks our dependence on the 'hero leader'. He claims it results in a vicious circle. The circle begins with a crisis, which leads to the search for a new CEO in whom all hopes are invested. The new CEO acts proactively and aggressively, and makes some dramatic short-term improvements such as cutting costs and improving productivity. Everyone then falls in line to please the new CEO, who does not suffer fools gladly. Employees comply rather than work hard to challenge the status quo, and a new crisis inevitably occurs. This vicious circle does not result in new thinking, organizational learning or renewal, or even growth, and in turn feeds our desire to find new hero leaders. See Figure 4.1.

Senge offers some stark truths about organization change, which counteract the reliance on top-level vision set out by Bennis and Kotter:

- little significant change can occur if it is driven from the top;

- CEO programmes rolled out from the top are a great way to foster cynicism and distract everyone from real efforts to change;

- top management buy-in is a poor substitute for genuine commitment and learning capabilities at all levels in an organization.

You can see Senge's point. How could one or two brave people at the top of an organization really be responsible for envisaging and tackling the enormous range of challenges that present themselves when fundamental change is attempted? He claims that we need to think about developing communities of interdependent leaders across organizations.

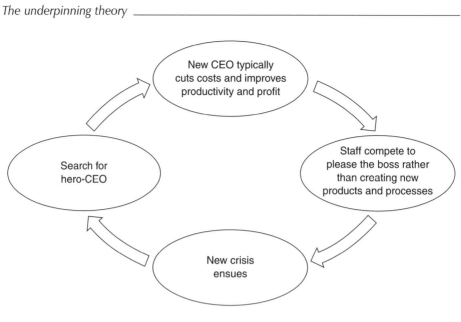

Figure 4.1 The search for a hero-CEO
Source: Senge *et al* (1999)

Different types of leaders have different types of role. He identifies three important, interconnected types of leader: local line leaders, executive leaders and network leaders.

Local line leaders

These are the front-line managers who design the products and services and make the core processes work. Without the commitment of these people, no significant change will happen. These people are usually very focused on their own teams and customers. They rely on network leaders to link them with other parts of the organization, and on executive leaders to create the right infrastructure for good ideas to emerge and take root.

Executive leaders

These are management board members. Senge does not believe that all change starts here. Rather, he states that these leaders are responsible for three key things: designing the right innovation environment and the right infrastructure for assessment and reward, teaching and mentoring local line leaders, and serving as role models to demonstrate their commitment to values and purpose.

Network leaders

Senge makes the point that the really significant organizational challenges occur at the interfaces between project groups, functions and teams. Network leaders are people who work at these interfaces. They are guides, advisers, active helpers and accessors (helping groups of people to get resource from elsewhere), working in partnership with line leaders. They often have the insight to help local line leaders to move forward and make changes happen across the organization.

The interconnections are hard to achieve in reality. We have observed the following obstacles to achieving smooth interconnections between the different roles:

- Executive leaders are busy, hard-to-get-hold-of people who can become quite disconnected from their local line leaders.

- Executive leaders and local line leaders rarely meet face-to-face and communicate by e-mail, if at all.

- Network leaders, such as internal consultants or process facilitators, are often diverted from their leadership roles by requests either to perform expert tasks or to implement HR-led initiatives.

- Network leaders may be busy and effective, but are usually under-valued as leaders of change. They often have to battle to get recognized as important players in the organization.

Senge's model recognizes the need for all three types of leader, and the need for connectivity between different parts of the organization if change is desired.

O'Neill: four key roles for successful change

Mary Beth O'Neill (2000) agrees with Senge's idea of communities of leaders, and identifies four specific leadership roles necessary for successful and sustained change efforts in organizations. She uses Daryl Conner's work on family therapy as her model for the change process, and identifies the important roles as sponsor, implementer, advocate and agent. See Table 4.4.

Table 4.4   Roles in a change process

Role	Description	Hint
Sponsor	Has the authority to make the change happen. Has control of resources.	Needs to have a clear vision for the change. Identify goals and measurable outcomes.
Sustaining sponsor	Sponsors change in own area, although top-level responsibility lies further up the hierarchy.	Must be careful not to transmit cynicism.
Implementer	Implements the change. Reports to sponsor. Responsible for giving live feedback to the sponsor on change progress.	Needs to listen, enquire and clarify questions with the sponsor at the start of an initiative.
Change agent	Facilitator of change. Helps sponsor and implementers stay aligned. Keeps sponsor on board. No direct authority over implementers.	Acts as data gatherer, educator, adviser, meeting facilitator, coach.
Advocate	Has an idea. Needs a sponsor to make it happen. Usually highly motivated.	Must make idea appealing to sponsor.

Source: adapted from O'Neill (2000)

Sponsor

The sponsor has the authority to make the change happen. He or she legitimizes and sanctions the change, and has line authority over the people who will implement the change and control of resources – such as time, money and people. There are also sustaining sponsors who are responsible for sponsoring change in their own area.

Good sponsors have a clear vision for the change. They identify goals and measurable outcomes for the initiative. Sustaining sponsors must be careful not to telegraph cynicism about the change to the team of implementers.

Implementer

Implementers are the people who must actually implement the change. They have direct line responsibilities to the sponsor. Their job is to provide the sponsor with live feedback from the change initiative. They can save the sponsor from tunnel vision, or from being surprised by obstacles that those closest to the change sometimes notice first.

Implementers are most effective when they listen, inquire and clarify their questions and concerns with the sponsor at the beginning of an initiative. This means they can commit to an effort rather than falsely complying early on and sabotaging later.

Change agent

A change agent is the facilitator of the change. He or she helps the sponsor and the implementers stay aligned with each other. The effectiveness of this role depends on the sponsor not abandoning the change agent to the implementers. The sponsor must not 'drop the ball'. When this happens the change agent can over-function, making the system ineffective and unbalanced, and the change temporary.

The change agent acts as data gatherer, educator, adviser, meeting facilitator and coach. Most often he or she has no direct line authority over the implementers, and is therefore in a naturally occurring triangle among sponsor–implementer–agent.

Advocate

An advocate has an idea about how a change can happen but needs a sponsor for his or her idea. All change needs to be sponsored.

Advocates are often passionate and highly motivated to make the change happen. They must remember the key factor, which is to get a sponsor. Without this, advocates become frustrated and demoralized. Shrewd advocates promote ideas by showing their compatibility with issues near and dear to sponsors' change projects and goals.

We have included Mary Beth O'Neill's definitions of these roles because they provide a clear framework for those approaching organizational change, and illustrate the range of leadership roles necessary for change to occur. Our experience is that people at all levels in organizations find this framework useful for kicking off and sustaining change, and for judging how well the community of leaders is supporting the change process. This model seems to provide the necessary amount of clarity in today's organizations, where hierarchy is unclear and jobs and projects overlap. There is often a need for a simple but flexible way of defining who does what in any process of change.

STOP AND THINK!

Q 4.5 Use Mary Beth O'Neill's four roles to analyse a change process in your organization. Who performed which role? How well were the roles performed? What contribution did the performance of these roles make to the level of success of the changes?

LEADERSHIP STYLES, QUALITIES AND SKILLS

Much has been written about leadership styles, qualities and skills. We have included two different ways of looking at this area to illustrate two complementary 'lenses'. The first comes from Goleman (2000) and the second from Cameron and Green (2008).

We have chosen the work of Goleman because our clients tend to find it illuminating and useful as a first stage 'ready-reckoner' regarding their leadership style. Goleman identifies a set of six 'relationship-oriented' styles for the leader to choose from in any situation – as if choosing from a set of golf clubs. Leaders we have worked with find this very useful, particularly when faced with new people challenges, either one-to-one or in a group context (see boxed examples). This set of six styles is underpinned by Goleman's work on emotional intelligence, which sets out the underlying competencies associated with successful leadership. This acts as a convenient checklist for those assessing their skills.

We have also chosen, in contrast, our own set of five leadership qualities which we believe leaders need to demonstrate in varying amounts when facing significant change. Derived from analysis and research in the field, we have found this set of qualities to be very easily digested and understood by the leaders with whom we've worked over the past few years. It also seems to offer a way – particularly in a leadership team setting – of inquiring more deeply into the type of leadership that's being called for according to the change challenges ahead, and therefore where leaders need to develop or 'step up'.

Goleman: leadership that gets results

In his quest to discover the links between emotional intelligence and business results, Daniel Goleman (2000) developed a set of six distinct leadership styles through studying the performance of over 3,800 executives worldwide. These six leadership styles, arising from various different components of emotional intelligence, are used interchangeably by the best leaders. He encourages leaders to view the styles as six golf clubs, with each one being used in a different situation. Goleman also found that each style taken individually has a unique effect on organizational climate over time, some positive and some negative. This in turn has a major influence on business results.

Goleman links the competence of leaders directly to business results, but also identifies the situations in which each style is effective:

- **Coercive style.** Only to be used sparingly if a crisis arises. This is a useful style to employ if urgent changes are required now, but must be combined with other styles for positive results long term. Negative effects such as stress and mistrust result if this style is overused.

- **Authoritative style.** Useful when a turnaround is required and the leader is credible and enthusiastic. This is the 'visionary' leadership style. Goleman indicates that this style will only work if the leader is well respected by his or her people, and is genuinely enthusiastic about the change required. He acknowledges the strongly positive effect of this approach, given the right prevailing conditions.

- **Affiliative style.** This style helps to repair broken relationships and establish trust. It can be useful when the going gets tough in a change process and people are struggling. However, it must be used with other styles to be effective in setting direction and creating progress.

- **Democratic.** This is an effective style to use when the team knows more about the situation than the leader does. They will be able to come up with ideas and create plans with the leader operating as facilitator. However, it is not useful for inexperienced team members as they will go round in circles and fail to deliver.

- **Pace-setting.** This style can be used effectively with a highly motivated, competent team, but does not lead to positive results long term if used in isolation. Overuse of this style alone results in exhausted staff who feel directionless and unrewarded. The leader needs to switch out of this style to move into a change process rather than simply drive for more of the same.

- **Coaching.** This is an appropriate style to use if individuals need to acquire new skills or knowledge as part of changes being made.

THE COERCIVE-AFFILIATIVE MANAGER

I realize on reflection that I have been using just two leadership styles all my working life. I am 54, and this has been something of a revelation. I have been using the coercive style together with the affiliative style. It never occurred to me to do it any other way. I would tell the staff how things would be, give them a dressing down, and make up afterwards by talking about the football or asking about the family.

No one would make suggestions or use their initiative, and no one ever seemed to learn anything new. I was completely in charge of an efficient but stagnant site.

It wasn't easy incorporating other styles, but once I had cracked the coaching style, things began to change. The staff began to see me as more accessible. Now my people trust me more, and they are prepared to take responsibility and to suggest things and to make changes. I use less energy to carry out my role, and can think more clearly about how best to lead.

General manager of a manufacturing plant

THE PACE-SETTING MANAGER

At first glance I thought I was using all six styles in the right measure. Then when I began to talk to my team about it, I realized that I was using the pace-setting style 85 per cent of the time. Even my attempts at being friendly (or affiliative) turned out to be pace-setting approaches. People described how a casual chat with me would end up feeling like an interrogation. People on the shop floor actively avoided me after a while. Or they spent ages preparing for an encounter with me.

Of course, all my star performers loved this style. They found it thrilling and stimulating. The others fell by the wayside as I had no time for coaching at all. My style became a self-fulfilling prophecy. The competent people did well, and those who needed to learn didn't get the airtime from me that they needed, so they failed.

I'm not saying that this has completely changed. But now I do recognize when I need to coach and when I need to pace-set. My actions are more aligned to my intentions, rather than being simply a question of habit.

Head teacher

See Table 4.5 for our summary of the six different styles and their uses.

Goleman: the importance of emotional intelligence for successful leaders

Underpinning Goleman's six leadership styles is his work on emotional intelligence (see Goleman, 1998). This is worth examining as it sets out all the competencies required to be a successful leader.

Goleman's research into the necessity for emotional intelligence is convincing. First, his investigation into 181 different management competence models drawn from 121 organizations worldwide indicated that 67 per cent of the abilities deemed essential for management competence were emotional competencies. Further research carried out by Hay/McBer looked at data from 40 different corporations to determine the difference in terms of competencies between star performers and average performers. Again emotional competencies were found to be twice as important as skill-based or intellectual competencies.

Table 4.5 Our summary of Goleman's six leadership styles

	Coercive	Authoritative	Affiliative	Democratic	Pace-setting	Coaching
Short definition	Telling people what to do when.	Persuading and attracting people with an engaging vision.	Building relationships with people through use of positive feedback.	Asking the team what they think, and listening to this.	Raising the bar and asking for a bit more. Increasing the pace.	Encouraging and supporting people to try new things. Developing their skills.
When to use this style	When there is a crisis.	When step change is required. When manager is both credible and enthusiastic.	When relationships are broken.	When the team members have something to contribute.	When team members are highly motivated and highly competent.	When there is a skills gap.
Disadvantages of this style	Encourages dependence. People stop thinking.	Has a negative effect if manager is not credible.	Not productive if it is the only style used.	May lead nowhere if team is inexperienced.	Exhausting if used too much. Not appropriate when team members need help.	If manager is not a good coach, or if individual is not motivated, this style will not work.

EMOTIONAL COMPETENCIES FOR LEADERS

Self-awareness

Knowing one's internal states, preferences, resources, and intuitions:

- *Emotional awareness: recognizing one's emotions and their effects.*
- *Accurate self-assessment: knowing one's strengths and limits.*
- *Self-confidence: a strong sense of one's self-worth and capabilities.*

Self-management

Managing one's internal states, impulses, and resources:

- *Self-control: keeping disruptive emotions and impulses in check.*
- *Trustworthiness: maintaining standards of honesty and integrity.*
- *Conscientiousness: taking responsibility for personal performance.*
- *Adaptability: flexibility in handling change.*
- *Achievement orientation: striving to improve or meeting a standard of excellence.*
- *Initiative: readiness to act on opportunities.*

Social awareness

Awareness of others' feelings, needs, and concerns:

- *Empathy: sensing others' feelings and perspectives, and taking an active interest in their concerns.*
- *Organizational awareness: reading a group's emotional currents and power relationships.*
- *Service orientation: anticipating, recognizing and meeting customers' needs.*

Social skills

Adeptness at inducing desirable responses in others:

- *Developing others: sensing others' development needs and bolstering their abilities.*
- *Leadership: inspiring and guiding individuals and groups.*
- *Influence: wielding effective tactics for persuasion.*
- *Communication: listening openly and sending convincing messages.*
- *Change catalyst: initiating or managing change.*
- *Conflict management: negotiating and resolving disagreements.*

> - *Building bonds: nurturing instrumental relationships.*
> - *Teamwork and collaboration: working with others toward shared goals.*
>   *Creating group synergy in pursuing collective goals.*
>
> *Source:* Goleman (1998), reproduced with permission of
> Bloomsbury Publishing, London

Goleman defined a comprehensive set of emotional competencies for leaders (see box above). He grouped these competencies into four categories:

1   self-awareness;

2   self-management;

3   social awareness; and

4   social skills.

Self-awareness, he says, is at the heart of emotional intelligence. To back this up, Goleman's research shows that if self-awareness is not present in a leader, the chance of that person being competent in the other three categories is much reduced.

THE IMPORTANCE OF SELF-MANAGEMENT

The managers that we work with often have high drive levels and are also very intelligent. When this combination of characteristics is present in an individual, that individual often experiences a lot of frustration. Other people are either too slow, or too relaxed, or simply 'not getting it'.

This was crystallized by a very dynamic and successful IT manager whom I worked with recently. When I went through her emotional intelligence feedback with her using HayGroup's Emotional Competence Inventory, her self-management scores were low, especially in the area of self-control. I asked her how often she felt frustrated in her work. She paused for a moment and then with a sudden realization she said, 'All the time'. Up until that point, she had not realized that there was an issue. This had just become a way of life. Others were experiencing her as bad tempered, moody and occasionally bullying. Then we started to talk about strategies for dealing with this.

Esther Cameron, 2003

A brief scan of the competence set will confirm that self-awareness, self-management and social awareness are all competencies that are not necessarily observable. We call this *inner leadership*. Only the social skills category contains obvious observable behaviours. We call this *outer leadership*.

In our experience those involved in leading change have to develop especially strong inner leadership because of the emotions arising from their own drive to achieve, coupled with potential resistance from many levels, and the discomfort involved in letting go of old habits. It is a very emotional landscape!

Daniel Goleman says that it is vital that leaders develop emotional competencies:

> In the new stripped-down, every-job-counts business climate, these human realities will matter more than ever. Massive change is constant; technical innovations, global competition, and the pressures of institutional investors are ever-escalating forces for flux. As organizations shrink through waves of down-sizing, those people who remain are more accountable – and more visible.

Whereas a bully, or a hypersensitive manager, might have gone un-noticed deep in many organizations 10 years ago, he or she is much more visible now.

Cameron and Green: five leadership qualities to support change

Since the first edition we have become very interested in the possibility that different leadership qualities may be required in different organizational change contexts. We searched the literature, and combined this with our knowledge of many different sets of leadership competences from organizations we work with. From this process we derived a set of five leadership qualities that cover the full set of possibilities using a clustering approach.

We invited research participants, all experienced managers or Organization Development professionals, to use their organizational wisdom to select the leadership qualities they thought would be most effective in a range of contexts. We wanted to find out if different leadership qualities, or combinations of qualities, appeared to match up to any particular contexts. We asked participants to select the one or two leadership qualities that they thought would be most effective in each of a range of organizational contexts.

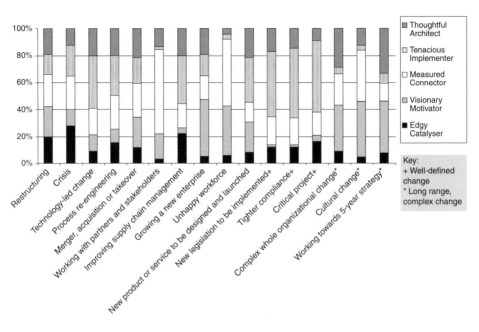

Figure 4.2 The five leadership qualities
Source: Cameron and Green (2008)

The summary of results appears in Figure 4.2. It is clear from this information that a wide range of roles are useful, and that combinations of roles
work well. There are some interesting patterns to notice about particular
contexts, but the overall message is that all the roles are useful at times.

In our book *Making Sense of Leadership* (2008), we describe our research,
set out the results and conclude that there are five qualities to select from
which leaders need to use flexibly if they are to be versatile performers.
Again, we concluded that there is no one right way, but there are some
guidelines.

The five qualities, shown in Figure 4.3 for a summary, are:

1   The Edgy Catalyser: focuses on creating discomfort to catalyse
    change.

2   The Visionary Motivator: focuses on engagement and buy-in to
    energize people.

3   The Measured Connector: focuses on sense of purpose and connec-
    tivity across the organization to help change to emerge.

4   The Tenacious Implementer: focuses on projects, plans, deadlines
    and progress to achieve results.

Figure 4.3 Summary of the five leadership qualities
Source: Cameron and Green (2008)

5   The Thoughtful Architect: focuses on frameworks, designs and complex fit between strategies and concepts to ensure that ideas provide a sound basis for change.

STOP AND THINK!

Q 4.6   Draw a pie chart that represents your own use of Goleman's six leadership styles. Are you using them in the right proportion? If not, what do you plan to do differently and why? Try this exercise again, but this time use the framework to help someone else to focus on his or her leadership style. Write up the conversation, indicating what insights the exercise provoked.

You can also try the exercise with the five leadership qualities.

DIFFERENT LEADERSHIP FOR DIFFERENT PHASES OF CHANGE

In this section we examine the different phases of the change process, to identify the need for a leader to perform different skills or activities during each phase. We do this by using three different but complementary models of the change process.

Cameron and Green: inner and outer leadership

In our own experience of working with leaders on change processes, it is important to establish phases of change so that plans can be made and achievements recognized. This phasing also enables a leader to see the need for flexibility in leadership style, as the change moves from one phase into another phase. We have identified both the outer leadership and inner leadership requirements of a leader of change for each phase; see Table 4.6.

Table 4.6 Leadership of change phase by phase, comparing inner and outer leadership requirements

Phase of change	Outer leadership – observable actions of the leader	Inner leadership – what goes on inside the leader
1. Establishing the need for change The leader illuminates a problem area through discussion.	Influencing, understanding, researching, presenting, listening.	Managing emotions, maintaining integrity, being courageous, being patient, knowing yourself, judging whether you really have the energy to do this.
2. Building the change team The leader brings the right people together and establishes momentum through teamwork.	Chairing meetings, connecting agendas, facilitating discussion, building relationships, building teams, cutting through the politics.	Social and organizational awareness, self-awareness, managing emotions, adaptability, taking initiative, having the drive to achieve, maintaining energy despite knock-backs.
3. Creating vision and values The leader works with the group to build a picture of success.	Initiating ideas, brainstorming, encouraging divergent and creative thinking, challenging others constructively, envisaging the future, facilitating agreement.	Strategic thinking, taking time to reflect, social awareness, drive to achieve, managing emotions.

Table 4.6 *continued*

Phase of change	Outer leadership – observable actions of the leader	Inner leadership – what goes on inside the leader
4. Communicating and engaging The leader plays his or her role in communicating direction, giving it meaning, being clear about timescale and letting people know what part they will be playing.	Persuading and engaging, presenting with passion, listening, being assertive, being creative with ways of communicating.	Patience, analysis of how to present to different audiences, managing emotions with regard to other people's resistance, social awareness, adaptability, empathy.
5. Empowering others The leader entrusts those who have been involved in the creation of the new vision with key tasks.	Clear target setting, good delegation, managing without micromanaging or abdicating, coaching.	Integrity, trust, patience, drive to achieve, steadiness of purpose, empathy.
6. Noticing improvements and energizing The leader stays interested in the process. This involves the ability to juggle lots of different projects and initiatives.	Playing the sponsorship role well, walking the talk, rewarding and sharing success, building on new ideas.	Steadiness of purpose, organizational and social awareness, empathy, managing emotions, drive to achieve.
7. Consolidating The leader encourages people to take stock of where they are, and reflect on how much has been achieved.	Reviewing objectively, celebrating success, giving positive feedback before moving on to what's next.	Social awareness, empathy, drive to achieve, taking time to reflect, steadiness of purpose.

Kotter: the importance of getting the early steps right

Kotter's eight steps to transforming your organization (see Chapter 3) form a comprehensive guide to tackling the process of change. Kotter says that good leaders must get all eight steps right. However, he predicts that the process will be a great deal easier if groundwork is done well.

In *Leading Change* (1996), Kotter describes some of the actions a leader needs to take during all eight steps. In Table 4.7 we give some of Kotter's suggestions for the first four steps, as they seem to necessitate the most direct action from the leader.

Table 4.7   Kotter's recommended actions for the first four change steps

Kotter's step	Recommended actions
1. Establishing a sense of urgency	Push up the urgency level. Create a crisis by exposing issues rather than protecting people from them. Send more data to people about customer satisfaction, especially where weaknesses are demonstrated. Encourage more honest discussion of these issues.
2. Creating the guiding coalition	Include enough main line managers, enough relevant expertise, enough people with good credibility and reputation in the organization and enough ability to lead. Avoid big egos and snakes (who engender distrust). Talk a lot together, build trust and build a common goal.
3. Developing a vision and strategy	Vision building is a messy, difficult and sometimes emotionally charged exercise. Take time to do the process properly and expect it to take months. It is never achieved in a single meeting.
4. Communicating the change vision	Keep the communication simple and use metaphor and analogy. Creativity is necessary to ensure that many different forms of communication are used to repeat the message, including leading by example. Use two-way discussions and listen to the feedback.

Rosabeth Moss Kanter: learning how to persevere

Rosabeth Moss Kanter (2002) highlights the need for keeping going in the change process, even when it gets tough. She says that too often executives announce a plan, launch a task force and then simply hope that people find the answers. Kanter's emphasis is different from Kotter's. She says the difficulties will come after the change is begun.

Kanter says that leaders need to employ the following strategies to ensure that a change process is sustained beyond the first flourish:

1   **Tune into the environment.** Create a network of listening posts to listen and learn from customers.

2   **Challenge the prevailing organizational wisdom.** Promote kaleidoscopic thinking. Send people far afield, rotate jobs and create interdisciplinary project teams to get people to question their assumptions.

3   **Communicate a compelling aspiration.** This is not just about communicating a picture of what could be; it is an appeal to better ourselves and become something more. The aspiration needs to be compelling as there are so many sources of resistance to overcome.

4   **Build coalitions.** Kanter says that the coalition-building step, though obvious, is one of the most neglected steps in the change process. She says that change leaders need the involvement of people who have the resources, the knowledge and the political clout to make things happen.

5   **Transfer ownership to a working team.** Once a coalition is formed, others should be brought on board to focus on implementation. Leaders need to stay involved to guarantee time and resources for implementers. The implementation team can then build its own identity and concentrate on the task.

6   **Learn to persevere.** Kanter says that everything can look like a failure in the middle. If you stick with the process through the difficult times (see box overleaf), good things may emerge. The beginning is exciting and the end satisfying. It is the hard work in the middle that necessitates the leader's perseverance.

7   **Make everyone a hero.** Leaders need to remember to reward and recognize achievements. This skill is often underused in organizations, and it is often free! This part of the cycle is important to motivate people to give them the energy to tackle the next change process.

> ## STICKY MOMENTS IN THE MIDDLE OF CHANGE AND HOW TO GET UNSTUCK
>
> - **Forecasts fall short.** *Change leaders must be prepared to accept serious departures from plans, especially when they are doing something new and different.*
> - **Roads curve.** *Expect the unexpected. Do not panic when the path of change takes a twist or a turn.*
> - **Momentum slows.** *When the going gets tough it is important to review what has been achieved and what remains – and to revisit the mission.*
> - **Critics emerge.** *Critics will emerge in the middle when they begin to realize the impact of proposed changes. Change leaders should respond to this, remove obstacles and move forward.*
>
> *Source:* Kanter (2002)

Bridges: leading people through transition

William Bridges (1991) has very clear ideas about what leaders need to do to make change work. Bridges says that what often stops people from making new beginnings in a change process is that they have not yet let go of the past. He sees the leader as the person who helps to manage that transition. We see this as a particularly useful frame of thinking when an inevitable change such as a merger, acquisition, reorganization or site closure is under way. In Chapter 3 we referred to his three phases of transition: ending, neutral zone and new beginning.

Leadership for the ending

Here is Bridges' advice for how to manage the ending phase (or how to get them to let go):

- Study the change carefully and identify who is likely to lose what.

- Acknowledge these losses openly – it is not stirring up trouble. Sweeping losses under the carpet stirs up trouble.

- Allow people to grieve and publicly express your own sense of loss.

- Compensate people for their losses. This does not mean handouts! Compensate losses of status with a new type of status. Compensate loss of core competence with training in new areas.

- Give people accurate information again and again.

- Define what is over and what is not.

- Find ways to 'mark the ending' (see box below).

- Honour rather than denigrate the past.

MARKING THE END

When a large publicly owned utility company in the UK split up into a myriad of small privatized units, there was a great sense of loss. Old teams and old friendships were breaking up. It was the end of an era. The organization held a wake, at which everyone moaned and complained and generally got things off their chest. There was much talk late into the night. The transition moved more smoothly after that event as people began to accept the reality and inevitability of the ending.

Leadership for the neutral zone

The neutral zone is an uncomfortable place to be. This is the time when, for instance, the reorganization has been announced but the new organization is not in place, or understood, or working. Anxiety levels go up and motivation goes down, and discord among the team can rise. This phase needs to be managed well, or it can lead to chaos. A selection of Bridges' tips for this phase are listed below (he itemizes 21 in his book):

- Explain the neutral zone as an uncomfortable time which, with careful attention, can be turned to everyone's advantage.

- Choose a new and more affirmative metaphor with which to describe it.

- Reinforce the metaphor with training programmes, policy changes and financial rewards for people to keep doing their jobs during the neutral zone.

- Create temporary policies, procedures, roles and reporting relationships to get you through the neutral zone.

- Set short-range goals and checkpoints.

- Set up a transition monitoring team to keep realistic feedback flowing upward during the time in the neutral zone.

- Encourage experimentation and risk taking. Be careful not to punish all failures.

- Encourage people to brainstorm many answers to the old problems – the ones that people say you just have to live with. Do this for your own problems too.

Leadership for the new beginning

Here are some of Bridges' ideas for this phase:

- Distinguish in your own mind the difference between the start, which can happen on a planned schedule, and the beginning, which will not.

- Communicate the purpose of the change.

- Create an effective picture of the change and communicate it effectively.

- Create a plan for bringing people through the three phases of transition, and distinguish it from the change management plan.

- Help people to discover the part they will play in the new system.

- Build some occasions for quick success.

- Celebrate the new beginning and the conclusion of the time of transition.

STOP AND THINK!

Q 4.7 Reflect on an organizational change in which you were involved. Did the 'sticky moments' suggested by Rosabeth Moss Kanter arise, and how were they dealt with? What could have been done differently by those leading the change?

Q 4.8 Imagine that the organization you work for as a line manager is about to be taken over by one of your key competitors. You have been told that everyone in your area will still have a job, but you will have to learn about the other organization's way of doing business and drop many of the products and services you deliver now. Use the William Bridges' tips to list some of the things you would need to start doing to enable the transition.

THE IMPORTANCE OF SELF-KNOWLEDGE AND INNER RESOURCES

Much is expected of a leader throughout a change process. It takes courage, a sense of purpose, the ability to manage your emotions, high integrity and a wide range of skills to lead change well. A great deal has been written about skills development, but what about self-knowledge and inner resources? How great a part does the inner life of the leader play in his or her ability to lead change, and how can this capacity be developed or improved?

We believe that this is the key to successful leadership; so does Daniel Goleman. See earlier in this chapter to read about his research into leadership success, which indicates that self-awareness forms the bedrock of the emotionally intelligent leader.

Bennis: the role of self-knowledge

Warren Bennis (1994) emphasizes the need to know yourself in order to become a good leader. He says that leaders must have self-knowledge if they want to be freed up sufficiently to think in new ways. Bennis claims that you make your life your own by understanding it, and become your own designer rather than being designed by your own experience. He itemizes four lessons of self-knowledge. These are:

- **One: be your own teacher.** Leaders assume responsibility for their own learning, and treat it as a route to self-knowledge and self-expression. No one can teach them the lessons they need to learn. Stumbling blocks can be denial and blame.

- **Two: accept responsibility and blame no one.** Do not expect other people to take charge or do things for you.

- **Three: you can learn anything you want to learn.** Leadership involves a kind of fearlessness, an optimism and a confidence.

- **Four: true understanding comes from reflecting on your experience.** Leaders make reflection part of their daily life. An honest look at the past prepares you for the future.

Bennis also notes the potential benefits of leaders recalling their childhoods honestly, reflecting on them, understanding them, and thereby overcoming the influence that childhood has on them. He quotes Erikson, the famed psychoanalyst, who says that there are eight stages of life, each with an accompanying crisis (see Table 4.8). Erikson claims that the way in which we resolve the eight crises determines who we will be. He also notes that we may get stuck at a particular stage if we do not manage to solve the crisis satisfactorily. For instance, many of us never overcome the inner struggle between initiative and guilt, and so we lack purpose.

Table 4.8 Development stages and their challenges

Stage	Crisis	Resolution	Conditions for optimal development
Infancy (0–18 months)	Trust vs mistrust	Hope or withdrawal	Mirroring Acceptance
Early childhood (18 months–3 years)	Autonomy vs shame and doubt	Will or compulsion	Security (routines and rituals)
Play age (3–5 years)	Initiative vs guilt	Purpose or inhibition	Clear boundaries Vision setting
School age (8–12 years)	Industry vs inferiority	Competence or inertia	Spectators Discipline
Adolesence (12–28 years)	Identity vs identity confusion	Fidelity or repudiation	Sampling Modelling
Young adulthood (28–40 years)	Intimacy vs isolation	Love or exclusivity	Maturity Identity
Adulthood (40–55 years)	Generativity vs stagnation	Care or rejectivity	Balance Mastery
Maturity (55+)	Integrity vs despair	Wisdom or disdain	Support Forgiveness

Source: adapted from Erik Erikson, in Bennis (1994)

As a leader you may need to overcome some of the habits you developed at an early age, which will be challenging but rewarding. Usually this process is accomplished via coaching, counselling or therapy depending on how deep you want or need to go.

Covey: the need for principle-centred leadership

Steve Covey is a writer and teacher who has had a tremendous effect on the psyche of UK and US managers. His book, *Principle-centred Leadership* (1992) was a *New York Times* bestseller for 220 weeks. His eight characteristics of principle-centred leaders (see box) and his seven habits (see below) are much quoted in management and leadership training courses. Again, his focus is on inner leadership; that is, on how to *be* rather than on what to *do*.

EIGHT CHARACTERISTICS OF PRINCIPLE-CENTRED LEADERS

1 *They are continually learning.*
2 *They are service-oriented.*
3 *They radiate positive energy.*
4 *They believe in other people.*
5 *They lead balanced lives.*
6 *They see life as an adventure.*
7 *They are synergistic.*
8 *They exercise for renewal on all four dimensions of human personality – physical, mental, emotional and spiritual.*

Source: Covey (1992)

Covey's organization runs workshops and programmes underpinned by a humanistic self-development approach. Unlike Bennis, he does not advocate revisiting your childhood to overcome difficulties, but encourages us to focus on visualizing a positive outcome and working with energy and enthusiasm towards it.

Covey's seven habits (Covey, 1989) connect the leader's outer habits with the inner capability, which he labels 'endowments':

Habit 1: Be proactive. Know what needs to be done and decide to do it. Do not be driven by circumstances. (Needs self-awareness and self-knowledge.)

Habit 2: Begin with the end in mind. Have a clear sense of what you are trying to achieve in each year, month, day, moment. (Needs imagination and conscience.)

Habit 3: Put first things first. This is about organizing how you spend your time in line with Habit 2. He talks about looking at level of urgency and level of importance of activities, and comments that we spend too much time responding to urgent issues. (Needs willpower.)

Habit 4: Think win-win. Manage all interactions with the assumption that mutually beneficial solutions are possible. (Needs an abundance mentality.)

Habit 5: Seek first to understand, then to be understood. Be prepared to clarify what other people are getting at before you put your point across. (Needs courage balanced with consideration.)

Habit 6: Synergize. Value differences in people and work with others to create a sum that is greater than the parts. (Needs creativity.)

Habit 7: Sharpen the saw. Avoid the futility of endless 'busyness'. Make time to renew. Covey says: 'Without this discipline, the body becomes weak, the mind mechanical, the emotions raw, the spirit insensitive, and the person selfish.' (Needs continuous improvement or self-renewal.)

STOP AND THINK!

Q 4.9 Identify the top five inner leadership strengths that you believe the headmaster or headmistress of an underperforming school needs to have. Use the ideas of Bennis and Covey in the section above, and consider also Goleman's emotional competencies. Justify your choices. How could these areas be developed if they were lacking?

Q 4.10 Reflect on your own leadership using Covey's seven habits. What are your strengths and weak areas?

Q 4.11 Imagine you have just been asked to lead a cultural change programme in a 10,000-strong organization based throughout Europe and the United States. The organization is a micro-electronics company that has grown through acquisition and now wants to strengthen its unique culture as one organization emphasizing commercial applications, customer service and innovation. Using the ideas presented in this chapter, describe the approach you would take to leading this initiative and explain why.

SUMMARY AND CONCLUSIONS

- Different metaphors of change lead to different assumptions about what good leaders do. We believe that the most effective ideas about change combine a number of metaphors, bringing the maximum benefits and avoiding the pitfalls of blinkered thinking.

- A popular notion of leadership is of the hero leader who leads from the front with determination, great vision and independence of mind.
  - Bennis places visionary leadership high on the agenda, and makes a point of distinguishing leadership from management. Kotter echoes this view.
  - Studies that compared the effects of 'transformational leadership' with those of 'transactional leadership' at the end of the 20th century indicated that charismatic and inspirational leadership were the elements that led most reliably to team success.
  - Howard Gardner's research into the minds of significant 20th-century leaders indicated that leaders who had great influence embodied stories and took care to connect well with their audiences.
  - Heifetz and Laurie and Jean Lipman-Blumen all argue against the need for visionary leadership. Heifetz and Laurie advocate adaptive leadership, which is about taking people out of their comfort zones, letting people feel external pressure and exposing conflict. Jean Lipman-Blumen instead emphasizes the need for leaders to ensure connectivity. She says leaders need to be able to perceive connections among diverse people, ideas and institutions even when the parties themselves do not.

- 21st-century organizations are different, and the pace of change is even faster. This has given rise to new ideas about where leaders need to put their energies. Perhaps this means less vision and more connectivity.

- Different metaphors of the change process imply different leadership roles. Senge advocates dispersed leadership, identifying three key types of leader in an organizational system. If these three roles are in place and are well connected, change will happen naturally. Mary Beth O'Neill names four key leadership roles in any change process.

- Inner leadership is about what goes on inside the leader. Outer leadership is about what the leader does. Outer and inner leadership are both important for achieving organizational change.

- Daniel Goleman defines six leadership styles. A leader can select the right style for the right situation, taking into account the necessary conditions for success and long-term consequences. Goleman's checklist of emotional intelligence competencies is useful for any leader wishing to be successful. These competencies include both inner and outer leadership elements.

- Cameron and Green identify five leadership qualities that leaders need to demonstrate in varying amounts according to the type of change challenge being faced. This set of five qualities is particularly useful to support a leadership team facing significant change challenges in identifying where team members need to develop their leadership skills or 'step up' in some way.

- Kotter says that the hard work must be put in early in the change process, while Rosabeth Moss Kanter says the hardest part comes in the middle and that perseverance is key. Bridges identifies specific leadership tasks during endings, the neutral zone and beginnings.

- Bennis and Covey both place high value on the inner life of leaders. Bennis emphasizes the need for self-knowledge, whereas Covey lists a set of principles and guidelines to help leaders to develop positive thinking patterns.

Leadership is a fascinating subject. We all have different experiences and different views about what makes a good leader, and many of these views are ones we hold quite strongly. There are many apparent contradictions here. It is always intriguing to see how leaders with very different styles can be equally successful. This observation can appear baffling to those wishing to make a rational assessment of what works in leadership and what does not.

So how do we get to the truth about leaders? Do our heroes give us useful clues? The hero leader is an enduring theme in discussions of leadership. Even the process of asking people to name their 'top leaders' encourages an individualist perspective, and automatically results in the naming of heroes. Perhaps this type of information is flawed, as it depends so much on the profile-raising skills of the leader, and his or her own personal brand. The facts concerning how these leaders demonstrated good leadership get lost in the general impression of success.

Leaders who offer a vision, or have a strong story, tend to be the most memorable. Their stories, or new ways of thinking, if taken on, may outlive the leader. Is this a sign of great leadership: when the story begins to live outside of the leader? There is also a strong sense that today's followers need more than just a good story. They need a credible story that stands up to scrutiny.

On the other hand, those who doubt the viability of the role of visionary leadership suggest that leaders need to focus instead on connecting agendas and highlighting painful challenges. Our view is that all these things are necessary to create change, including the articulation of an attractive vision. Just read the words of Martin Luther King again to feel the power of a well-articulated vision. Other things need to be in place too: the timing has to be right, and the vision has to be accepted by followers.

The leader of change has to be courageous and self-aware. He or she has to choose the right action at the right time, and to keep a steady eye on the ball. However, the leader cannot make change happen alone. A team needs to be in place, with well-thought-out roles, and committed people who are in for the duration, not just for the kick-off.

One thing is certain: the going will not be smooth.

5

The change agent

INTRODUCTION

The objective of this chapter is to look at the role of the change agent in supporting the management of change. It looks at the change agent, rather than the leader, in terms of the nature of the role – whether it is internal or external to the organization, the focus, the competencies needed, and some of the deeper psychological aspects. It will look at what goes on inside the change agent – thoughts, decision making, feelings – and also the outwardly observable effective behaviours.

The purpose of the chapter will be to understand:

- models of change agency;
- the consulting process and the role of the change agent within it;
- change agent tools and frameworks;
- the competencies of the change agent;
- deeper aspects of being a change agent.

MODELS OF CHANGE AGENCY

Chapter 4 looked at leading change and touched on the particular role of the change agent and defined it in O'Neill's (2000) terminology as:

> A Change Agent is the facilitator of the change. He/she helps the Sponsor and the Implementers stay aligned with each other.

> The Change Agent acts as data gatherer, educator, advisor, meeting facilitator and coach. Most often he or she has no direct line authority over the implementers and is therefore in a naturally occurring triangle among sponsor-implementer-agent.

Caldwell (2003), in researching the role of the change agent, recognized the shift over the last few decades away from a planned approach to change, which often required or was exemplified by a top-down approach. He saw different approaches that organizations were beginning to adopt to meet unprecedented levels of change – for example, the growth in the use of management consultants specializing in change management; the realization that more emergent approaches to change might be necessary; and the conflation of the concept of leadership with change management. Caldwell developed a fourfold classification covering leadership, management, consultancy and team models (see Table 5.1), which were all supported by extensive reference to research in the field.

Each of these models will bring their own challenges and perhaps different emphases on the core skills needed.

STOP AND THINK!

Q 5.1 Reviewing Caldwell's framework, can you identify different change scenarios that you have experienced or observed that use all or some of the leadership, management, consultancy and team models?

Q 5.2 In what ways was the use of the model(s) effective and ineffective?

Table 5.2 shows the key strengths of each of these models and some of the areas of potential concern.

Table 5.1   Models of change agency

Leadership models	Change agents are identified as leaders or senior executives at the very top of the organization who envision, initiate or sponsor strategic change of a far-reaching or transformational nature.
Management models	Change agents are conceived as middle level managers and functional specialists who adapt, carry forward or build support for strategic change within business units or key functions.
Consultancy models	Change agents are conceived as external or internal consultants who operate at a strategic, operational, task, or process level within an organization, providing advice, expertise, project management, change programme coordination, or process skills in facilitating change.
Team models	Change agents are conceived as teams that may operate at a strategic, operational, task, or process level within an organization and may include managers, functional specialists and employees at all levels, as well as internal and external consultants.

Source: Caldwell (2003)

In the previous chapter we looked at a number of leadership models and to some extent the management model. The management model is an interesting one because those with line management responsibility, often the middle manager, have a special role to play in the vast majority of change initiatives. Balogun (2003) suggests that:

> Managers at middle levels in organizations may be able to make a strategic contribution… middle managers fulfil a complex 'change intermediary' position during implementation… [they] engage in a range of activities to aid their interpretation of the change intent. This interpretation activity then informs the personal changes they attempt to undertake, how they help others through change, how they keep the business going during the transition and what changes they implement in their departments.

Table 5.2 Key strengths of Caldwell's four models and potential concerns

	Key strengths	Things to watch out for
Leadership models	Clear sponsorship and clear direction. Power and authority to 'make change happen'. Stakeholders can see the commitment of senior management to the change.	Potential for the change to be too top-down and have too directive an approach. If leaders are unresponsive there is the potential for 'voices from below' not to be heard and those with different views to be seen as resistors.
Management models	The ability to translate strategic vision to more local actions. Much nearer the 'coal face' so greater knowledge of what works and what doesn't. Ability for more immediate feedback.	Capacity and capability issues for middle managers given their necessary attention on business as usual as well as the changes. They may be ill-equipped with the necessary skills and resources. Senior managers can abdicate responsibility.
Consultancy models	Ability to coach and advise and work in partnership with the organization. Change management expertise and experience in a multitude of settings. Can use their objectivity to the full as they have (ideally) no personal (career or job-related) investment in the solutions. Can take more of a whole systems view.	Can be detached with no demonstrable commitment to the area undergoing change. Staff might feel 'done to'. May have no power or authority to progress the changes or no explicit or implicit 'licence to operate'. Driving for delivery (in order to invoice!) Diminishing others with their expertise. May be limited skills transfer into the organization.
Team models	Have the 'requisite variety' of people on the team. Both change management expertise and business knowledge. Have a greater network into the organizational system.	Can replicate the organizational dysfunction by becoming fragmented and dysfunctional themselves. Can become insular and isolated from the rest of the organization. They can feel superior and believe they know best.

The consultancy model is probably the one that allows more latitude for an emergent approach rather than a purely programmatic approach to change. Partly this is due to the psychological and contractual distance that the consultants may have, and partly due to the fact that they are not so embedded in the organization to be part of both the change and the organization after the change. Positioned where they are, the effective consultant can support leaders to provide a containing environment for reflection and emergence to occur, even within the midst of the pressure to deliver.

The research from Prosci (2003, 2007) and Green (2007a) supports the view that the team model – properly configured – is a critical part of change management success. Prosci sees the need for an 'exceptional change management team taking the form of an experienced credible team who maintained good internal working relations and also net-worked into the organization' together with dedicated resources. Green highlights the importance of the change team being convened from representative parts of the organization including those with change management expertise together with knowledge of the business areas and the business processes, with attention also given to the effective functioning of the change team itself.

One could argue that a fifth model, perhaps a meta-model, might be called for, where there is a more holistic approach, maybe a 'responsibility-taking model' where all four Caldwell models are in evidence and aligned, and key players work together across the whole system.

THE CONSULTING PROCESS

Whichever of Caldwell's models you use, there needs to be strong contracting between the change agent and the leadership line, which is best supported by a clear consulting process. It makes sense to identify the stages of the classical consulting process to establish such a framework, and this section will look at each of these stages, together with the typical features and imperatives of each stage.

Before we look at the process itself it is worth understanding the types of roles a change agent can play within it. Block (2000) sees that there can be three types of role that the change agent can play in the consulting process:

1   **The Expert** – someone who is brought in because other people in the organization need someone who knows what to do and how to do it. The organization doesn't have the capability without the expert, so this is a directive role.

2   **The Extra Pair of Hands** – someone who is brought in to help out because the organization doesn't have the capacity. This is a more compliant role and the subject of direction.

3   **The Collaborative Role** – someone who has expertise and experience in the change field. They can collaborate with people within the system to make sense jointly of the situation and what needs to be addressed. They can work alongside people to facilitate the process of change and support leaders to step up to what's required of them.

There is further consideration of these roles in Chapter 11.

Of course it is important in the initial stages of any change process to establish which type of role is being asked for and indeed ensure that there is agreement at the beginning and throughout the process that the role's integrity is maintained. It is also important to establish that the change agent has the capacity and the capability to fulfil the chosen role.

Block helpfully suggests that the primary tasks of the consultant are to:

● establish a collaborative relationship;

● solve problems so that they stay solved; and

● ensure attention is given to both the technical/business problem and the relationships.

Different commentators delineate the stages of the consulting process in different ways (see Table 5.3) but generically they can be described as an entry stage, followed by contracting, diagnosing, implementing and evaluating (Lacey, 1995).

Table 5.3   Stages of the consulting process

Kubr (1986)	Lacey (1995)	Huffington *et al* (1997)	Block (2000)	Cummings and Worley (2009)	Cheung-Judge and Holbeche (2011)
Entry	Entry	Scouting	Entry and contracting	Entry and contracting	Entry/initial contact
Diagnosis	Contracting	Entry	Discovery and dialogue	Diagnosing organizations	Data collection
Action Planning	Diagnosing	Contracting	Feedback and the decision to act	Diagnosing groups	Data analysis
Implement-ation	Implement-ing	Data gathering	Engagement and implement-ation	Collecting and analysing diagnostic information	Feedback
Termination	Evaluating	Diagnosis	Extension, recycle, or termination	Feeding back diagnostic information	Action planning
		Planning		Designing interventions	Action taking
		Intervention		Leading and managing change	Evaluation
		Evaluation		Evaluating and institutionalizing organizational development (OD) interventions	Termination
		Withdrawal			

Skills at each stage

The consulting process suggests that different sets of knowledge, cognitive skills and behaviours are needed at different stages in the consulting process. Table 5.4 summarizes the work of a number of researchers who suggest what is required of the change agent at each stage.

Table 5.4   The consulting process and the range of knowledge, skills and behaviours

Consulting phase	Indicative knowledge, skills and behaviours
Entry	**Interpersonal** Communication skills – particularly spirit of inquiry and deep and active listening Impact and influence Build trust and commitment Interpersonal and relationship skills Ability to appraise the match between the client and the consultant and decision whether to 'enter the system' Ability to establish an initial relationship with the client and build the basis for involvement **Analytic** Strategic and analytic skills Political sensitivity to the system and stakeholder groupings Change readiness assessment Application of relevant frameworks and models **Personal** In touch with own feelings re the client, organization and project Pragmatism (art of the possible) Coping with mixed motivation on the part of the client and dealing with their concerns about exposure and the loss of control **Project management** Project planning
Contracting	**Interpersonal** Relationship building Ability to use every intervention as part of the discovery process Clarifying expectations **Analytic** Understanding of the whole system and network of stakeholders Development of an effective proposal – goals, recommended actions (preliminary), responsibilities and accountabilities, strategies for achieving end state, fees, terms and conditions Establishment of monitoring methods and evaluation criteria **Personal** Understand the levels of motivation and engagement for the project and within the change agents

Table 5.4 *continued*

Consulting phase	Indicative knowledge, skills and behaviours

Contracting **Project management**
Ability to co-generate achievable objectives and metrics
Clarity of scope – what is and isn't in the project
Clear governance framework
Project management methodology and skills
Resource management
Developing a mutually agreed contract, clarifying expectations
 and the way of working

Diagnosis **Interpersonal**
Understanding of the operating environment, different
 organizational elements, and strategic imperatives
Plan the data collection jointly with the client
Ability to coach, facilitate and tutor others in the diagnostic methods
Ability to feed back to client, and develop a joint understanding
Ability to feed back relevant, understandable, descriptive,
 significant and verifiable information in a timely, even if
 perhaps tentative, way
Facilitation of different stakeholders in understanding of data,
 option generation, and securing of agreement for action
Action planning by self, and team and client
Facilitating group meetings
Gathering 'sensing data' through interview and conversations –
 information gleaned from observational and intuitive awareness
Involve the client in interpreting the data collected

Analytic
Stakeholder mapping
Mapping of political domain
Understanding different and appropriate diagnostic models at an
 organizational, group, team and individual level
Diagnostic skills and an ability to interpret data
Ability to measure the organization's efficiencies and effectiveness
Critical analysis of feedback data
Generation of viable options for action
An understanding of the multi-faceted nature of the organization
 and the degree of complexity of the system
Understanding the various elements of the Change Kaleidoscope
An assessment of the organization's readiness for change
Identification of specific interventions together with who will be
 doing what and how it may be evaluated
Distinguish between the presenting problem and the underlying
 problem
Elicit and describe both the technical/business problem and how
 the problem is being managed

Table 5.4   _continued_

Consulting phase	Indicative knowledge, skills and behaviours
Diagnosis	**Personal** Presentation techniques Dealing with political climate Resisting the urge for complete data Seeing all contact with the client as an intervention Identifying and working with different forms of resistance Presenting personal and organizational data Not taking client reactions personally Ask questions about the client's own role in causing or maintaining the situation Ask questions about what others in the organization are doing to cause or maintain the presenting or target problem Recognize the similarity between how the client manages you and how they manage their own organization **Project management** Ability to make sense of the data and translate into manageable action and project plans
Intervening	**Interpersonal** Continued collaborative working in terms of sense making, action planning and interventions Ensure shared responsibility between client and consultant, while ensuring that organizational leaders are leading Continued transfer of knowledge from consultant to client and attention to internal capability building Focus more on engagement over mandate and persuasion Design more participation than presentation **Analytic** Thought and methodological leadership in the range of interventions Alignment between theoretical insight and designed methods Ability to design interventions informed by the various elements of the Change Kaleidoscope Ability to choose interventions on organizational, group, team and individual levels that fit Development of creative and innovative ideas and interventions

Table 5.4 *continued*

Consulting phase	Indicative knowledge, skills and behaviours

Intervening **Personal**

Alert to feedback and consequences of interventions and other changes in the system

Using self as instrument for understanding

Providing containment and creation of a facilitating environment or supporting leaders in doing so

Have an open mind and a stance of curiosity especially when 'resistance' is experienced

Encourage difficult public exchanges

Put real choice on the table

Change the conversation to change the culture

Project management

Sensible sequencing of interventions

Learning and development interventions delivered by skilled trainers and management developers

Evaluating **Interpersonal**

Ability to show how evaluation is a key aspect in the whole change process

Analytic

Ability to co-design, implement and monitor evaluation methods and metrics

Financial acumen to evaluate costs and benefits of interventions

Assessing the success of the interventions across a range of appropriate measures and agreement on the need for further action or exit

Personal

Be open to the idea that all feedback is valid data

Project management

Ensuring different stakeholder groups have clarity about the objectives and whether they have been achieved

Recognizing that evaluation begins at contracting stage and developing shared understanding of what can be achieved together with a realistic set of evaluation methods and, if no further action is required, managing the termination of the work while leaving the system with an enhanced capacity to manage change by itself in the future

Adapted from Block (2000), Cheung-Judge and Holbeche (2011), Cummings and Worley (2009) and Huffington *et al* (1997)

Differences between internal and external change agents

Some organizations rely on outside help whilst others believe that they have the change agency capacity in-house. Although the core competencies of internal and external change agents are similar it is worth considering some of the differences between the two, partly so one can consider what may be best for any particular change situation, and partly so that the change agent can understand some of the nuances. Lacey (1995), in Table 5.5, identifies some of these different factors.

Table 5.5   Differences between internal and external consultants

Consulting process	Internal change agent	External change agent
Entry	Ready access to clients Ready relationships Knows company jargon Understands root causes Time efficient Congenial phase Obligated to work with everyone Steady pay	Source (find) clients Build relationships Learn company jargon 'Presenting problem' challenge Time consuming Stressful phase Select client/project according to own criteria Unpredictable outcome
Contracting	Informal agreements Must complete projects assigned No out-of-pocket expenses Information can be open or confidential Risk of client retaliation and loss of job at stake Acts as third party (on behalf of client), or pair of hands	Formal documents Can terminate project at will Guard against out-of-pocket expenses Information confidential Loss of contract at stake Maintain third-party role
Diagnosing	Has relationship with many organization members Prestige determined by job rank and client stature Sustain reputation as trustworthy over time Data openly shared can reduce political intrigue	Meet most organization members for the first time Prestige from being external Build trust quickly Confidential data can increase political sensitivities

Table 5.5   *continued*

Consulting process	Internal change agent	External change agent
Intervening	Insist on valid information, and internal commitment; free and informed choice – people can choose to participate or not – is a luxury Run interference for client across organizational lines to align support ('allowed' to engage with other parties of the organization if need be)	Insist on valid information, free and informed choice, and internal commitment Confine activities within boundaries of client organization
Evaluating	Rely on repeat business, pay rise, and promotion as key measures of success Can see change become institutionalized Little recognition for job well done	Rely on repeat business and customer referral as key measures of project success Seldom see long-term results

Source: Lacey (1995)

We can see that throughout the course of the assignment both internal and external consultants will have challenges, but often of a different nature. Huffington *et al* (1997) building on the work of Basset and Brunning (1994) suggest some criteria for when internal and external consultants may be indicated for a particular project:

- *Internal*: when there is a need to work longer term with the outcomes of the change; when there is an internal driver to use or rely upon internal capacity or capability; when internal knowledge of the system now and into the future is required; when engagement with the wider groupings will be improved with internal change agents; and when there is a belief that ownership should clearly be internal.

- *External*: when there is the need for a major organization-wide change especially when there is high-level senior management involvement or sponsorship; when the changes are of a complex nature with limited capacity or capability within; when there is a need for an external, more objective, perspective; and when the situation requires an intervention by people with no conflicts of interest, loyalty or prejudice.

STOP AND THINK!

Q 5.3   Review Table 5.4, 'The consulting process and the range of knowledge, skills and behaviours' and identify some areas of strength and some areas you need to develop. For the latter draw up a number of possible next steps you could take to improve.

Q 5.4   Review Table 5.5, 'Differences between internal and external consultants' and list the pros and cons of using each type for a particular change intervention you have in mind. What are the implications for the organization and the key questions for the change agent?

CHANGE AGENT TOOLS AND FRAMEWORKS

By definition a change agent is seeking or supporting some sort of organizational change in, for example the strategy, the structure, the systems and processes, the people, their capabilities, the management style, and the shared values all within the context of the organizational culture. The change agent crafts interventions that either align with the current culture – the way things are done around here – or are deliberately countercultural, introducing and role-modelling new ways of behaving. Often the change agent has to facilitate people and the organization going into the unknown, with the known knowns being a clear boundary to the scope of the project, but with the final destination as yet unclear, to be fleshed out or discovered.

Whether the focus is at an individual, team or organizational (or large group) level, the change agent supports leaders to make people aware of the specific or general direction of change; is able to support the organization and implementation of the changes; is able to support leaders to mobilize necessary stakeholder groups and accompany them through the transition; and finally ensure that leaders focus on some integration of the process (Green, 2007a).

In the first four chapters we looked at change from the perspective of the individual, the team and the organization as well as different ways of leading change. We can summarize what the agent of change needs to be focusing on by building on the key elements of each of those chapters.

Facilitating individual change

As we saw in Chapter 1, a key aspect for individuals is the necessity to undo some current ways of seeing and behaving and learn new ways. Indeed Schein points out that a key task is to balance the anxiety people feel about surviving this change with the paralysing effect of the anxiety felt about being able to learn new ways of doing things. The critical task therefore is to help people through the learning cycle. To do this, both the change agent and the individual need to be aware of their levels of competence and indeed incompetence.

At a global level, and taking into account Virginia Satir's dictum that change happens 'one person at a time', one needs to ensure that individuals are clear about what practical steps need to be taken to ensure they are ready and able to step into the changes. At an emotional level they may need to be assisted in understanding the choices available to them and helped through the change curve. For this to happen the change agent can draw upon his or her knowledge of what motivates people and then ensure that an appropriate suite of psychological interventions are available to use. These can be informed by the behavioural, cognitive, psychodynamic or humanistic principles and indicative interventions discussed in Chapter 1.

Increasingly the authors believe that tough conversations and high-quality dialogue are key factors in helping the facilitation of change at every level within the system. These two factors need to be supported by a range of organizational development interventions, relying more on inter-relatedness and discovering meaning, such as balancing advocacy with inquiry and catalytic questions.

Based on the work of Scoular (2011), Table 5.6 looks at some of the different questions that the change agent may use – be it the leader, the line manager or the (internal/external) consultant – at the stages Prochaska *et al* (2006) postulate people go through when approaching and reacting to change – precontemplation, contemplation, preparation, action and maintenance.

In the more emergent types of change there may well need to be a good understanding of the consequences of the action, and rather than just 'maintenance' there may well need to be a considered response, which in itself would most likely follow the cycle again from precontemplation onwards.

To help people move through these stages, in a similar way to helping people move through the stages of the change curve, an understanding of people's learning styles, their motivation levels and their personality

Table 5.6 Questions for stages of change

Stage		Questions
Precontemplation	Not intending to act. Questions can only raise awareness.	• How could things be better? • What are the implications of not changing?
Contemplation	Intending to act, but ambivalent. Questions should still raise awareness, and acknowledge the ambivalence (don't confront the resistance). Can also gently test their concerns – using 'R' (Reality) of GROW.	• So on the one hand, this could be helpful, but on the other you're concerned it might not work? • I'm hearing a choice here, between… and… is that right? • You said the new strategy is a 'total disaster', would it be helpful to explore that – or not at this point?
Preparation	Intending to act soon. Questions are still raising awareness, and transitioning towards action.	• So how could you explore this further? • What might you broadly want to achieve? • Any thoughts on how you might go about it?
Action	*Acting:* Questions are helping to plan action and monitoring results. 'O' and 'W' of GROW. *If relapse:* Emphasize this is normal, and as in GROW, go back to whatever was missed and rebuild the process. *Maintenance* may need to continue for life. If Exit happens, celebrate!	• What specifically could you do? Etc • How did that work out? So how will you adjust the plan?

The GROW Model of Coaching stresses the importance of having a clear Goal, an understanding of current Reality, the generation of Options, and an exploration of the Will or Way forward.

Adapted from Prochaska *et al* (2006) and Scoular, A (2011)

type are all important. Schein's (see Chapter 1) ideas for overcoming resistance will also help. Likewise, having enough strategies drawn from the four psychologies in Table 1.6 (representative interventions to facilitate the change process) is crucial. *How* the change agent does this – for example drawing on Rogers' positive regard, facilitating environment, etc – will be explored later in this chapter.

Facilitating team change

In addition to the complexity of dealing with one or more individuals, the change agent also needs to deal with groups of individuals experiencing change, usually within their previously defined teams. This presents both challenges and opportunities. Reviewing Chapter 2 you will recognize that it is important to understand the current state and status of the teams involved in change and the future state and status desired by those engaged in the change, from both a task and psychological perspective:

- Identifying the nature of the team and what might need to change in its structure, format and the role it will perform.

- Understanding how much of a team and teamworking are now needed (the more complex the decisions and uncertain the context, the more teamworking is needed).

- Understanding what the requirements are in terms of changes to the team's five elements (Glaser and Glaser, 1992):
    - team mission, planning and goal setting;
    - team roles;
    - team operating processes;
    - team interpersonal relationships; and
    - inter-team relations.

- And through this process ensuring that the team and its members address the issues of new team formation and realignment – (re)forming, storming, norming and performing.

Times of change and uncertainty can put considerable stress on individuals and teams, and often individuals' survival instincts can take precedence over the team's cohesion. It is at these times that the unconscious processes and phenomena alluded to can be observed.

Responses can include team fragmentation, with individuals going off in different directions with their own personal agendas, and also 'Group

Think' where the embattled team creates an island fortress oblivious and impervious to outside influences. Bion's (1961) basic assumptions may also be much in evidence.

It is of paramount importance to have the ability to observe unconscious processes, to have an understanding of these team dynamics, to be able to facilitate team movement through these states and to be able to create a 'holding environment' for team functioning. The change agent needs to be aware of these phenomena and be able to help the organizational leadership in dealing with them.

Understanding individual and team MBTI types and Belbin team roles can also be extremely useful during these times. Additionally, MBTI-trained facilitators can assist individuals and teams who are 'in the grip' – manifesting atypical parts of their personalities during times of change and stress.

Table 2.3 'Effective and ineffective teams' and Table 2.7 'Teams going through change', highlighted key aspects for the change agent to be noticing and addressing. Chapter 6 also explores how to enable teams' functioning during organizational change with a four-stage team alignment model and a comprehensive table (6.4): 'Addressing team change during restructuring', which is valid in any change involving teams.

Facilitating organizational change

In the Introduction to Part Two you will see two diagrams which graphically represent the strategic change process. One is a rather linear, more planned approach to change. The second is represented as more fluid and perhaps more emergent. Whichever framework you employ, the role of the change agent in facilitating organizational change does require an understanding of both, and the skills necessary to be able to negotiate oneself and others through the challenges presenting themselves each step of the way.

Using Balogun and Hope Hailey's 'Change Kaleidoscope' (2004) (see Figure 5.1) you can begin to see the different aspects of change that the change agent needs to be able to diagnose and assess to decide what type of interventions might be feasible. This framework would most likely sit more comfortably in the planned approach to change. However the more emergent the situation the more complexity there is, and this framework can help reduce, to some degree, the feelings of chaos which might abound.

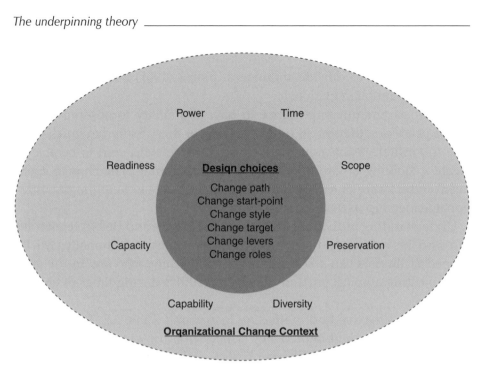

Figure 5.1   Change Kaleidoscope

Contextual choices

- **Time.** How quickly is change needed? Is the organization in crisis or is it concerned with longer-term strategic development?

- **Scope.** What degree of change is needed? Realignment or transformation? Does the change affect the whole organization or only part of it?

- **Preservation.** What organizational assets, characteristics and practices need to be maintained and protected during change?

- **Diversity.** Are the different staff/professional groups and divisions within the organization relatively homogeneous or more diverse in terms of values, norms and attitudes?

- **Capability.** What is the level of organizational, managerial and personal capability to implement change?

- **Capacity.** How much resource can the organization invest in the proposed change in terms of cash, people and time?

- **Readiness for change.** How ready for change are the employees within the organization? Are they both aware of the need to change and motivated to deliver the changes?

- **Power.** Where is power invested within the organization? How much latitude for discretion does the unit need to change and the change leader possess?

Design choices

- **Change path:** the type of change to be undertaken in terms of the nature of the change and the desired end result.

- **Change start-point:** where the change is initiated and developed, which could be summarized simplistically as top-down or bottom-up, but there are other choices.

- **Change style:** the management style of the implementation, such as highly collaborative or more directive.

- **Change target:** the target of the change interventions, in terms of people's attitudes and values, behaviours or outputs.

- **Change levers:** the range of levers and interventions to be deployed across four subsystems – technical, political, cultural and interpersonal.

- **Change roles:** who is to take responsibility for leading and implementing the changes.

Reading the chapter on organizational change you would have realized the many different approaches and choices that the change agent engages with and the levels of complexity of the situation. Notwithstanding that, there are some key practices to engage in. Understanding the culture of the organization underpins much of what one then has to work with or work against.

If the changes are totally within the 'boundary' of the current cultural practices, how one manages change will no doubt be aligned to the values and the behaviours of the prevailing culture. If, however, the reason or rationale for change is to shift the culture in some way, or the culture needs to be shifted to enable other changes to occur, then the interventions and the role-modelling of the change agent will need to be aligned with either the current culture or the preferred one. Table 5.7 highlights these possible choices.

The four metaphors that we have used to illustrate different cultures and ways of doing things will assist in determining the stance that you take and what you may need to do differently to move towards a different culture. Likewise, both Goffee and Jones (1998) and Cameron and Quinn (2011) offer models of organizational culture (both across two

Table 5.7 Choices of intervention based on the nature of the cultural change

Organization change required	Possible choices	Change agent stance
Change within current culture norms (local restructure, geographic expansion, etc)		Role-modelling based on current ways of doing things including management style, degree of consultation, decision-making processes, etc
Change outside current culture norms (diversification requiring new way of working, partnership working, etc)		Role-modelling based on new ways of doing things including management style, degree of consultation, decision-making processes, etc
Culture change itself (eg new ways of doing things to meet external or internal drivers for change)		Role-modelling based on effective change management practices including management style, degree of consultation, decision-making processes, etc

axes resulting in four possible cultures, or parts thereof) (see Figures 5.2 and 5.3). The authors of both these models provide sets of interventions which help the shift from one culture to another.

For example with Goffee and Jones, if the change agent were involved in a change that included moving the organization from a more Fragmented culture to a more Communal one, it would make sense for the change agent's style and the interventions to be highly participative, with reward structures being targeted to encourage teamworking and partnership.

With Cameron and Quinn's cultural framework, if the change agent were involved in a change that included moving the organizational from a more Hierarchical culture to an Adhocracy, it would make sense for them to be role-modelling creative and innovative ways of doing things, checking what the customers wanted, and allowing considerable autonomy in the shaping of the change process and the final outcome.

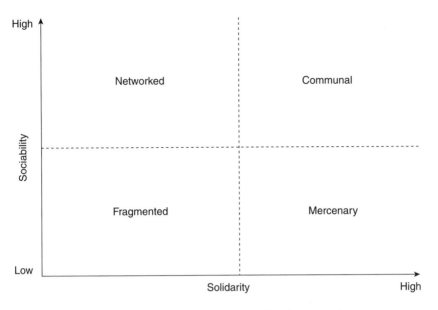

Figure 5.2   Organizational cultures (1)
Source: Goffee and Jones (1998)

Figure 5.3   Organizational cultures (2)
Source: Cameron and Quinn (2011)

Exploring the notion of culture, and the assumptions that lie beneath the surface, helps trigger reflections of your assumptions, as change agent, about culture and about the nature of change itself, which can subconsciously skew your approach.

An important aspect of the change agent's role is to be able to be both sufficiently close to the change to understand how it is going and what now needs to be done, and sufficiently detached – up on the balcony – to be able to see the system at work. Change agents need to move between those two positions, to engage in both active reflection and reflective activity and to make meaningful decisions about the change.

STOP AND THINK!

Q 5.5 As you work through the various phases of the consulting process, where do your strengths lie and what knowledge, skills and understanding do you need to develop?

Q 5.6 Think of a current or future change you are involved in: what are the individual, team and organizational challenges that you face?

Q 5.7 What cultural sensitivities do you need to be aware of and how might you plan your interventions to be aligned with the current or future culture?

COMPETENCIES OF THE CHANGE AGENT

In the previous section we saw the myriad of different things that change agents need to be aware of and skilled at if they want to be effective at an individual, team and organizational level across a range of different organizational cultures and throughout the life cycle of the consulting process. In Part Two we look at specific change situations, which may also require specific knowledge, skills and understanding.

Making Sense of Change Management was written to develop readers' knowledge in areas such as individual psychology, group dynamics and organization behaviour. In addition it aims to introduce, describe and discuss many if not all of the key influences and influencers in the field of change along with the most widely regarded theories and models of change together with emerging ideas.

It is appropriate to look at the range of competencies that might be required of the skilled change agent, and to ascertain which are essential and which are nice to have. Cummings and Worley (2009) have produced a definitive list of the knowledge and skill requirements of the organization development practitioner (see Table 5.8), which correspond well with those of the change agent.

The change agent will, in addition, need to have a good understanding of how business works, together with knowledge (or a knowledgeable partner) in the field of Human Resources. The final aspect referred to by

Table 5.8 Knowledge and skill requirements of the organization development practitioner

Existing system – Knowledge	How systems change over time – Knowledge	How systems change over time – Skills

Organization behaviour
A. Organization culture
B. Work design
C. Interpersonal
    relations
D. Power and politics
E. Leadership
F. Goal setting
G. Conflict
H. Ethics
	Organization design
	Decision-making process
	associated with
	formulating and aligning
	HR systems; information
	systems; reward systems;
	work design; political
	systems; culture; etc.
	A. The concept of fit and
	    alignment
	B. Diagnostic and design
	    model for sub-systems
	C. Key thought leaders in
	    organization design
		*Managing the consulting
		process*
		A. Entry
		B. Contracting
		C. Diagnosing
		D. Designing
		    interventions
		E. Implementation
		F. Managing emergent
		    issues
		G. Evaluation

Individual psychology A. Learning theory B. Motivation theory C. Perception theory	*Organization research* Field research; interviewing; content analysis; change evaluation processes; quantitative and qualitative methods.	*Analysis/diagnosis* Inquiry into the system's effectiveness at an individual, group and organization-wide level. Ability to understand and inquire into one's self.

Group dynamics
A. Roles
B. Communication
    processes
C. Decision-making
    process
D. Stages of group
    development
E. Leadership
	System dynamics
	Understanding of how
	systems evolve and
	develop over time; how
	systems respond to
	planned and unplanned
	interventions.
		*Designing/choosing
		appropriate and relevant
		interventions*
		Understanding how to
		select, modify, or design
		effective interventions
		that will move the
		organization from its
		current state to its
		desired future state.

Table 5.8 *continued*

Existing system – Knowledge	How systems change over time – Knowledge	How systems change over time – Skills
Management and organization theory A. Planning, organizing, leading, and controlling B. Problem solving and decision making C. Systems theory D. Contingency theory E. Organization structure F. Characteristics of environment and technology G. Models of organization and system	*History of organization development* A. Human relations movement B. National Training Lab C. Survey research D. Quality of life E. Tavistock Institute F. Key thought leaders G. Humanistic values H. Statement of ethics	*Facilitation and process consultation* Ability to assist an individual or a group towards a goal. Ability to inquire into individual and group processes so that the client system (organization) maintains ownership of the issue, increases the capacity for reflection on the consequences of its behaviours and actions, and develops a sense of increased control and ability.
Research methods/statistics A. Measures of central tendency B. Measures of dispersion C. Basic sampling theory D. Basic experimental design E. Sample inferential statistics	*Theories and models of change* A. Basic action research model B. Change topologies C. Lewin's model D. Transition models, etc	*Developing client capability* The ability to conduct a change process so that the client is better able to plan and implement a successful change process in the future, using technologies of planned change in a values-based and ethical manner.
Comparative cultural perspectives A. Dimensions of national culture B. Dimensions of industry culture C. Systems implications		*Evaluating organization change* The ability to design and implement a process to evaluate the impact and effects of change intervention, including control of alternative explanations and interpretations of performance outcomes.

Table 5.8 *continued*

Existing system – Knowledge	How systems change over time – Knowledge	How systems change over time – Skills
Functional knowledge of business A. Interpersonal communication (listening, feedback, and articulation) B. Collaboration/ working together C. Problem solving D. Using new technology E. Conceptualizing F. Project management G. Present/education/ coach		

From Cummings/Worley (2009) *Organization Development and Change*, International Edition, 9e. © 2009 South-Western, a part of Cengage Learning, Inc. Reproduced by permission. www.cengage.com/permissions.

Cummings and Worley is the skills set acquired through management development and interpersonal training together with a serious attempt at ongoing personal learning and development.

Having looked at generic competencies applied across all change situations we can now approach this from a different perspective. Léon de Caluwé and Hans Vermaak (2004) have categorized approaches to change in a somewhat similar way to the four organizational metaphors we have used throughout this book. They use the notion of five paradigms or lenses, each tagged with a colour, through which change can be approached:

- *Blue – change through design* is the programmatic or planned approach to change, which can be mapped on to the Machine metaphor.

- *Yellow – change through addressing interests* is mainly focused on aligning stakeholders to the overarching aims. This can be mapped on to the Political Systems metaphor.

- *White – change through emergence* corresponds to the Flux and Transformation metaphor.

- *Green – change through learning* fits very well with the Organism metaphor.

- *Red – change through people* focuses on ensuring that an HR expert manages the practical side of people management, together with the realization of the need to manage people through the emotional aspects of psychological transition. This paradigm can principally be overlaid onto the Machine and Organism metaphors.

One of the reasons why the five paradigms approach is so useful is that de Caluwé and Vermaak suggest what role the change agent should be playing together with the necessary knowledge, skills and attitudes (see Table 5.9).

Table 5.9 Paradigms and the necessary knowledge, skills and attitudes

Paradigm and role	Knowledge	Skills	Attitude

Blue – Design
Expert
Specialist
Competence
The right solution
The best solution
Full responsibility for
  implementation
Plan, Do, Review
	Project
	  management
	Relevant subject
	  knowledge
	SWOT analysis
	Processes, systems
	  and projects
		Project management
		Planning and control
		Analytic thinking
		Research methods
		Presentation techniques
			Results-oriented
			Decisiveness
			Independence
			Intelligence
			Accuracy
			Dedication

Yellow – Addressing
Interests
Power broker
Mediator
Negotiator
Looks for solutions
  with a chance
Art of the possible
	Strategy
	Top structure
	Stakeholder
	  analysis
		Network identification
		Understanding and using
		  power
		Conflict resolution
		Influencing
		Strategic interventions
			Independence
			Stability
			Self-control
			Self-confidence
			Perseverance
			Flexibility
			Diplomacy

White – Emergence
Spotter
Catalyst
Sets out general
  direction and
  principles
Energizes
Holds up a mirror
	Chaos theory
	Systems theory
	Complexity
	Psychology
		Pattern recognition
		Challenging the status quo
		Dealing with conflicts
		Creating dialogue
		Dealing with uncertainty
			Independence
			Authenticity
			Self-assured
			Honesty
			Flexibility
			Self-confidence
			Spiritual
			Empathy

Table 5.9 *continued*

Paradigm and role	Knowledge	Skills	Attitude
Green – Learning Facilitator Coach Mentor Communicator	Learning theories Educational theories OD thinking	Designing and facilitating learning situations Creating an open and safe environment Coaching, listening, feedback Role model	Trustworthiness Creativity Openness Flexibility Self-confidence Inspirational
Red – People Manager of Human Resource HR procedure expert Involvement and engagement Motivator	Management science HRM Motivation theories People and performance	HRM policies and procedures Communication planning Teamworking Discussion facilitation Motivating	Carefulness Flexibility Trustworthiness Decisiveness Loyalty Steadfastness

Adapted from de Caluwé, L and Hans Vermaak, H (2003) *Learning to Change: A guide for organization change agents*, Sage, CA

The implications of this are that the change agent will need to craft his or her objectives and interventions in a way that is congruent with the prevailing culture to ensure some traction, even if at a later date interventions from different paradigms are warranted. For example, managing change within the blue paradigm will call for a clear set of objectives that have been established at the outset, a set of rational interventions conducted by a competent specialist and in a very planned and orderly manner. The box below described implications across the five paradigms and four change metaphors.

IMPLICATIONS AND DIFFERENT ROLES OF LEADERS AND CHANGE AGENTS

Entering into a change process when operating within one of the four change metaphors or five paradigms has implications for how you construct your change process and what sort of role you need to play.

Using the machine metaphor or the 'change through design' paradigm will entail a rigorous project management approach with a leadership style that is one of architect and grand designer. The terrain is about efficiency and effectiveness of project planning processes and their well-oiled implementation. It's about an unambiguous mapping out of the plan to get from A to B and the careful planning, managing, monitoring and controlling of this process.

The political metaphor and 'change through addressing interests' will require a greater focus on managing stakeholders, the informal organization and ensuring that key players are brought on board and potential winners are motivated enough and potential losers' needs are managed. The terrain for the change agent within this paradigm is all about power and the harnessing of it. The change agents themselves have to have perceived power as well as requiring powerful sponsors.

The organism metaphor requires the change agent to be monitoring the environment and taking the pulse of the organization. A key focus will be to create an enabling environment where people can learn to become responsive to the environment and the changes that are necessary. And it is also necessary to be aware of the process in order for responses and reactions and adaptations to be factored in as the change proceeds.

The flux and transformation metaphor and the 'change through emergence' paradigm recognize that change cannot be explicitly managed, but rather needs to emerge. The tensions, the conflicts, the hot spots within the organization and those on the boundary are where the change agent is focused. Once again the role is one of enabling emergence rather than directing and controlling it. The concepts of setting parameters, acting as a container and reminding people of core values are critical to this process.

The 'change through learning' paradigm draws on the key ideas from the Organizational Development movement originating in the 1960s and the writers and researchers of the Learning Organization. Coaching, training and group and team facilitation are all ways of providing opportunities for learning to take place.

The 'change through people' paradigm is situated between the learning paradigm and the interest paradigm. It recognizes the need to include, involve and engage with all stakeholders, but principally managers and staff in order to create solutions which address the important issues. Given that change happens through people, winning the hearts and minds of the people is clearly a key factor in this. Affiliative and democratic management styles, human resource management and a collaborative culture are strong indicators of change agents operating within this paradigm.

Green (2007a)

STOP AND THINK!

Q 5.8 Review Table 5.8, 'Knowledge and skill requirements of the organization development practitioner', highlight the knowledge and the skills that you consider to be essential and produce a mini personal development plan for those aspects you consider you need to develop.

DEEPER ASPECTS OF BEING A CHANGE AGENT

In this section we look at some of the difficulties that a change agent may encounter in his or her work at a deeper level. Although you may have been enlisted to assist the organization, that doesn't mean that the organization or its constituent parts will want to change or welcome your interventions. The organization and its protagonists can 'act out' in terms of dysfunctional behaviour. This has been well documented by authors such as Argyris (1990), Egan (1994) and Kets de Vries (2001). We will look at organizational defence mechanisms and then how you can better equip yourself to address these issues and work well within the organizational system and create an environment that is conducive to growth and development.

Overcoming organizational defences

Chris Argyris in his book *Overcoming Organizational Defenses: Facilitating organizational learning* (1990) highlights a challenge that most change agents will encounter during their organizational work – organizational defensive routines and how to overcome them. He defines organizational defensive routines as:

> Actions or policies that prevent individuals or segments of the organization from experiencing embarrassment or threat. Simultaneously they prevent people from identifying and getting rid of the causes of the potential embarrassment or threat. Organizational defensive routines are antilearning, overprotective, and self-sealing.

Both he and Peter Block (2000) provide familiar examples in action:

'I don't mean to interrupt you but…' or, 'I don't want to upset you… but', which translates as: 'I don't want you to feel bad about my interrupting you or upsetting you but actually that is exactly what I intend to do.'

'Thank you for your feedback…' translates as: 'I really didn't like it'; 'That's a very interesting idea…' when actually I'm clear that I won't be using it.

And finally: 'That's a great proposal… let me go away and think about it' – meaning there is no way we will accept it.

These could perhaps be categorized as everyday examples but once embedded in the culture the malaise of organizational defensive routines has far greater import. Many actions – particularly of the senior management – will not be questioned, and especially in times of change people lower down an organization can see the truth or parts of the truth of a situation but are afraid to point out, for example, the emperor's new clothes or the fault lines in the strategy.

Argyris suggests that 'organizational defensive routines make it highly unlikely that individuals, groups, inter-groups and organizations will detect and correct the errors that are embarrassing and threatening' because the fundamental rules are to:

1   bypass the errors and act as if they were not being done;

2   make the bypass undiscussable; and

3   make its undiscussability undiscussable.

To challenge the undiscussable feels like a very high-risk strategy, even at the best of times, but when uncertainty prevails during times of change, the risks can be even higher. And these phenomena are more likely precisely during times of change… and the change agent is in the 'privileged' position of being able to spot and point out these phenomena. In order to do so the change agent will need to have a high degree of self- and social awareness and be skilled at creating the right environment within which to intervene.

Self as instrument

If we were to adopt the mechanistic view of managing change, the change agent would be the rational expert with specialist knowledge who would plan the change process and the process itself would run according to plan, if properly executed. The feedback mechanisms would be through project reviews, and cost, quality and time measurements. The change agent would be taking an objective stance in this and any intervention would be based on rational analysis of evidence-based information – operating within the rational, change through design paradigm.

In our experience however, the world doesn't work like this. From science we know that the 'observer effect' will have the potential of making the act of observing a determinant of the outcome. Likewise in information systems, if a process is electronically monitored the process itself will potentially be influenced by the monitoring. And importantly we know from the 'Hawthorne effect' (Mayo, 1949) that people will change their behaviour simply when they are put under the spotlight by being observed by external researchers or consultants.

One of Freud's definitions of psychoanalysis was the procedure for the investigation of mental processes that are almost inaccessible in any other way – that is the unconscious phenomena in human interaction. As such it is one way of being able to understand the more irrational aspects of human behaviour. Table 5.10 lists a number of psychoanalytic terms which describe phenomena that not only manifest themselves on the analyst's couch but are very much alive in the world of individual, team and organizational change.

Table 5.10   Psychoanalytic terms useful in the change agent's practice

Psychoanalytic term	
Transference	The process by which emotions and desires originally associated with one person, such as a parent or sibling, are unconsciously shifted to another person, especially to the analyst
Projection	The attribution of one's own attitudes, feelings, or suppositions to others
Counter-transference	The psychoanalyst's displacement of emotion onto the patient or more generally the psychoanalyst's emotional involvement in the therapeutic interaction

For example, people might transfer their very positive parental feelings onto the consultant and imagine that the consultant will have the power, authority and magic to take away all the pain and fix things. Or they might see you as the autocratic despotic father figure who is to be feared and shied away from. They can also transfer any negative feelings that they have for the management onto the consultancy team.

In the same way that the client system might be impacted by the change agent entering the system, the question can be asked whether the change agents themselves can be impacted by being in the client system and, if so, how might this look? We need to enter the realm of depth psychology and psychoanalysis to aid our understanding. Freud and Jung, both in their own ways, suggested that communication between therapist and patient operated not only on the rational, conscious level, but also on the unconscious level. Patients would, for example, project their own, cut-off feelings onto the therapist and also transfer feelings associated with other (significant) figures in their lives onto the therapist. The therapist in turn would have feelings about the client. These Jung labelled as 'counter-transference'. Initially this was seen as unresolved issues within the therapist's own psyche, but has later become relevant in terms of feelings that the therapist is 'holding' for the patient – that is, feelings that don't belong to the therapist at all but tell him or her something about the inner world of the patient.

Jung was adamant that therapists needed a rigorous analysis themselves to ensure that they could see clearly what their issues were and what were legitimately the patient's and therefore 'grist for the mill' of the therapeutic work. Hanna Segal (quoted in Bell, 1997) did issue a health warning though by saying: 'Counter-transference can be the best of servants but is the most awful of masters.' She meant that change agents need to be able to own what is theirs, in terms of what is being experienced, rather than merely seeing it as part of the client system. Seeing it as part of the client system and seeking to understand what that means are crucial, but one should always be looking inward too, ensuring that intense feelings are not part of one's own psychopathology. Because change can produce intense emotional reactions and some people may not want to admit or live with those feelings, they can unconsciously project these onto the consultant who, to them may then appear as, for example, bored, irritated or angry.

The important thing to note here is that when people do this, they do so unconsciously and then react to you as if you were exhibiting those attributes and feelings. As the consultant you therefore need to be aware of other people's reactions and behaviours, especially when they appear to be at odds with your reality.

The consultant might find himself, for example, uncomfortably aligned with a group that is being scapegoated, that is perceived as troublesome or difficult. Given the job of helping its members to 'improve', he may come to feel that his choice is to fight back on their behalf against the unfair projections, or he may join in and come to believe the projections and blame the members of the group for their shortcomings.

Czander and Eisold (2003)

This is where being in touch with your own feelings is so important, and feelings of counter-transference can help. When you have strong positive or negative feelings – and indeed when you are feeling nothing at all – it is wise to ask yourself whether these could be someone else's in the client system and what that might mean for them, for you and for the project.

Developing observational skills of self and others is extremely important if you want to use yourself as an instrument of change. Cheung-Judge (2001) suggests that:

> In practice, owning the self means devoting time and energy to learning about who we are, and how issues of family history, gender, race and sexuality affect self-perception. It means also identifying and exploring the values by which we live our lives, as well as developing our intellectual, emotional, physical and spiritual capacities.

She is clearly proposing that to be effective in this kind of work one has to work 'on oneself' as well as developing the technical and inter-personal skills necessary to interact with confidence and competence.

This is further endorsed when one looks at what Nevis (1987) calls the five basic roles played by the (Gestalt) consultant:

1   to be totally attentive to the client system through detailed observations of both the specific and the patterns;

2   to be aware of one's own experience of feelings, sensations and thoughts and to appropriately share these constructively and thereby establish one's presence;

3   to focus on where the energy or lack of it is in the client system and the emergence of or lack of issues for which there is energy and to be able to catalyse the energy to enable action to happen;

4   to facilitate clear and meaningful contact between parts of the client system, including the change agent;

5   to help the group achieve heightened awareness of its process in completing the tasks in front of it.

Cheung-Judge recommends that you have to:

• develop lifelong learning habits (in both the technical and inter-personal aspects of the role);

- work through issues of power (which clearly manifest when dealing with multiple stakeholders in times of change and uncertainty);

- build emotional and intuitive self-awareness (through understanding one's strengths, weaknesses, blind spots and areas of anxiety, and developing emotional intelligence); and

- have a serious commitment to self-care (in the form of looking after yourself, body, mind and spirit, nurturing your support networks and developing practices of reflection and self-renewal).

Nevis suggests that the change agent be focused on the interpersonal aspects of intervening in the client system highlighting the fact that it is:

> *interaction with the client* as a means through which movement toward improved organizational functioning will occur. Specifically, the practitioner models a way of approaching problems and, through interest in the attractiveness of this way of being, hopes to mobilize the energy of the client.

Tolbert and Hanafin (2006) see the need for the change agent to develop a sense of presence, which they believe to be one of the key enablers for genuine interaction to occur. They define presence as representing 'the translation of personal appearance, manner, values, knowledge, reputation, and other characteristics into interest and impact… Presence is use of self with intent.' They highlight the principles of presence (see Table 5.11).

We will return to the notion of 'presence' in Chapter 11 when we look at leaders' ability to deal with uncertainty.

Creating the holding environment

> *If only we can wait, the patient arrives at understanding creatively and with immense joy… The principle is that it is the patient and only the patient who has the answers.*
>
> Winnicott (1965)

Individual and group psychoanalytic practitioners and psychologists such as Bion (1961), Winnicott (1965) and Bowlby (1980, 1988) stressed the importance of the change agent's ability to create a psychological safe place – a holding environment, a facilitating environment – which is a container for change to be explored and developed, in which individuals

Table 5.11   Principles of presence

Be honourable
  Align personal assumptions, values, beliefs, behaviour
  Stand for something; take a position
  Dare to be different (or similar)
  State the obvious
  Speak the unspeakable

Be an effective agent of change
  Be an awareness expert
  Facilitate enhanced interaction among members of the client system and
    with self
  Teach basic behavioural skills
  Model a methodology for solving problems and for dealing with life in general
  Cultivate conditions for the client to experiment with new behaviour
  Help the client complete work and achieve closure on unfinished business

Be curious
  Stay in a space of perpetual wonderment
  Show genuine interest in the client
  Be interested in self
  Explore the nature of relationships between self and client and among
    individuals in the client system

Tolbert and Hanafin (2006) Use of Self in OD Consulting, Chapter 4 in *The NTL Handbook of Organization Development and Change,* Jones, B and Brazzel, M (eds) © 2006. Reproduced with permission of John Wiley & Sons Inc.

and groups can be more at ease with their uncertainty and anxiety about the changes they are experiencing. The principles of presence described above will engender the creation of a holding environment. We will return to the idea of 'containment' from a leadership perspective in Chapter 11.

Creation of such an environment has physical and tangible as well as psychological aspects; one example of both is the idea of boundaries – boundaries such as clarity about project scope, meetings times, and a clearly defined set of operating procedures and ground rules in which people can be together, share feedback together and learn together. This then transcends into an environment where anxieties and concerns can be explored without the fear of their getting out of control or being talked about outside destructively.

Much of what Carl Rogers wrote about (see Chapter 1) is in fact concerned with creating such an environment for learning, development and change. His three conditions to bring about growth and development are genuineness and congruence; unconditional positive regard; and empathetic understanding.

Heifetz and Linsky (2002), recognizing that change will inevitably move people away from their comfort zones and cause disquiet and unease, stress the importance of developing a holding environment 'to contain and adjust the heat that is being generated by addressing difficult issues or wide value differences'. They define a holding environment as:

> a space formed by a network of relationships within which people can tackle tough, sometimes divisive questions without flying apart. Creating a holding environment enables you to direct creative energy toward working out the conflicts and containing passions that could easily boil over.

This can be created in one-to-one, team and larger group situations by attention to a number of facets, particularly the need to create a tangible as well as psychological safe space. This requires stability, continuity and reliability – things which of course are often lacking in times of change. However, the change agent can engender these through the careful use of structures, boundaries, routines, communications and attentive listening. The change agent can be a constant, reliable and stable presence within the organization and specifically in meetings, conversations and role-modelling. Heifetz and Linsky give some practical examples of ways that a holding environment can be created or strengthened:

Shared language.

Shared orienting values and purposes.

History of working together.

Lateral bonds of affection, trust and camaraderie.

Vertical bonds of trust in authority figures and the authority structure.

At the micro level for a working group, a meeting room with comfortable chairs, a round table, and rules of confidentiality and brainstorming that encourage people to speak their minds.

Kahn (2001) writes at length about the holding environment. He draws the parallel with the nature of adult relationships of friendship by quoting Klein (1987):

They produce speculations, explanations, and suggestions of their own for us to consider, and much else. In times of crisis they are especially important, sustaining us while we encounter and explore new things, encouraging us to carry on, holding us when we temporarily lose our footing in the stress of reorganizing our concepts. They take care of us and step in when, in the course of the temporary disorganization that new developments may bring, we are about to do something permanently detrimental to our interests.

According to Kahn, holding environments are created with the juxtaposition of opportunity, desire and competence – three elements that the change agent needs to ensure. He lists the facilitating conditions for a holding environment:

- *Optimum range of anxiety* – there is no need when people are not unduly worried about the changes being proposed; and if individuals have too much stress and anxiety, which are creating dysfunction, then additional professional support may be required.

- *Trusting movements towards others* – clearly if the organization has a culture that has created trust, a holding environment is that much easier to create. Creating trust in the organization is a prerequisite for this type of work, and can be seen to be an important initial stage.

- *Available, competent holding* – this requires the physical and psychological availability of trusted colleagues or advisers who have sufficient competence and a balance of objectivity and empathy.

- *Competent receiving* – so that those who need support do not become overly dependent and have the maturity to receive support while maintaining their self-reliance and resilience.

- *Resilient boundaries* – time and space are required for the holding environment and these need to be created out of what may be a pressured work situation with people juggling 'business as usual' and the changes.

- *Positive experiences and outcomes* – the more that these environments are seen to work and be a force for positive outcomes, the more trust will be placed in the process, which in turn will strengthen the process.

Kahn cites three crucial dimensions of holding behaviours and suggests 12 behaviours that will help; see Table 5.12.

Table 5.12 Kahn's dimensions of holding behaviours

Dimension	Task	Behaviours	Receiver experiences
Containment	Create safe, reliable environment enabling the other's expression of strong emotions and impulses	*Accessibility* – remain in the vicinity of the other person, allowing time and space for uninterrupted contact and connection *Attention* – actively attend to the other's experiences, ideas, and expressions; show comprehension with eye contact, verbal and nonverbal gestures *Inquiry* – probe for the other's experiences, thoughts and feelings *Compassion* – show emotional presence by displaying warmth, affection, and kindness *Acceptance* – accept the other's thoughts and feelings without judgement; bear painful affect without withdrawal; resist own impulses to react in evaluative, non-accepting ways	Receiver feels cared for, symbolically held, witnessed, joined, not alone, accompanied
Empathetic acknowledgement	Create empathetic context that affirms the other's sense of self as knowable, worthwhile, and understandable, laying the groundwork for the resumption of ego functioning	*Curiosity* – acknowledge the other's individuality by inquiring about and accepting the other's unique experiences of situations *Empathy* – become imaginatively engrossed in and identify with the other's experiences *Validation* – communicate positive regard, respect, and appreciation to the other; reflect back and confirm the other's positive qualities	Receiver feels valued and acknowledged through attention and curiosity; feels self-accepting through the other's acceptance and empathy

Table 5.12 *continued*

Dimension	Task	Behaviours	Receiver experiences
Enabling perspective	Create context in which the other can recover sense of primary work task and reengage ego functioning on behalf of that task; involves separating the other from their emotional experiences and creating space for rational thought and action	*Sense-making* – help other make sense of experiences and situations through focus on individual and contextual factors *Self-reflection* – use own experiences about other and of situation as useful data *Task focusing* – help the other focus on controllable elements of situation and the primary task rather than on unproductive, anxiety-arousing elements *Negotiated interpretation* – help the other develop actionable interpretations of situations and experiences based on critical thinking about tasks	Receiver feels less bound up emotionally, less anxiety, and more accepting of self in relation to situation; has clearer understanding of personal and contextual factors; is reoriented toward task; and has more capacity for self-regulated, competent thought and action

Source: Kahn, W A (2001) Holding Enviroments at Work, *Journal of Applied Behavioural Science*, September, **37**(3)

Klonsky (2010) in her doctoral research on how leaders enable the undiscussables to be discussed, found a clear link between creating a holding environment within the organization and the ability of the organization to surface undiscussables and to address the issues that they pertain to. The leaders displayed 'relational authenticity' through a demonstration of such qualities as awareness of others, active listening, acting with care, building community, empathy, growing employees' capacity, inspiring trust and acting respectfully.

Supervision and shadow consultancy

Hawkins and Smith (2006) define supervision as:

> The process by which a coach/mentor/consultant with the help of a supervisor, who is not working directly with the client, can attend to understanding better both the client system and themselves as part of the client–coach/mentor/consultant system and transform their work.

Some of the key aspects of supervision that Hawkins and Smith identify include:

- space for reflection on the work in progress;
- to review interactions and interventions and help develop them further;
- to be offered advice and/or expertise to better equip the supervisee;
- to monitor progress and receive both process and content feedback;
- to have a critical friend who can support and challenge;
- to not be scapegoated and isolated;
- to reflect upon one's own psychological reactions to the intensity of the project and individuals within it;
- to make sense of the project and the client system and develop additional approaches;
- to plan further interventions and maintain one's professionalism.

(Adapted from Hawkins and Smith, 2006)

This type of supervision is a real support for individual practitioners and their reactions to intervening in the client system. In addition there is a whole discipline that has emerged called 'shadow consultancy', which addresses the same arena but has advantages when there is a consultancy team engaged on a project and the 'shadow consultant' can act as an additional resource outside of the client and (to some extent) the consultant system. We use 'shadow' here in the context of shadowing. Hawkins and Smith define it as:

> The process by which a consultant (or team of consultants) with the help of an experienced shadow consultant, who is not working directly with the client, attends to understanding better the client system and themselves as part of the client/consultant system. Systemic shadow consultancy focuses on the interconnections between what the consultant(s) need to shift in themselves; their relationship with the client system; and in the client system – in order to be more successful.

Apart from ensuring ongoing professional development at both a task and process level, supervision and shadow consultancy can also surface 'parallel processes' – the re-enactment  within the consultant-supervisor relationship of phenomena that are being played out within the client system. As such this space is fertile ground for exploring first-hand the client system and its conscious and unconscious processes.

Encountering the organizational shadow and defence systems, using oneself as an instrument and creating and nurturing a holding environment can be intense experiences and psychologically draining. On assignments where there are substantial elements of the shadow being present, where undiscussables are not being discussed, where there is a highly political culture, or where the task within the system is complex, supervision and shadow consultancy can mean the difference between a successful project and failure, between maintaining one's sanity or burning out.

> Within organizations the shadow manifests in many ways – it's the hidden, the unspoken, the undiscussable, the power plays, all the things that sap the energy from an organization and divert it from achieving its objectives and addressing the issues that are holding it back.
>
> Green (2007a)

Looking after yourself as the change agent so you can effectively engage with the client's issues and challenges has been a key theme of this chapter. It is wise, if not essential, to ensure that you have access to your own adviser, coach or supervisor in addition to developing your technical expertise and competency and working on yourself to ensure development of interpersonal skills and all-round emotional intelligence. When engaging in difficult, complex assignments there are (inevitably) degrees of organizational dysfunction. Lone consultants and indeed whole teams of consultants can get mired in the very dysfunction they were brought in ostensibly to address.

TIME FOR SUPERVISION?

What are some of the indications for when a change agent might need supervision?

- When you have strange dreams – for example of King Kong climbing the tower block of the organization's HQ where you are working...
- When you feel 'out of sorts' or 'not yourself' for no apparent reason...
- When you have intense feelings (or lack of feelings) while engaged on an assignment...
- When whatever you say to the client they just don't get it...
- When you start having conflict in the consultancy team...
- When you feel totally inadequate and have lost the confidence to continue...
- When everyone is being very compliant...
- When lots of people are gossiping to you about other people in the organization...
- When the CEO gets very angry with some feedback you give him or her...

STOP AND THINK!

Q 5.9 Which aspects of this section 'Deeper aspects of being a change agent' do you find intriguing and what might you do to develop your expertise in those particular areas?

Flawless consulting

Finally, being a change agent can be a challenging role requiring not only high degrees of knowledge, skills and understanding but also high degrees of emotional intelligence and resilience. Peter Block, in his book *Flawless Consulting* (2000) defines the act of consulting as an act of love – 'the wish to be genuinely helpful to another... To use what we know, or feel, or have endured in a way that lightens the weight on another' and he continues by suggesting that attention always needs to be paid to two processes: being as authentic as you can be at all times with the client; and attending directly, in words and actions, to the business of each stage of the consulting process.

Amongst a plethora of practical advice for the consultant and the consulting process there are a number of particularly important points that are useful for this chapter. In keeping with the section on 'self as instrument' on page 206, Block also highlights that you should be using your experience in the project within the organization as an important part of the data-gathering process:

> The client manages you, the consultant, the same way the client manages other resources and people. If you want to understand the client's management style, you simply have to observe how you are treated. Are you feeling controlled, listened to, supported, treated with respect or disdain? Are the decisions with the client collaborative or one-way? Is the client open to options or forever on one track? Your observations and experience about the client are valid data. Paying close attention to how you are managed by the client early in the project gives you more guidance on what to explore in determining how the technical business problem is being managed.

In addition he has wise words to keep you sane by adopting a number of stances:

- Choose learning over teaching – rather than step into the expert role of dispensing wisdom, endeavour to work collaboratively with members of the organizational system to facilitate their learning about how things work and their roles in the process.

- See learning as a social adventure – which requires the elements of doubt and risk and inquiry to be present, a mutual journey of discovery which is enabled by valuing 'struggle over prescription, questions over answers, tensions over comfort, and capacities over needs and deficiencies'.

- Know the struggle is the solution – allow for the insight that perhaps there is not necessarily one or indeed any clear answer. Consulting around change will often involve looking at the tensions between choosing one thing over the other (more or less control, more or less centralization, for example). The solution emerges from grappling with the issues.

- See the question as more important than the answer – as Heifetz and Linsky (2002) observe, leaders don't know all the answers, but they ask the right questions.

- Mine the moments of tension for insight – in the change process, when there is tension, conflict or resistance you should investigate more thoroughly the situation. The energy or lack of energy will tell you a lot about the organization and the changes.

- Focus on strengths rather than deficiencies – in the spirit of appreciative inquiry there is growing evidence that the more you focus on what is going right rather than what is wrong, and your strengths rather than your weaknesses, the more you'll be able to leverage far more of the innate capabilities within the organization.

- Take responsibility for one another's learning – which is another way of saying one needs to breed collaboration rather than competition in the system and proactively facilitate connection-making and organization-wide learning.

- Let each moment be an example of the destination – paraphrasing Mahatma Gandhi, Block is saying that if you are in the process of creating culture change, that moment-to-moment activity and being should reflect the culture that you wish to create. It is not just something that happens in the future, but in every action that you take.

- Include ourselves as learners – given the particular 'take' of this chapter, it is clear that one cannot enter into a change situation knowing all that needs to be done to 'fix' the situation. The change process itself is a learning process, and the change agent will be amongst those who might need to learn the most as actions are carried out and consequences are made, and the change agent reviews and reflects and learns to intervene in a different way.

- Be authentic – in the way we manage ourselves and in our connection to our clients.

STOP AND THINK!

Q 5.10 Jaap Boonstra, in *Dynamics of Organizational Change and Learning* (2004) asks a series of penetrating questions of change agents that help raise self-awareness, challenge assumptions, and identify potential areas for further growth and development.

Read through the list of questions below and see which ones you feel able to answer clearly and which ones you find difficult. Take time out to review and reflect and then note down your answers and, if necessary, draw up a plan to more fully address the issues that arise:

- Why am I working in the field of organizational change and learning?

- Towards what purpose am I working in change and learning?

- What are my assumptions about organizations, change, and learning?

- What kind of paradoxes and dilemmas do I experience when working in change management and how do I deal with them?

- How do I define success (and failure) in organizational change?

- What is my own theoretical framework and what are the implications for me and others I am working with?

- How do I relate to different theoretical frameworks?

- What are the principles that guide my choices and actions?

- How do I interact with senior management?

- What is the nature of my relationship with others in the field of change and learning?

- What roles do I prefer for change managers and consultants?

- How do I view power and resistance in change management?

- What power do I have, how do I use it, and what are the ethical values that guide my choices?

- What do interaction and communication mean for me in change and learning?

- How do I view the notion of participation in change and learning?

- How do I choose specific interventions and why some more often than others?

- What knowledge and added value to my profession do I have to offer?

- How can I contribute to sharing insights and knowledge with participants, practitioners, and scholars?

Adapted from Boonstra (2004)

These questions will repay further reflection during your next change project.

SUMMARY AND CONCLUSIONS

O'Neill (2000) defined the change agent as 'data gatherer, educator, advisor, meeting facilitator, coach. Most often he or she has no direct line authority over the implementers.' Caldwell (2003) suggests there are four models of change agency:

1   leadership;

2   management;

3   consultancy; and

4   team.

The classical consulting process comprises various stages:

1   entry;

2   contracting;

3   diagnosis;

4   implementation; and

5   evaluation.

In the consulting process you may be asked to perform one of three roles:

- The Expert.

- The Extra Pair of Hands.

- The Collaborative Role.

You can perform these either as an internal or external agent, but be aware of the differences.

Block (2000) suggests that the two processes you need to always pay attention to are: being as authentic as you can be at all times with the client; and attending directly, in words and actions, to the business of each stage of the consulting process.

At each stage of the consulting process you need to ensure you have the necessary Interpersonal, Analytic, Personal and Project Management skills.

In order to intervene in a client system at an individual, team and organizational level you need to evaluate the culture and tailor your interventions to be either aligned or counter-culture. Frameworks to use may include:

- Change Kaleidoscope (Balogun and Hope Hailey, 2004)
- Goffee and Jones' *Character of the Corporation* (1998)
- Cameron and Quinn's *Competing Values Framework* (2011)
- The four organizational metaphors (Morgan, 1986)
- The change five paradigms (Léon de Caluwé and Hans Vermaak, 2004)

Areas of competency and skill for the change agent should include:

- organization behaviour;
- individual psychology;
- group dynamics;
- management and organization theory;
- research methods/statistics;
- comparative cultural perspectives;
- functional knowledge of business;
- organization design;
- organization research;
- system dynamics;
- history of organization development;
- theories and models of change;
- managing the consulting process;
- analysis/diagnosis;
- designing/choosing appropriate and relevant interventions;
- facilitation and process consultation;
- developing client capability;
- evaluating organization change.

For the deeper aspects of being a change agent you need to understand the importance of:

- overcoming organizational defences;
- using the self as an instrument;
- creating the holding environment;
- supervision and shadow consultancy.

Part Two

The applications

*Strategy is the pattern or plan that integrates an organization's major
goals, policies and action sequences into a cohesive whole.*

James Quinn (1980)

In Part One we looked at change and the management of change from
three different perspectives: the individual, the team and the organization. We also examined the roles, styles and skills needed to become
a successful leader of change and a further chapter looked at the role
of the change agent.

In Part Two we now look more closely at four different organizational
change processes or applications, offering tips, frameworks and examples
which illustrate how best to support change and apply tools and techniques in each of these different contexts:

- structural change;
- mergers and acquisitions;
- cultural change;
- project- and programme-led change.

We look at what differentiates these changes, identify which approach to managing organizational change is the most relevant, look at the implications for change managers and leaders and give tips and resources for managers in these situations.

In this introduction we briefly review the strategic change process, identifying the elements that make a strategic change process successful.

STRATEGIC CHANGE PROCESS

When we look at Figure II.1, or probably more realistically Figure II.2, we can see that typically the whole process begins with an internal or external trigger for change. In a way we compartmentalize the universe in order to make sense of it. This whole book is an attempt to make order out of the chaos we sometimes feel around change. It is very rare that anyone could say for sure that this change began on that particular day or at that particular meeting. But in our ideal universe these triggers for change make us take a long hard look at the market or industry we are in, examine our customer and stakeholder relationships, and scrutinize our organizational capability. And as a result we review where we want to be, how we want to get there and what we need to do to get there. We develop our new vision, mission and values.

Now all sorts of changes may need to happen as a result of this exercise, but typically we will need to adjust one or all of the following:

- the organizational structure;
- the commercial approach;
- the organizational culture;
- the relevant processes.

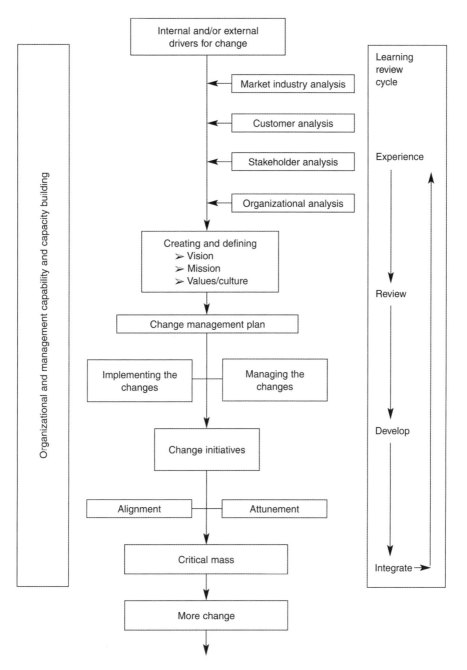

Figure II.1   The strategic change process (1)

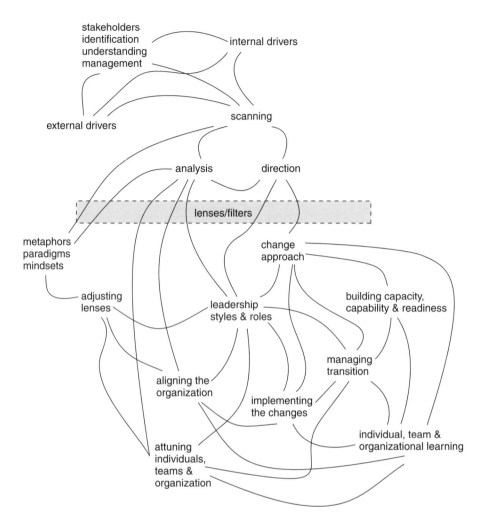

Figure II.2   The strategic change process (2)

OVERVIEW OF STRUCTURE

We tackle all four types of change identified above. In Chapter 6 we tackle structural changes head on. This is because we observe how many strategic changes result in structural changes, and we wanted to write something helpful about how to make this approach work well. Chapter 7 tackles mergers and acquisitions, and deals with change situations when competitors or suppliers (and indeed customers) are brought into the organization. Although it is not specifically addressed, many of the issues raised are pertinent to partnering as well. Chapter 8 focuses on cultural change, and specifically deals with: why culture is important; the key role of values; how to facilitate culture change; and emerging cultural trends. Finally, Chapter 9 is focused on the effectiveness of project- and programme-led approaches to change given that these tools and techniques are now so widely used.

Other important aspects of the change process

There are six other essential characteristics of successful strategic change initiatives:

1 **Alignment** is an important feature of a successful change initiative. This is about ensuring that all the components of the change plan are an integrated whole. This means that they have an internal integrity but are also linked into the whole organizational system and beyond, if necessary.

2 **Attunement** is important too. This is about mirroring the preferred organizational culture, and ensuring that all aspects of the change are carried out in line with organizational values and with sufficient attention to the human side of change.

3 **Critical mass** is vital. The aim of a change management plan is to develop momentum and build sustainability. This occurs when a sufficiently critical mass of people are aligned and in tune with senior management.

4 **Building organizational capacity, capability and readiness.** Change management capacity and capability within organizations vary dramatically. Even organizations that seem to go through constant change do not necessarily have this as a key competency within their people. Our contention is that the more the senior management recognizes the need to develop this capability within itself and a significant proportion of its managers, the sooner change can become a way of life and not something to be feared, shunned and avoided.

5 **Encouraging individual, team and organizational learning.** Change managers should be well supported with training and coaching if they are to be successful. Some succeed without this, but they are the

exception. Usually the demands of implementing change, together with a need to keep the day-to-day requirements of the job going, mean that everything gets done in a rush, without pausing to review, develop or integrate. The habit is then set: managers hop from experience to experience without learning very much. Learning it clearly doesn't stop at an individual level. Mentoring, reviewing and feedback mechanisms help the change process and also build ongoing change capability.

6 **Mindset**. The whole of the change process will operate within a certain mindset or prevailing culture. It is important to understand that all our observations, calculations and decisions will be influenced by the lens through which we look.

As you go through the following chapters, it may help to refer back to Figures II.1 and II.2 as you think through how each type of change can be achieved successfully as part of an organization-wide strategic change.

6

Restructuring

These words, spoken two millennia ago, might be very familiar to some of you. They certainly are to us, and we believe they are as insightful now as they were then. However, even though these words have been much quoted, organizations do not necessarily take any notice of them!

Although some managers are now getting this process right, most people's experience of restructuring is negative. People often roll their eyes and say, 'Not again', 'It failed', 'Why didn't they manage it better?', and 'Why can't they leave us to just get on with the job?'

Restructuring as a theme for change might seem a little strange because restructuring as a key strategic objective is not particularly meaningful;

surely we should be looking at the reasons behind the change. There are a number of important points here:

- It seems that restructuring becomes the solution to a variety of organizational issues, and in that sense we need to look at the restructuring process itself as it impacts on so many people's lives.

- Given that managers and staff are restructured so often, it is important to understand the dynamics of restructuring, what typically goes wrong and what a good process looks like.

- In our view restructuring should be the last option considered by management rather than the first. It is often a method for not addressing the organizational issues that it seeks to resolve.

- Many of the tools are useful in other change situations.

This chapter looks at:

- the reasons for restructuring;
- the restructuring processes:
    - strategic review and reasons for change;
    - critical success factors, design options and risk assessment;
    - learnings from previous projects and best practice;
    - project planning and project implementation;
    - monitoring and review;
- restructuring from an individual change perspective – the special case of redundancy;
- enabling teams to address organizational change.

In the UK the Chartered Institute of Personnel and Development (CIPD) is running an ongoing research project, 'Organising for Success in the 21st century' (www.cipd.org.uk) looking at current and future themes of restructuring in organizations today. It stresses the importance to companies of this process:

> [When] DuPont announced its reorganization in February 2002, its stock price rose 12 per cent, putting a valuation on the new organization design of $7 billion (£4.5 billion). Less fortunate was the reception of Procter and Gamble's... launched in 1999 by the company's new chief executive, Durk

Jager, this reorganization had a $1.9 billion (£1.2 billion) budget over six years. Within 18 months, the perceived difficulties... had cost Jager his job.

On a macro level, the survey found that during the 1990s the top 50 UK companies moved from having on average one major reorganization every five years to having one every three years. On a micro level, individual managers had personally experienced seven reorganizations within their organizations. Not all of the seven were major organization-wide change, some were more local. Nonetheless managers encountered various challenges as a result: managing the changes within themselves, managing the changes within their staff, ensuring that both large-scale and minor changes were aligned to the wider organizational strategies, and last but by no means least, delivering on business as usual and ensuring staff were motivated to deliver on business as usual.

REASONS FOR RESTRUCTURING

We are concerned in this chapter with the dynamics of change and restructuring, less so with why the organization or part thereof is being restructured. Restructuring can occur for numerous reasons:

- downsizing or rightsizing (market conditions or competitiveness);

- rationalization or cost-cutting (market conditions or competitiveness);

- efficiency or effectiveness (drive towards internal improvement);

- decentralization or centralization (drive towards internal improvement);

- flattening of the hierarchy (drive towards internal improvement);

- change in strategy (strategy implementation);

- merger or acquisition (strategy implementation);

- new product or service (strategy implementation);

- cultural change (strategy implementation);

- internal market re-alignment (strategy implementation);

- change of senior manager (leadership decision);

- internal or external crisis (unforeseen/unplanned change).

We believe that restructuring should only take place as a result of a change in strategy. It should have a clear rationale and should be done in conjunction with other parallel changes such as process change and culture change. Of course this is not always the case. Sometimes other events kick off restructuring processes, such as a new boss arriving, a process or product failure, an argument, a dissatisfied client or an underperforming person or department. In these cases it is sometimes difficult for employees to curb their cynicism when changes in structure seem to be a knee-jerk reaction that lacks direction, appears cosmetic and fails to lead to any real improvement.

We look at specific cases of restructuring such as mergers and acquisitions, cultural change and rebranding, and IT-based change in the other application chapters.

THE RESTRUCTURING PROCESS

Whereas some of the other change scenarios we discuss in this book are more problematic (for instance, culture change and merger/acquisition), on the surface a restructuring of the organization should be a relatively straightforward affair. If we recollect the organizational change metaphors, the restructure could be quite neatly placed into the machine metaphor.

The key beliefs of the machine metaphor are:

- Each employee should have only one line manager.
- Labour should be divided into specific roles.
- Each individual should be managed by objectives.
- Teams represent no more than the summation of individual efforts.
- Management should control and there should be employee discipline.

This leads to the following assumptions about organizational change:

- The organization can be changed to an agreed end state by those in positions of authority.
- There will be resistance, and this needs to be managed.

Change can be executed well if it is well planned and well controlled.

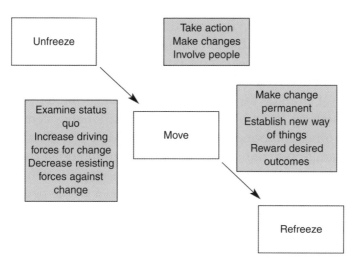

Figure 6.1 Lewin's three-step model
Source: Lewin (1951)

Within this metaphor we could perhaps draw on Kurt Lewin's three-step process of organizational change (see Figure 6.1). The first step involves unfreezing the current state of affairs. This means defining the current state, surfacing the driving and resisting forces and picturing a desired end state. The second step is about moving to a new state through participation and involvement. The third step focuses on refreezing and stabilizing the new state of affairs by setting policy, rewarding success and establishing new standards. Clearly an organizational restructuring process could follow this model. There is a current state that needs unfreezing and a perceived end state that is required. The main focus therefore is the need to ensure that movement between the former to the latter state is as smooth and quick as necessary.

However, our experience when facilitating organizational change is that a restructuring process will not be successful if it is focused solely on generating organizational structure charts and project plans. It is disappointing to note that the CIPD research (CIPD, 2003) suggests that organizations typically devote much more time during restructuring to areas other than human resources. The finance and systems functions accounted for double the time and attention that HR issues received. Anyone managing or experiencing restructuring knows that there are many other factors to consider. The politics of the situation and the psychological needs of managers and staff play a key role. It is also important to ensure that the restructuring process is positioned as a framework to enable the organization to do something it has not done before, rather than simply as a tool for changing the structure around.

It is therefore useful to remind ourselves of Nadler and Tushman's congruence model, which derives from the political and organism metaphors. One of the key aspects of the congruence model is that if you change something in one part of the organizational system, the whole system and other component parts are affected. If you do not factor this into your change equation you may well face unintended consequences. For example, restructuring in one part of the organization means that people in other areas may well have to develop a whole new set of relationships. Very often little is done to communicate the changes, let alone actively work to foster new working relationships.

The authors have witnessed numerous restructures in a variety of public and private sector organizations, and have concluded that perhaps the best way to approach the restructuring process is as a mixture of the machine and organism metaphors. Beckhard and Harris' change formula (1983) is useful here:

$$C = [ABD] > X$$

C = Change
A = Level of dissatisfaction with the status quo
B = Desirability of the proposed change or end state
D = Practicality of the change (minimal risk and disruption)
X = 'Cost' of changing.

According to this formula, there are three important factors in any restructuring. First, the reasons, timing and rationale for the restructure must be made very clear. Second, the end goal or vision must be communicated in an appealing way. Third, the whole exercise must appear doable by being well planned and well implemented. For the majority of individuals the overwhelming experience is one of upheaval. The cost of changing is high. It is therefore imperative that the benefits are accentuated and then planned for in the most authentic and genuine way possible.

In Figure 6.2 we outline our generic approach to restructuring, which can be tailored to individual circumstances. We highlight areas of potential problems and also suggest ways of making it a more effective process.

Strategic review and reasons for change

Any attempt to restructure needs to have a clear communicable rationale. This will typically come from a review of strategy that highlights the need

Strategic review

⇓

Reasons for change

⇓

Critical success factors

⇓

Design options

⇓

Risk assessment

⇓

Learning from previous
projects

⇓

Learning from best
practice

⇓

Project plan

⇓

Project implementation

⇓

Continuous monitoring
feedback and adjustment

⇓

Review

Figure 6.2   A generic approach to restructuring

to address a specific issue relating to the internal or external business environment. In the CIPD research cited above, restructuring was often undertaken to improve customer responsiveness, gain market share or improve organizational efficiency. Key drivers in the private sector were 'typically performance declines, mergers and acquisitions and a change of chief executive. In the public sector, key drivers are the need for new collaborations and legislative and regulatory change, though chief executive changes are again important.'

Critical success factors

Planning a structure requires the generation of critical success factors, design options and a risk assessment. The purpose of a restructure is to align the organization to better achieve its strategy. Critical success factors are important to define, because if they are met they will ensure success for the new structure and by implication the strategy. Although identification of these key factors is an important prerequisite to any restructuring, this task is not necessarily clear-cut. The factors themselves will depend on the organizational strategy, its culture, its market, its infrastructure and its internal processes.

In the box we give an example from a local government authority that needed to reorientate itself to have a much greater customer and citizen focus. One of the explicit strategies was to restructure the organization in a way that would dissolve the traditional departmental boundaries and their associated destructive tensions and unhelpful silo mentality.

CRITICAL SUCCESS FACTORS FOR A LOCAL AUTHORITY

Public service users (and relevant stakeholders), not providers, are the focus

Will this structure result in clear, measurable deliverables to the customers and citizens?

To what extent have we consulted with our customers?

New working relationships are accommodated such as community leadership, neighbourhood working and political management arrangements

Does the structure reflect and support key changes in the political arrangements and thinking?

A realistic interaction is demonstrated between policy planning in all its forms, business development and financial planning at every level

Does the structure enable clear links between the different types of plans and the relevant timescales?

Better prioritization of objectives and decision making on workloads and resourcing can take place

Does the structure enable clarity around the authority's strategic objectives?

Are there linkages across the organization?

Is there clarity as to who is accountable for what?

Are there supporting processes that manage potentially conflicting priorities?

Individuals are clear about their responsibilities and accountabilities and can act in an empowered way

Does the structure enable better application of the performance management system?

Are individual and team development needs identified and resourced to meet business outcomes?

> **A performance and feedback culture is developed across the organization, internally and externally**
>
> Does the structure help strengthen the performance and feedback culture?

Design options

Once it has been decided what factors it is important for the restructure to meet, it is important to demonstrate that these are better achieved through this structure rather than any other one.

Design options are the different ways in which the particular organization can be structured. It is not within the scope of this book to discuss in depth the different types of organizational structure – readers are encouraged to read an overview in _Organization Theory,_ edited by D S Pugh (1990). However, we are interested not only in the general impact of restructuring but also in any specifics relating to a move from one type of structure to another. Miles and Snow (1984) detailed the evolution of organizational structure and its relationship to business strategy:

- an entrepreneurial structure when there is a single product or service, or local/regional markets;

- a functional structure when there is a limited, standardized product or service line, or regional/national markets;

- a divisional structure when there is a diversified, changing product or service line, or national/international markets;

- a matrix structure when there are standard and innovative products or services, or stable and changing markets;

- a dynamic network when there is the need for product or service design or global changing markets.

The majority of organizations are structured according to an entrepreneurial, functional, divisional or matrix structure. All have their advantages and their limitations, as outlined in Table 6.1.

Table 6.1 Advantages and limitations of different types of organization structure

Structure	Entrepreneurial	Functional	Divisional by product, geography or both	Matrix
Main features	Organized around one central figure. Totally centralized; no division of responsibility.	Organized around tasks to be carried out. Centralized.	Divisions likely to be profit centres and may be seen as strategic business units for planning and control purposes. Divisions/business units headed by general managers who have responsibility for their own resources. Decentralized.	Double definition of profit centres. Permanent and full dual control of operating units – though one will be generally more powerful than the other. Authority and accountability defined in terms of particular decisions.
Situations where appropriate	Simple companies in early stages of their development.	Small companies, few plants, limited product or service diversity. Relatively stable situations.	Growing in size and complexity. Appropriate divisional/business splits exist. Organizations growing through mergers and acquisition. Turbulent environments. When producing a number of different products or services. Geographic splits with cultural distinctions in company's markets.	Large multi-product, multinational companies with significant interrelationships and interdependencies. Small sophisticated service companies.

	(1)	(2)	(3)	(4)
Advantages	Enables the founder, who has a logical or intuitive grasp of the business, to control its early growth and development.	Controlled by strategic leaders/chief executive. Relatively low overheads. Efficient. Clearly delineated external relationships. Specialist managers develop expertise. Relatively simple lines of control. Can promote competitive advantage through the functions.	Spreads profit responsibility. Enables evaluation of contributions of various activities. Motivates managers and facilitates development of both specialists and generalists. Enables adaptive change. CEO concentrates on corporate strategy. Growth through acquisition easier. Can be entrepreneurial. Divestment can be managed more easily.	Decisions can be taken locally, decentralized within a large corporation, which might otherwise be bureaucratic. Optimum use of skills and resources – and high-quality informed decisions, reconciling conflicts within the organization. Enables control of growth and increasing complexity. Opportunities for management development.
Limitations	Founder may have insufficient knowledge in certain areas. Only appropriate up to a certain size.	Succession problems – specialists not generalists are created. Unlikely to be entrepreneurial or adaptive. Profit responsibility exclusively with CEO. Becomes stretched by growth and product diversification. Functional managers may concentrate on short-term routine activities at the expense of longer-term strategic developments. Problems of ensuring coordination between functions – rivalry may develop. Functional experts may seek to build mini-empires.	Conflict between divisions for resources. Possible confusion over locus of responsibility (local or head office). Duplication of efforts and resources. Divisions may think short-term and concentrate on profits. Divisions may be of different sizes and some may grow very large. Evaluation of relative performances may be difficult. Coordination of interdependent divisions and establishing transfer pricing may be difficult.	Difficult to implement. Dual responsibilities can cause confusion. Accounting and control difficulties. Potential conflict between the two wings, with one generally more powerful. High overhead costs. Decision making can be slow.

Source: summarized from Thompson (2001)

Risk assessment

As you can detect from the limitations described for each of the organizational structures, there are risks attached to the restructuring process. Those identified here are obviously generic risks; however, each organization will need to identify the specific risks associated with moving from one structure to another. The management therefore needs to understand fully the nature of these risks. As a concrete example we have included in the box excerpts from a risk assessment generated for a medium-sized company that had decided to move from a function-oriented organization to a divisionalized structure incorporating five product-based business units together with a centralized 'shared services' and financial control unit.

RISKS OF NEW STRUCTURE

Structure and interdependencies

Business unit structures will require some level of consistency (shape, size, roles and responsibilities, reporting lines, etc) amongst themselves to ensure that they can be adequately serviced from the centre.

Being very clear about the boundaries of the businesses we are in. That is, boundaries of the markets and boundaries between the business units.

There needs to be clarity of role and responsibility between the central services, shared services and business units.

Shared services/central service effectiveness

Shared services and, to a slightly lesser degree, central services need to be closely aligned culturally and process-wise with the business units that they interact with, to encourage efficient and effective management across the boundary.

How support services are devolved, shared and centralized requires careful planning to ensure cost-effective, efficient and productive functions.

Corporate identity

The corporate identity will be dissipated and may not be replaced.

In some areas staff's 'affinity' will be significantly diminished – how can this be managed?

Synergies

Synergies may be harder to exploit (eg deploying e-commerce solutions across business units).

Cost

Costs are likely to increase if we move to devolved support functions – what are the specific proposals that will increase income?

Cost inefficiency is a risk – the structure will inevitably lead to some duplication of costs across the business units. The structure is not ideal from a cost point of view.

Root cause

We may not address some true causes of problems that we have by thinking that we are dealing with them by restructuring.

The task for the management team was to generate an honest list, assess the degree of risk (probability × impact) and agree actions to minimize the risks. In addition, and as an example of good practice, a risk assessment was also completed for the process of managing the change as well as the changes themselves, as listed in the box.

RISKS INHERENT IN MANAGING CHANGE

Management of change

The organization will spend another six months to a year with the 'eye off the ball'.

There is a lack of change/implementation expertise and skills.

The executive management team tends to get 'bored with the detail' quickly and therefore may lose interest and impetus and let both the transition and the transformation peter out.

Communications

Staff may see this as 'yet another restructure' not tackling the real problems, and therefore become demotivated.

People

We need to ensure the best people possible for each job. We need to ensure that we keep the people we want to keep.

Management of synergies

Loss of knowledge – we need to capture and transfer knowledge of, for example, strategy formulation and implementation.

> We need to ensure best practice in one part of the company is transferred across the company.
>
> **Roles, responsibilities and interdependencies**
>
> Risk of business units declaring 'UDI' and not fully engaging with central services and company-wide issues.
>
> We need to ensure those in the centre are motivated and their performance measured. We need to establish levers other than the policeman role and the threat of regulators, etc.

Learning from previous projects and best practice

Clearly you do not have to reinvent the wheel when it comes to restructuring. Given the propensity for restructuring that most organizations have, you and your colleagues will have a reservoir of knowledge as to what has worked before. You will also know quite a lot about what has not worked! Now is the time to check back to see what the learnings are from previous change projects. If your organization has not formally retained this knowledge, a requisite variety of managers and staff can quite easily generate such a list. We include an example list (see box). The headings are the central themes that emerged during the session. These were the most relevant issues for the organization under review. Yours might well be different.

In terms of best practice there are many resources: this book for example, a wide range of literature, professional bodies and consultancy firms. It is important to get the right balance between what has worked elsewhere and what will work in your organization. And there is no guaranteed formula for that.

LEARNINGS FROM PREVIOUS CHANGE PROJECTS

Change management/project management

Preparation

Utilize previous learning from projects.
Check for false assumptions.
Always, always do a potential problem analysis.
Look for design faults at an early stage and throughout.
Significant top-level commitment.

Communication

Induction for all in the change.
Ensure earliest possible involvement of stakeholders.
Take the board with you.
Ensure cohesion across organization.
Harness energy and enthusiasm across organization.

Objectives

Lack of focus produces failures.
Link the hard and soft interventions and measures.
Have clear objectives.
Differentiate between the what and the how.
Specific behaviour objectives help.

Implementation

It helps to have people who have been through similar projects before.
Network of people and resources.
Dedicated project management.
Multidisciplinary approach.
Build the change management team.

Monitoring

Build in a process of automatic review.
Always evaluate, financially and otherwise.
To ensure sustainability, have follow-through.

Leadership and strategy

Vision, mission and values need to be overt, obvious, communicated and followed.
Ensure alignment to strategy.

People

Don't let line managers duck the issues – build responsibilities and accountabilities into the process.
Requires involvement of people – as part of buy-in, and they can actually help!
Requires communication with people.
Be honest with people.
All the new teams need to be motivated and built.
Get the right people in the right jobs.

Profitability

Always cost the initiative.
Be clear where the value is added.
Separate infrastructure investment from return on investment.
Check for false assumptions.

Project planning and project implementation

Leadership

The restructuring process can create considerable turbulence within an organization, its managers and its staff. In the box is a copy of a note to a chief executive shortly after a restructuring process had begun. It clearly identifies the state of confusion that people throughout the organization were experiencing.

MEMO TO CEO DESCRIBING THE EFFECT OF CHANGE ON STAFF

People were still very much in the throes of the changes – many clearly still affected on an emotional level by the restructuring process and all highlighting areas that need clarifying going forward.

People thought that there was a tremendous energy surrounding the changes – seeing lots of activity and lots of change being managed at a rapid pace. The downside to this was the sense that it was too fast and out of control, certainly outside of their control.

The majority of people felt positive at the ideas introduced at a high level by the strategy. Some saw it as new and exciting, others as providing one clear direction and having a certain theoretical clarity. However, the overwhelming feeling was a sense that while the Vision was fine, there was a real lack of clarity around how it would be translated into a living workable strategy. They needed something not only motivating to aim for but also something quite specific.

Coupled with people's sense of the pace of change, many reported that not only was the direction somewhat hazy, but they saw different managers going off in different directions.

There was a certain resignation to the fact that the organization was going round and round – a 'here we go again' attitude – a sense that they had been here before and wondering whether this time would be any different.

They recognized that the direction might be clearer from the top; perhaps they were not in the right place to be seeing the bigger picture. Some people complained of having too little information, while others complained of having too much information. Although one could say that staff going through change may never be satisfied – or that management will always get it wrong (damned if you do, damned if you don't) – the key question is 'How do we deliver the right message, at the right time, to the right people, through the right medium?'

> Coupled with this theme of communication was the perceived need to provide answers to the many questions people have when they are experiencing (psychologically) the chaos of change. Often people were left with no one to ask, or asking questions of managers who either didn't know or were themselves preoccupied with their own reactions to changes they were going through.
>
> In summary, and from an emotional perspective, the effect of combining the various themes described above is quite a heady one. People have reported feelings of being lost and confused, anxious and worried, degrees of uncertainty and puzzlement, an inability to piece the jigsaw together and, to some, the tremendous strain of having to wait while the changes were revealed. Points to note here include the feeling of having no control over their destiny and also watching as others (often their managers) were suffering the traumatic effects of the changes which they themselves might have to suffer at some stage.

This is often at the very time that 'business as usual' efforts need to be redoubled. The tasks of those leading the restructure are to ensure that business as usual continues; that people are readied for operating within the new structure; and that the transition from the old structure to the new is smooth and timely.

Attention to both the task and people sides of the process is imperative. Depending on people's predisposition, normally one will take precedence over the other. There is a need to ensure that plans are in place for all the necessary processes that are part of the change:

- communication plans: what, to whom, when and how;
- selection/recruitment plans: clear guidelines for both those undergoing selection, their managers and interested onlookers. These should include criteria for selection, information about the process, timescales and rationale behind the process;
- contingency plans: necessary if key people are unavailable at critical times or if timescales look like slipping.

Future direction and strategy

For many people the strategy and future direction behind a restructure are hazy. This is very often a case of too much vision and not enough pragmatism, but sometimes a case of too much pragmatism and not enough vision! A balance is needed.

In any restructure it is imperative to describe a positive future as well as to explain fully the rationale behind it, how it links to the strategy, how it will work in practice, how it differs from what went before, how it is better than what went before and what the benefits will be from it.

Communication

Communication in any change is absolutely essential. However, communications are often variable. There is sometimes too much communication, but more often too little too late. An added problem is communication by e-mail. This is such a useful mechanism when managers need large numbers of people to receive the same information at the same time, but it is so impersonal and so heartless when delivering messages of an emotional and potentially threatening nature.

A more tailored or personalized approach is better. The greater the access to people who know the answers to the important questions, the better. It is useful to compile and communicate FAQs (frequently asked questions) but do not expect this to be the end of the story. Just because you think you have told someone something it does not mean to say he or she has heard it, assimilated it or believed it. People do strange things under stress, like not listening. And they need to see the whites of your eyes when you respond!

Key questions in people's minds will be:

- What is the purpose of the restructure?
- How will it operate in practice?
- Who will be affected and how?
- What are the steps along the way, including milestones and timescales?
- How will new posts be filled and people selected?
- What happens to the others?
- Where do you go to get help and how do you get involved?
- What is the new structure and what are the new roles?
- What new behaviours will be required?
- Will training and development be provided?

Communication needs to be well planned, and these plans need to be clear about how to get the right information to the right people at the right time through the right medium (for the recipient). This includes well-presented briefing notes for managers if they are to be the channel for further communication. It is also worth checking for understanding before these messengers are required to communicate the message.

Change in any form can trigger a number of emotional responses. If the messages can be personalized the recipient is more likely to receive them in a positive frame of mind. Personalized messages such as face-to-face and one-to-one communications are especially relevant when an individual may be adversely affected by the change.

Different communities of interest have different needs when it comes to communications. Some people will need to be involved, some consulted and some told. It is important that the right people get the appropriate level of communication. It is important for them and it is important for those around them. If your manager is seen to be ignored, what does it say about the value of your work section?

Thought needs to be given to the recipients of the communication. Those responsible for communicating need to ask:

- What are their needs for information?

- What is their preferred form of communication?

- When is the best time for them to be communicated with?

For example, people in a contact centre may not have the time to read endlessly long e-mails informing them of changes in other parts of the business. However, they would probably like to be told face-to-face of events that will involve changes to their management structure, or the introduction of a new way of working.

To prevent the rumour mill growing it is important that communication is timely, and reaches each of the chosen communities at the agreed time. Start–stop–start again communications do not help either. A continuing flow of communication will engender more confidence in the change process.

Implementation process

The complexity of the restructuring task is often underestimated. Timescales are often not met. Staff directly affected by the change and potentially facing redundancy are subjected to undue stress because the whole process takes too long to complete.

Managing people's expectations is key. If you announce a plan, it needs to be adhered to, or changes to the plan clearly communicated.

Supporting mechanisms

To make the restructuring as smooth as possible and ensure that the new structure gets up and running quickly, a number of support mechanisms need to be in place.

Visible managerial support

A key response of people going through the process is that their management was often ineffectual at managing change during this period. This is not necessarily the manager's fault. Many experience having to go through a selection process themselves, many do not seem to get adequately briefed as to the nature of the changes, and some either lose their jobs or get appointed to new positions and so do not or cannot provide the necessary support through change.

Management styles across an organization can also be variable. Often there is a reduced rather than increased management visibility at these times.

People can see a restructure as just that – a change in structure, rather than an internal realignment that would help them and the business focus on, for example, their customers and with a different way of doing things. It is the role of the manager to translate the purpose of the restructure into an understandable and viable way of doing things differently.

Continued communication of the purpose

There needs to be an ongoing planned and 'personalized' communication programme to ensure the right people get the right information at the right time in the right format for them. People need to be told and involved in how the organization will be operating differently in the future. In these two-way communications staff and managers' perspectives need to be listened to and, where valid, they need to be addressed.

Clear selection process

During any selection process certain things need to be in place: first, a selection process plan that is agreed, is sensible, has an inner integrity, is consistent, equitable and scheduled; and second, clear guidelines for those undergoing selection, their managers and interested onlookers. These should include criteria for selection, information about the process, timescales, and the rationale behind the process.

Senior management attention

In most instances where senior management are involved, their presence is generally appreciated, even if the restructure is perceived as a negative change. The more people see the commitment of senior management the better; by attending meetings, visiting departments, branches or contact centres to explain the rationale, and facing the staff.

Constructive consultation

Different organizations will have different ways of involving staff in changes. We believe that if middle managers and staff have a say in the planning of change, some of the inconsistencies and incongruities emerging from the change are picked up and addressed at a much earlier stage. If there is more input and involvement at an earlier stage from those managers who have a responsibility to manage the changes, this too has an impact on the success of the change.

Monitoring and review

Monitoring and review is not something just to be done at the end of the process and written up for the next time. If you have adopted the machine approach to restructuring, perhaps you may think that once the plan is in place, all it needs is a robotic implementation. Of course organizations are not entirely mechanistic, and individuals and groups going through change can react in all sorts of ways. The restructuring plan needs to be monitored constantly to see how both the task and people aspects of the plan are progressing. Feedback loops need to be built into the plan so that senior managers and those responsible for implementation have their fingers on the pulse of the organization.

In our discussion of individual change (see Chapter 1) we remarked that a certain amount of resistance to proposed changes is to be expected. Just because people resist change does not mean to say that you are doing it wrong! It is a natural, healthy human reaction for individuals and groups to express both positive and negative emotions about change. Managers can help this process along by encouraging straight talk.

Also, just because people resist change it does not mean to say that they have got it wrong! They might well see gaps and overlaps, or things that just are not going to work. Listening to the people who will have to make the new structure work is not only a nice thing to do, it is useful and constitutes effective use of management time.

The process of monitoring and review should begin at the planning stage and be an important part of the whole process, right through to the point where you evaluate the effectiveness of the new structure in the months and years after implementation.

RESTRUCTURING FROM AN INDIVIDUAL CHANGE PERSPECTIVE: THE SPECIAL CASE OF REDUNDANCY

This section looks at redundancy and how it affects those made redundant and those who survive. David Noer spent many years working with individuals in organizations and supporting them through change. He has captured much of this experience in his book, *Healing the Wounds: Overcoming the trauma of layoffs and revitalizing downsized organizations* (1993). Although, as the title suggests, the book is primarily focused on redundancy, there is much of benefit to anyone who wants to tackle organizational change and change management. The recent recession has resulted in a new spate of redundancies, initially in the private sector but increasingly within the public sector.

Noer's research is useful for illuminating the short-, medium- and long-term impact of change. He also suggests how a manager can intervene on a number of levels to help smooth and perhaps quicken the change process.

Table 6.2 looks at the individual and organizational short- to long-term impact that redundancy can have. Many of these feelings are not

Table 6.2 The individual and organizational short- to long-term impact of redundancy

	Individual impact	Organizational impact
Short to medium term	Psychological contract broken	Reduced risk taking
		Reduced motivation
	Job insecurity	Lack of management credibility
	Unfairness	
	Distrust and sense of betrayal	Increased short-termism
		Dissatisfaction with planning and communication
	Depression, stress, fatigue	Anger over the process
	Wanting it to be over	
	Guilt	Sense of permanent change
	Optimism	Continued commitment
Medium to long term	Insecurity	Extra workload
	Sadness	Decreased motivation
	Anxiety	Loyalty to job but not to company
	Fear	
	Numbness	Increased self-reliance
	Resignation	Sense of unfairness regarding top management pay and severance
	Depression, stress, fatigue	

Source: summarized from Noer (1993). Reprinted by permission of Jossey-Bass

necessarily disclosed: some are acted upon, others just experienced internally but with a clear effect on morale and motivation. Table 6.3 suggests a breakdown of what feelings are disclosed and undisclosed. You might notice that many of the feelings found among those going through this process are precisely the same ones that Kübler-Ross described in her work on the change curve (1969).

Dealing with redundancy: Noer's model

Noer sees interventions at four different levels when dealing with redundancy in an organizational context. Most managers only progress to level one, whereas Noer suggests that managers need to work with their people at all four levels (see Figure 6.3).

Table 6.3 Disclosed and undisclosed feelings about redundancy

Feelings	Disclosed	Undisclosed
Held in	Fear, insecurity and uncertainty. Easier to identify and found in every redundancy situation.	Sadness, depression and guilt. Often not acknowledged and hidden behind group bravado.
Acted out	Unfairness, betrayal and distrust. Often acted out through blaming others and constant requests for information.	Frustration, resentment and anger. Often not openly expressed but leak out in other ways.

Source: summarized from Noer (1993). Reprinted by permission of Jossey-Bass

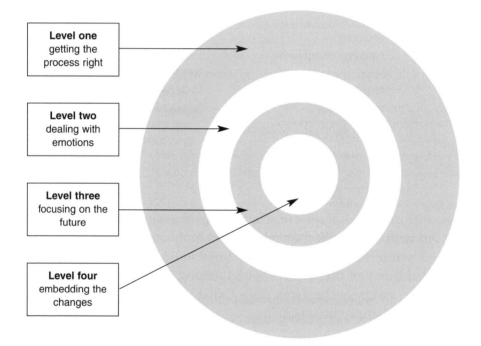

Figure 6.3 Noer's four-level redundancy intervention model
Source: Noer (1993)

Level one: getting the implementation process right

Level one interventions are all about getting the process of change right. In any change process there needs to be a good level of efficient and effective management. This includes a communication strategy and a process that is in line with organizational values.

Noer suggests that once the decision is made to effect redundancies, it needs to be done cleanly and with compassion. This requires open communication – 'over-communicating is better than under-communicating' – emotional honesty and authenticity.

Although this is just level one, it is hard to get it absolutely right!

Level two: dealing with emotions

Once you have attended to getting the task process right, the next level is getting the emotional process right. This involves dealing with the disclosed and undisclosed feelings mentioned above. Let us be frank: a lot of people are not very good at this. For many, allowing the release of emotions and negative thoughts about the situation feels like they are opening a hornet's nest. Managers need some support and a considerable amount of self-awareness if they are to handle this well.

There are many ways that managers can facilitate this process, with either one-to-one meetings or team meetings.

This level is about 'allowing time for expressions of feelings about the situation plus implications for the future and next steps for moving on'.

Level three: focusing on the future

The change curve indicates that a period of inner focus is followed by a period of outward focus. Noer's research suggests that once levels one and two have been dealt with, the organization now needs to focus on those surviving the redundancy. This is aimed at 'recapturing' their sense of self-control, empowerment and self-esteem. Those who have been made redundant need to go through a process of regaining their self-worth and focusing on their strengths; those remaining need to do the same.

There should be plenty of organizational imperatives for this to happen! But once again, let it be a considered approach rather than haphazard. The organization would not have gone through the changes that it has without a clear need to do so. It remains to those left to address that need – be it cost-efficiency, productivity, culture change or merger. The more that individuals and teams can be involved in shaping the organization's future, the greater will be the engagement and commitment, and the greater the chances of success.

Level four: embedding the changes

Level four interventions occur at a whole-system level. One option – the *laissez-faire* or reactive one – is to pretend that nothing much has changed. In terms of Satir's model, as described by Weinberg (1997), the organization can fail to really address or redress the situation. It could:

- try to reject foreign elements;
- try to accommodate foreign elements in its old model;
- try to transform the old model to receive foreign elements, but fail.

Any of these options creates a scenario in which the changes are not sustainable. Noer suggests embedding any changes made into the new way of working. This includes:

- creating structural systems and processes that treat and/or prevent survivor syndrome symptoms;
- redefining the psychological contract – being clear about what the new deal now is between employer and employee;
- enacting and embodying the new culture and its values if that is one of the stated objectives;
- ensuring all HR practices and management style are aligned with the espoused culture.

Key lessons that Noer teaches us are:

- to address change on both the task and people level;
- to pay attention, not only to what individuals and groups are going through now, but also the tasks necessary to move the organization along; to use these tasks to engage people as they come out of the more negative aspects of the change curve;
- to take the opportunity of the turbulence of the situation to embed in the organization those structures, systems and processes that will be necessary to sustain the changes in the longer term.

ENABLING TEAMS TO ADDRESS ORGANIZATIONAL CHANGE

Teams are often strongly impacted by restructuring processes. Their composition changes, or they have a new leader, or maybe they have a new purpose. There needs to be a process for quickly establishing individual and team roles, responsibilities and priorities.

Issues that teams and groups have to contend with during periods of organizational change brought about by restructuring include:

- loss of individual roles and jobs;

- new individual roles and jobs;

- loss of team members;

- new team members;

- new team purpose and objectives;

- new line manager;

- new organizational or departmental strategy.

Any of these can cause individual members of a team, or the team as a whole, to experience a range of emotions and new ways of thinking about their organization, their colleagues and their own career.

Teams need to develop so that their contribution to the organizational changes can be as good as possible as quickly as possible.

From our consultancy experience we find one particular framework useful for newly restructured teams. This framework (see Figure 6.4) encompasses a number of the issues we have highlighted. We encourage teams to work through the four-part framework in order to establish quickly the sense of team cohesion necessary for tasks to be accomplished in a meaningful and collaborative way. This is best done in a workshop format.

We have found that if a team spends time to focus both on the people and task side of this process, it will be able to deal with the transition less turbulently than one that has not.

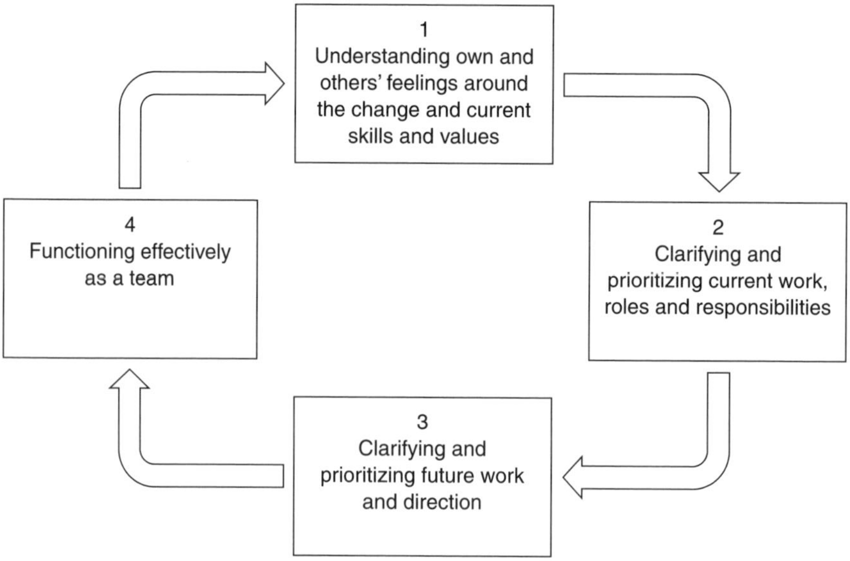

Figure 6.4 The four-stage team alignment model

Four-stage team alignment

1 *Understanding one another's skills, feelings and values.* It is useful for the team to acknowledge its own journey to where it is today. This means talking about the individuals, the team and other influential parts of the organization, and the processes of change that have been gone through to arrive at the current situation. How much of this it is necessary to acknowledge will depend upon the scale of change and the story so far.

2 *Clarifying and prioritizing current work.* The team needs to clarify the current level of demand, and must work together to satisfy current customer needs.

3 *Clarifying and prioritizing future work and direction.* If teams are facing a large change agenda, they can easily become overwhelmed unless activities are phased and planned. Do-ability must be convincing. Teams need to take stock of their current agenda, ensure it is understood, and agree priorities, responsibilities and timing.

4 *Functioning effectively as a team.* The impact of stages 1 to 3 can be extremely demanding on a team. The team needs to develop clarity about its roles, dynamics, practicalities of meetings, phasing of its development activities, communication and follow-through. Most

teams will have deficiencies and development needs in one or more areas. Teams need to assess where they need to improve and focus on those areas as a priority.

The specific outcome of this process for individuals and teams is greater clarity about the practical changes that need to happen and how necessary transformations can be managed.

You will have seen from the chapters on individual and team change that all individuals and teams undergoing change will progress through various stages. The four-stage team alignment model above attempts to address some of the key points from those chapters. Table 6.4 brings all the key team factors together as a useful reference.

CONCLUSION

Restructuring is an ever-present phenomenon in today's organizations, and the process itself can be deeply unrewarding for those who initiate and those who experience it. We have drawn together ideas in Table 6.4, from both a task and a people perspective, which will increase the chances of achieving a smoother journey. However, it must be emphasized that turbulence is one thing you will not avoid. How you manage it will be the test of how well you can lead change.

Table 6.4 Addressing team change during restructuring

	Forming		Storming	
	Task (orientation)	**People (dependency)**	**Task (organization)**	**People (conflict)**
Team purpose	Establish purpose of change and team objectives in relation to change.	Ensure understanding and commitment from team around change purpose on an intellectual and emotional level.	Ensure clarity around purpose of change and team objectives in relation to change.	Check out individual purpose engagement to enrolment, enlistment, compliance, resistance. Discuss differences.
Team roles	Establish roles and responsibilities of whole team and individual members.	Ensure individuals understand their roles and those of others. Establish whether there are any overlaps or grey areas.	Ensure clarity of roles and responsibilities of whole team and individual members.	Establish degree of comfort with individual roles and establish levels of support and challenge required. Highlight areas of team tension.
Team processes	Highlight the need for team processes.	Establish ground rules for team working.	Establish processes for decision making, problem solving, conflict resolution if not already in place.	Check out levels of trust and agreement. Surface areas of team tension.

Team relations	Highlight the need for team processes.	Establish ground rules for team working.	Ensure team is agreed on purpose, objectives, roles and processes.	Build safe environment for team to openly express thoughts and feelings.
Inter-team relations	Establish dependencies on and with other organizational groupings.	Highlight the need to establish protocols with key organizational groupings.	Establish process for communicating with other organizational groupings.	Engage with other groupings on how they will work together.
MBTI™*	Ensure balance between high-level vision and more tangible and specific objectives.	Balance between acknowledging the business case for the change and individuals' feelings about the change.	Ensure balance between tying agreements down and keeping options open.	Ensure that different types are understood and potential pitfalls and communication barriers.
Key Belbin roles	Co-ordinator, shaper, plant, implementer.	Co-ordinator, team worker.	Co-ordinator, resource investigator.	Co-ordinator, team worker, monitor-evaluator.
Organizational focus	Ensure alignment of team goals to organizational change objectives.	Ensure team members engage on an intellectual and emotional level with organizational goals.	Ensure team structure, roles and responsibilities fit with proposed changes and organizational ethos.	Ensure commitment to organizational goals and operating in line with values.

Table 6.4 *continued*

	Norming		Performing	
	Task (orientation)	People (dependency)	Task (organization)	People (conflict)
Team purpose	Review progress on team purpose and objectives; adjust as necessary.	Review progress; recognize achievement.	Review progress on team purpose and objectives; adjust as necessary.	Review team performance against purpose; recommit as necessary.
Team roles	Review roles and responsibilities; adjust as necessary.	Review progress; recognize achievements and development areas.	Review roles and responsibilities; adjust as necessary. Develop strategies for improving performance.	Review individual role performance and structure; recognize achievement and provide development.
Team processes	Review team processes; adjust as necessary.	Review team processes; adjust as necessary.	Review team processes; adjust as necessary. Develop strategies for improving performance.	Review level of team efficiency; adjust as necessary. Develop strategies for improving performance.
Team relations	Review team relations; attend to if necessary.	Review progress; recognize achievement.	Review team relations; attend to if necessary. Develop strategies for improving performance.	Reflect upon level of team effectiveness. Develop strategies for improving performance.

Inter-team relations	Review level of inter-team working; plan negotiations if necessary.	Review level of inter-team working; engage others in negotiating better relations if necessary.	Implement actions from review if necessary. Develop strategies for improving performance.	Continue to foster good working relations with other organizational groupings.
MBTI™*	Review predominate team type; take appropriate managerial action, if necessary.	Review team strengths and weaknesses and develop blind spots.	Balance time between reviewing past performance and planning future changes.	Balance time between individual and team needs, past performance and future planning.
Key Belbin roles	Monitor-evaluator, shaper, implementer, completer-finisher.	Co-ordinator, monitor-evaluator, team worker.	Shaper, (plant), monitor-evaluator, completer-finisher.	Co-ordinator, monitor-evaluator, team worker.
Organizational focus	As team begins to experience less turbulence, review alignment with organizational goals and check team performance against milestones.	Ensure team model values and espoused behaviours within and outside of team.	Ensure team in all of its five elements is performing at an effective level.	Ensure team is operating effectively across organizational boundaries.

* MBTI™ = Myers-Briggs Type Indicator™

Mergers and acquisitions

This chapter addresses the specific change scenario of tackling a merger or an acquisition. We pose the following questions:

- Why do organizations get involved in mergers and acquisitions (M&As)? Are there different aims and therefore different tactics involved in making this type of activity work?

- M&A activity has been very high over the last 15 years, and on a global scale. We must have learnt something from all this activity. What are the conclusions?

- Can the theory of change in individuals, groups and organizations be used to increase the success rate of M&As, and if so, how can it be applied?

The chapter has the following four sections:

1   the purpose of M&A activity;

2   lessons from research into successful and unsuccessful M&As;

3   applying the change theory: guidelines for leaders;

4   conclusions.

THE PURPOSE OF MERGER
AND ACQUISITION ACTIVITY

We begin with a short history of M&As. It is useful to track the changes in direction that M&A activity has gone through over the last 100 years to achieve a sense of perspective on the different strategies employed. Gaughan (2010) refers to six waves of M&A activity since 1897 (see box).

THE SIX WAVES OF MERGER AND ACQUISITION ACTIVITY

First wave (1897–1904): *horizontal* combinations and *consolidations* of several industries, US dominated.

Second wave (1916–29): mainly *horizontal* deals, but also many *vertical* deals, US dominated.

Third wave (1965–69): the *conglomerate* era involving acquisition of companies in different industries.

Fourth wave (1981–89): the era of the *corporate raider*, financed by junk bonds.

Fifth wave (1992–2001): larger *mega mergers*, more activity in Europe and Asia. More *strategic* mergers designed to complement company strategy. Emerging market acquirers built through acquisitions and consolidations of smaller companies, eg Mittal and Tata Group.

Sixth wave (2005–08): shareholder activism. Private equity. Leveraged buy-outs. Subprime crisis in 2007 leading to recession in 2008.

Source: adapted from Gaughan (2010)

It is important to classify types of M&A to gain an understanding of the different motivations behind the activity. Gaughan (2010) points out that there are three types of merger or acquisition deal: a horizontal deal involves merging with or acquiring a competitor, a vertical deal involves merging with or acquiring a company with whom the firm has a supplier or customer relationship, and a conglomerate deal involves merging with or acquiring a company that is not a competitor, a buyer or a seller.

So why do organizations embark on a merger or acquisition? The main reasons are listed below.

Growth

Most commercial M&As are about growth. Merging or acquiring another company provides a quick way of growing, which avoids the pain and uncertainty of internally generated growth. However, it brings with it the risks and challenges of realizing the intended benefits of this activity. The attractions of immediate revenue growth must be weighed up against the downsides of asking management to run an even larger company.

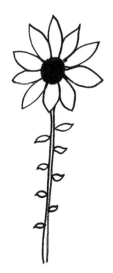

Growth normally involves acquiring new customers (for example, Vodafone and Airtouch), but can be about getting access to facilities, brands, trademarks, technology or even employees.

Synergy

Synergy is a familiar word in the M&A world. If two organizations are thought to have synergy, this refers to the potential ability of the two to be more successful when merged than they were apart (the whole is greater than the sum of the parts). This usually translates into:

- growth in revenues through a newly created or strengthened product or service (hard to achieve);

- cost reductions in core operating processes through economies of scale (easier to achieve);

- financial synergies such as lowering the cost of capital (cost of borrowing, flotation costs);

- more competent, clearer governance (as in the merger of two hospitals).

However, there may be other gains. Some acquisitions can be motivated by the belief that the acquiring company has better management skills and can therefore manage the acquired company's assets and employees more profitably and more successfully in the long term.

M&As can also be about strengthening quite specific areas, such as boosting research capability or strengthening the distribution network.

Diversification

Diversification is about growing business outside the company's traditional industry. This type of merger or acquisition was very popular during the third wave in the 1960s (see box). Although General Electric (GE) has flourished by following a strategy that embraced both diversification and divestiture, many companies following this course have been far less successful.

Diversification may result from a company's need to develop a portfolio through nervousness about the earning potential of its current markets, or through a desire to enter a more profitable line of business. The latter is a tough target, and economic theory suggests that a diversification strategy to gain entry into more profitable areas of business will not be successful in the long run (see Gaughan, 2010, for more explanation of this).

A classic recent example of this going wrong is Marconi, which tried to diversify by buying US telecoms businesses. Unfortunately, this was just before the whole telecoms market crashed, and Marconi suffered badly from this strategy.

Integration to achieve economic gains or better services

Another increasingly common motive for M&A activity is to achieve horizontal integration. A company may decide to merge with or acquire a competitor to gain market share and increase its marketing strength.

Public sector organizations may merge purely to achieve cost savings (often a guiltily held motivation) or to enhance partnership working in the service of customers.

Vertical integration is also an attraction. A company may decide to merge with or acquire a customer or a supplier to achieve at least one of the following:

- a dependable source of supply;

- the ability to demand specialized supply;

- lower costs of supply;

- improved competitive position.

Defensive measures

Some mergers are defensive and are a response to other mergers that threaten the commercial position of a company.

Pressure to do a deal, any deal

There is often tremendous pressure on the CEO to reinvest cash and grow reported earnings (Selden and Colvin, 2003). He or she may be being advised to make the deal quickly before a competitor does, so much so that the CEO's definition of success becomes completion of the deal rather than the longer-term programme of achieving intended benefits. This is dangerous because those merging or acquiring when in this frame of mind can easily overestimate potential revenue increases or costs savings. In short, they can get carried away.

Table 7.1   Comparison of reasons for embarking on a merger or acquisition

Reason for M&A activity	Advantages	Disadvantages	Organizational implications
Growth	Immediate revenue growth pleases shareholders. Reduction in competition (if other party is competitor). Good way of overcoming barriers to entry to specific areas of business.	More work for the top team. Hard to sustain the benefits once initial savings have been made. Cultural problems often hard to overcome, thus potential not realized.	Top team required to make a step change in performance. New arrivals in top team. Probably some administrative efficiencies. Integration in some areas if beneficial to results.
Synergy	May offer significant easy cost-reduction benefits. Attractive concept for employees (unless they have 'heard it all before').	More subtle forms of synergy such as product or service gains may be difficult to realize without significant effort. Cultural issues may cause problems that are hard to overcome.	Top teams need to work closely together on key areas of synergy. Other areas left intact.

Table 7.1 _continued_

Reason for M&A activity	Advantages	Disadvantages	Organizational implications
Diversification	May offer the possibility for entering new, inaccessible markets. Allows company to expand its portfolio if uncertain about current business levels.	Economic theory suggests that potential gains of entering more profitable profit streams may not be realized. May be hard for top team to agree strategy due to little understanding of each other's business areas.	Loosely coupled management teams, joint reporting, some administrative efficiencies, separate identities and logos.
Integration	Buyer or supplier power automatically reduced if other party is buyer or supplier. More control of customer demands or supply chain respectively. Better partnership desired for public sector organizations. Reduction in competition (if other party is competitor). Increase in market share/ marketing strength.	More work for the top team. In the case of horizontal integration (other party is a competitor), cultural problems often hard to overcome, thus potential not realized. Complex 'dual' structures often result to spare egos.	Integrated top team, merged administrative systems, tightly coupled core processes, single corporate identity, better partnership working, pooled resources, better services.
Defensive measure	Enhance the company's commercial position in the face of weighty competition.	May be very unexpected for staff and low performance can result from confusion.	If managed well, it leads to greater commercial strength.
Deal doing	Seductive and thrilling. Publicity about the deal augments the CEO's and the company's profile.	The excitement of the deal may cloud the CEO's judgement.	Anyone's guess!

We have taken several different sources, all of which propose a set of rules for M&As, and distilled these into five learning points:

1   communicate constantly;

2   get the structure right;

3   tackle the cultural issues;

4   keep customers on board;

5   use a clear overall process.

Communicate constantly

In the excitement of the deal, company bosses often forget that the merger or acquisition is more than a financial deal or a strategic opportunity. It is a human transaction between people too. Top managers need to do more than simply state the facts and figures; they need to employ all sorts of methods of communication to enhance relationships, establish trust, get people to think and innovate together and build commitment to a joint future. They also need to use all the avenues available to them such as:

- company presentations;
- formal question and answer sessions;
- newsletters;
- team briefings;
- notice boards;
- newsletters;
- e-mail communication;
- confidential helplines;
- websites with questions and answer sessions;
- conference calls.

COMMUNICATE CONSTANTLY

The top team had been working on the acquisition plans for over four months. Once the announcement was eventually made to all employees I just wanted to get on with things. I had so much enthusiasm for the deal. There was just endless business potential.

The difficulties came when I realized that not everyone shared my enthusiasm. My direct reports and their direct reports constantly asked me detailed questions about job roles and terms and conditions. It was beginning to really frustrate me that they couldn't see the big picture.

I found I had to talk about our visions for the future and our schedule for sorting out the structure at least five times a day, if not more. People needed to hear and see me say it, and needed me to keep on saying it. I learnt to keep my cool when repeating myself for the fifth time that day.

MD of acquiring company

Devine (1999) of Roffey Park Management Institute says that managers with M&A experience tend to agree that it is impossible to over-communicate during a merger. They advocate the use of specific opportunities for staff to discuss company communications. They also advise managers to encourage their people to read e-mails and attend communication meetings, watching out for those who might be inclined to stick their heads in the sand. Managers need to be prepared as regards formal communications:

- Develop your answers to tricky questions before you meet up with the team.

- Expect some negative reactions and decide how to handle these.

- Be prepared to be open about the extent of your own knowledge.

Carey (2000) says it is necessary to have constant communication to counteract rumours. He advises: 'When a company is acquired, people become extremely sensitive to every announcement. Managers need to constantly communicate to avoid the seizure that may come from over-reaction to badly delivered news.'

In company communications, it is very important to be clear on time-scales, particularly when it comes to defining the new structure. People want to know how this merger or acquisition will affect them, and when. Carey says: 'Everyone will be focused on the question "what happens to me?" They will not hear presentations about vision or strategic plans. They need the basic question regarding their own fate to be answered. If this cannot be done, then the management team should at least publish a plan for when it will be done.'

PRODUCTIVITY LEVELS DURING TIMES OF CHANGE

A very interesting statistic I once read says that people are normally productive for about 5–7 hours in an eight-hour business day. But any time a change of control takes place, their productivity falls to less than an hour.

Dennis Kozlowski, CEO Tyco International, quoted in Carey (2000)

In the public sector this challenge is even greater because of extended timescales. The National Audit Office recommends that regular communications need to be clear about what has been decided and what has yet to be decided.

Get the structure right

THE IMPORTANCE OF DECISIONS ABOUT STRUCTURE

At the time we thought it best to keep everyone happy and productive. Both the merged companies had good production managers, so we decided to ask them to work alongside each other, to share skills and learn a bit about the other person's way of working.

We thought this was the best idea to keep production high, and to promote harmony and learning. However, in the end it turned out to be highly unproductive. It was a huge strain for the two individuals involved in both cases. They thought they were being set up to compete, despite protestations that this was not so. Both began to show signs of stress.

> *This structural decision (or rather indecision) also slowed the integration process down as people wanted to stay loyal to their original manager. They studiously avoided reporting at all to the new manager from the other company. Joint projects ended in stalemate and integration of working standards was almost impossible to achieve.*
>
> HR director, involved in designing structure for merger

Structure is always a thorny issue for merging or acquiring companies. How do you create a structure that keeps the best of what is already there, while providing opportunities for the team to achieve the stretching targets that you aspire to?

Carey makes the point that it is essential to match the new company structure to the logic of the acquisition. If, for example, the intention was to fully integrate two sales teams to provide cost savings in administration and improve sales capability, then the structure should reflect this. It is tempting for senior managers to avoid conflict by appointing joint managers. Although this may work for the managers, it does not usually work for the teams. Integration becomes hard work as individuals prefer to keep reporting lines as they were.

Structure work should start early. Carey advises managers to begin working on the new structure before the deal is closed. Some companies use an integration team to work on this sort of planning. These people are in the ideal position to ask the CEO, 'What was the intended gain of this acquisition?' and, 'How will this structure support our goals?'

It is important that promotion possibilities provided by merger or acquisition activity are seen as golden opportunities for communicating the goals and values of the new company. Feldmann and Spratt (1999) warn against 'putting turtles on fence posts'. They emphasize the importance of providing good role models, and encourage senior managers to promote only those who provide good examples of how they want things to be. They say 'do not compromise on selection by indulging in a quota system (two of theirs and two of ours)'. And do not be tempted to fudge roles so that both people think they have got the best deal. This will only result in arguments and friction further down the line.

In public sector mergers a decision-making vacuum should be avoided by making it clear who is responsible for each phase, even if officers are not finally in position.

Tackle the cultural issues

Cultural incompatibility has often been cited as a problem area when implementing a merger or acquisition. Merging a US and a European company can be complicated because management styles are very different. For instance, US companies are known to be more aggressive with cost cutting, while European companies may take a longer view. Reward strategy and degree of centralization are also areas of difference. Jan Leschly, then-CEO of SmithKline Beecham, says in 'Lessons for master acquirers' (in Carey, 2000), 'The British and American philosophies are so far apart on those subjects they're almost impossible to reconcile.'

David Komansky, CEO of Merrill Lynch until 2003, made over 18 acquisitions between 1996 and 2001. In the same *HBR* article (Carey, 2000), he says:

> It's totally futile to impose a US-centric culture on a global organization. We think of our business as a broad road within the bounds of our strategy and our principles of doing business. We don't expect them to march down the white line, and, frankly, we don't care too much if they are on the left-hand side of the road or the right-hand side of the road. You need to adapt to local ways of doing things.

The amount of cultural integration required depends on the reason for the merger or acquisition. If core processes are to be combined for economies of scale, then integration is important and needs to be given management time and attention. However, if the company acquires a portfolio of diverse businesses it is possible that culture integration will only be necessary at the senior management level.

The best way to integrate cultures is to get people working together on solving business problems and achieving results that could not have been achieved before the merger or acquisition. In 'Making the deal real' (Ashkenas *et al*, 1998), the authors have distilled their acquisition experiences at GE into four steps intended to bridge cultural gaps:

1   Welcome and meet early with the new acquisition management team. Create a 100-day plan with their help.

2   Communicate and keep the process going. Pay attention to audience, timing, mode and message. This does not just mean bulletins, but videos, memos, town meetings and visits from management.

3   Address cultural issues head-on by running a focused, facilitated 'cultural workout' workshop with the new acquisition management team. This is grounded on analysis of cultural issues and focused on costs, brands, customers and technology.

4   Cascade the integration process through, giving others access to a cultural workout.

Roffey Park research (Devine, 1999) confirms the need to tackle cultural issues. This research shows that culture clashes are the main source of merger failure and can cost as much as 25–30 per cent in lost performance. They identify some of the signs of a culture clash:

- people talk in terms of 'them and us';

- people glorify the past, talking of the 'good old days';

- newcomers are vilified;

- there is obvious conflict – arguments, refusal to share information, forming coalitions;

- one party in the merger is portrayed as 'stronger' and the other as 'weaker'.

Therefore an examination of existing cultures is normally useful if there is even a small possibility that cultural issues will get in the way of the merger or acquisition being successful. This is a good exercise to carry out in workshop format with the teams themselves at all levels. The best time to look at cultural issues is when teams are forming right at the start of the integration. It breaks the ice for people and allows them to find out a bit about each other's history and company culture.

TACKLING THE CULTURAL ISSUES

The managers from company A described their culture as:

- fairly formal;
- courteous and caring;
- high standards;
- lots of team work;
- clear roles.

Company B added:

- precise;
- good reputation.

The managers from company B described their culture as:

- highly informal;
- a bit disorganized;
- relationships are important;
- customer focused;
- fast and fun.

Company A added:

- flexible roles;
- lack of hierarchy.

New culture – what did they need:

- role clarity;
- adaptability;
- high standards;
- customer focus;
- responsiveness;
- enjoyment;
- team work.

What might be the difficult areas:

- Balancing clarity of roles with adaptability – culture clash?
- Achieving high standards without getting too formal.
- Being responsive while keeping to high standards.
- Working as one team, rather than two teams.

Action plan:

1 Define flexible roles for all management team. Must be half page long.

2 Highlight areas where standards need to be reviewed.

3 Audit customer responsiveness and set targets.

4 Tackle each of the above by creating small task force with members from both companies.

Output from a management team meeting focusing on building a new culture

Cultural differences can be looked at using a simple cultural model such as the one offered in *Riding the Waves of Culture: Understanding cultural diversity in business* by Fons Trompenaars and Charles Hampden-Turner (1997); see Figure 7.1 for our representation of the various scales. People from each merger partner mark themselves on these scales and openly compare scores. In the workshop it is useful to ask the team to predict what kind of difficulties they might have as they start to work together, and to make an action plan to address these. We have run several such workshops, and in these we strongly encourage people to try to work together to define the new culture. This can be challenging work, especially

Cultural dimensions		
Rule versus relationships	Universalist Focus on rules	Particularist Focus on relationships
The group versus the individual	Individualism More use of 'I'	Communitarianism More use of 'We'
The range of feelings expressed	Neutral Do not reveal thoughts and feelings	Affective Reveal thoughts and feelings
The range of involvement	Specific Direct	Diffuse Indirect
How status is accorded	Achievement oriented Use titles only when relevant to task	Ascription oriented Extensive use of titles

Figure 7.1 Trompenaars and Hampden-Turner's cultural dimensions

Source: Trompenaars and Hampden-Turner (1997)

if the acquisition or merger is perceived as hostile, but necessary work if any sort of integration is desired.

Roffey Park's advice is:

- Identify the key tactics used by team members to adhere to their own cultures.

- Identify cultural 'hot-spots', highly obvious differences in working practices that generate tension and conflict.

- Using a cultural model, get team members to explore the traits of their cultures; ask them what was good or bad about their former cultures.

- Get your people to identify cultural values or meanings that are important to them and that they wish to preserve.

- Challenge team members to identify a cluster of values that everyone can commit to and use as a foundation for working together.

Keep customers on board

> Customers feel the effects first... They don't care about your internal prob-
> lems, and they most certainly aren't going to pay you to fix them.
>
> (Feldmann and Spratt, 1999)

'It's very easy to be so focused on the deal that customers are forgotten. Early plans for who will control customer relationships after the merger or acquisition are essential,' says Carey (2000). Devine (1999) adds weight to this by commenting:

> Mergers are often highly charged and unpredictable experiences. It is all too easy to take your eye off the ball and to forget the very reason for your existence. Ensure that your team concentrates on work deliverables so that everyone remembers that there is a world outside and that it is still as competitive and pressurized as ever. Help everyone to realize that your competitors will be on the lookout for opportunities to exploit any weaknesses arising from the merger. You might find that in the face of an external threat, cultural differences shrink in importance.

Some of our experiences as consultants contradict the idea that increased focus on the customer can help a team to forget cultural differences. The opposite effect can happen, where teams and individuals from the two original merging companies use customer focus to further accentuate cultural difficulties:

- sales people fight over customers and territory;

- managers blame each other rather than help each other when accounts are lost;

- people from company A apologize to customers for the 'shortcomings' of people from company B rather than back them up.

This lesson accentuates the need to tackle cultural issues early, as well as to define clear ground rules for working with customers as one team.

HOW TO KEEP CUSTOMERS ON BOARD

One of our first actions was to embark on a series of customer visits that involved a senior sales person from both the merging companies. This allowed us to learn how to work together, and fast! It reassured customers and allowed us to deliver a clear message:

- *we were now one company;*
- *there would be a single point of contact going forward;*
- *the merger was amicable and well managed.*

Sales manager from merged retail company

AVOIDING THE SEVEN DEADLY SINS

Feldmann and Spratt (1999) identify seven deadly sins in implementing a merger or acquisition. Their book goes on to describe in detail how to ensure that you avoid these problems:

- **Sin 1: Obsessive list-making.** Don't make lists of everything that needs to be done – it is exhausting and demoralizing. Instead, use the 80:20 rule. Focus on the 20 per cent of tasks that add the most value.

- **Sin 2: Content-free communications.** Don't send out communications that contain only hype and promotion. Employees, customers, suppliers and shareholders all have real questions, so answer them.

- **Sin 3: Creating a planning circus.** Use targeted task forces, rather than a hierarchy of slow-paced committees.
- **Sin 4: Barnyard behaviour.** Unless roles and relationships are clarified, feathers will fly in an attempt to establish the pecking order. Simply labelling the hierarchy will not sort this one out.
- **Sin 5: Preaching vision and values.** If you want cultural change, you have to work at it. It will not happen through proclamation.
- **Sin 6: Putting turtles on fence posts.** Ensure that the role models you select for promotion provide good examples of how you want things to be. Do not compromise on selection by indulging in a quota system (two of theirs and two of ours).
- **Sin 7: Rewarding the wrong behaviours.** Sort out compensation and link it to the right behaviours.

Use a clear overall process

The pitfalls associated with planning and successfully executing a merger or acquisition imply that it is important to have an overarching process to work to. GE's Pathfinder Model is summarized in Table 7.2. It acts as a useful checklist for those involved in acquisition work (more in Ashkenas *et al*, 1998). This model, derived through internal discussion and review, forms the basis for GE's acquisitions programme.

USE A CLEAR PHASED PROCESS

It's easy to get sucked into mindless list generation. There is an extraordinary amount of stuff to be done when you merge with another company. The trouble is that list making is very tiring, and the lists have to be numbered and monitored, which takes time and effort. We found that it was much simpler to develop a phased process than to list everything that needed to be done. We then created a timeline with obvious milestones such as 'structure chart delivered', or 'terms and conditions harmonized'. This helps people to keep on track without creating a circus of action planning and reporting.

Organization development manager talking about
the merger of two management consultancies

Table 7.2   Adapted version of GE's Pathfinder Model

Preacquisition	• Assess cultural strengths and potential barriers to integration. • Appoint integration manager. • Rate key managers of core units. • Develop strategy for communicating intentions and progress.
Foundation building	• Induct new executives into acquiring company's core processes. • Jointly work on short- and long-term business plans with new executives. • Visibly involve senior people. • Allocate the right resources and appoint the right people.
Rapid integration	• Speed up integration by running cultural workshops and doing intensive joint process mapping. • Conduct process audits. • Pay attention to and learn from feedback as you go along. • Exchange managers for short-term learning opportunities.
Assimilation	• Keep on learning and developing shared tools, language, processes. • Continue longer-term management exchanges. • Make use of training and development facilities to keep the learning going. • Audit the integration process.

Source: Ashkenas _et al_ (1998).

The National Audit Office recommends specialist programme management help to ensure continued business as usual, and to tackle HR, finance and particularly pensions issues.

APPLYING THE CHANGE THEORY: GUIDELINES FOR LEADERS

Which elements of the theories discussed in earlier chapters can be used to inform those leading M&A activity? We make links with ideas about individual, team and organizational change to help leaders channel their activities throughout this turbulent process. In addition, we refer to the previously mentioned research into successful mergers and acquisitions by Roffey Park Institute (Devine, 1999), which offers some useful guidelines for organizational leaders.

Managing the individuals

M&As bring uncertainty, and uncertainty in turn brings anxiety. The question on every person's mind is, 'What happens to me in this?' Once this question is answered satisfactorily, each individual can then begin to address the important challenges ahead. Until that time, there will be anxiety. Some people will be more anxious than others, depending on their personal style, personal history and proximity to the proposed changes. And if people do not like the look of the future, there will be a reaction.

The job of the leader in a merger or acquisition situation is, first, to ensure that the team know things will not be the same any more. Second, he or she needs to ensure people understand what will change, what will stay the same, and when all this will happen. Third, the leader needs to provide the right environment for people to try out new ways of doing things.

Schein (see Chapter 1) claims that healthy individual change happens when there is a good balance between anxiety about the future and anxiety about trying out new ways of working. The first anxiety must be greater than the second, but the first must not be too high, otherwise there will be paralysis or chaos.

In a merger or acquisition situation there is very little safety. People are anxious about their futures as well as uncertain about what new behaviours are required. This means the leader has to create psychological safety by:

- painting pictures of the future (visioning);
- acting as a strong role model of desired behaviours;
- being consistent about systems and structures.

But not by:

- avoiding the truth;
- saying that nothing will change;
- hiding from the team;
- putting off the delivery of bad news.

Chapter 1 addressed individual change by first introducing four schools of thought:

- behavioural;

- cognitive;

- psychodynamic;

- humanistic.

The behavioural model is useful as a reminder that reward strategies form an important part of the M&A process and must be addressed reasonably early. The cognitive model is based on the premise that our thinking affects our behaviour. This means that goal setting and role-modelling too are important.

However, the psychodynamic approach provides the most useful model to explain the process of individual change during the various stages of a merger or acquisition. In Table 7.3 we use the Kübler-Ross

Table 7.3 Stages of merger or acquisition process and how to manage reactions of staff

Stage	Employee experience	Management action
Merger or acquisition is announced	Shock. Disbelief. Relief that rumours are confirmed.	Give full and early communication of reasons behind, and aims of this merger or acquisition.
Specific plans are announced	Denial – it's not really happening. Mixture of excitement and anxiety. Anger and blame – 'This is all about greed', 'If we'd won the ABC contract we wouldn't be in this position now.'	Discuss implications of the merger or acquisition with individuals and team. Give people a timescale for clarification of the new structure and when they will know what their role will be in the new company. Acknowledge people's needs and concerns even though you cannot solve them all. Be patient with people's concerns. Be clear about the future. Find out and get back to them about the details you do not know yet. Do not take their emotional outbursts personally.

Table 7.3 *continued*

Stage	Employee experience	Management action
Changes start to happen – new bosses, new customers, new colleagues, redundancies, building	Depression – finally letting go of two companies, and accepting the new company. Acceptance.	Acknowledge the ending of an era. Hold a wake for the old company and keep one or two bits of memorabilia (photos, T-shirts). Delegate new responsibilities to your team. Encourage experimentation, especially with new relationships. Give positive feedback when people take risks. Create new joint goals. Discuss and agree new groundrules for the new team. Coach in new skills and behaviours.
New organization begins to take shape	Trying new things out. Finding new meaning. Optimism. New energy.	Encourage risk taking. Foster communication at all levels between the two parties. Create development opportunities, especially where people can learn from new colleagues. Discuss new values and ways of working. Reflect on experience, reviewing how much things have changed since the start. Celebrate successes as one group.

model from Chapter 1 to illustrate individual experiences of change and effective management interventions during this process of change.

Managing the team

Endings and beginnings are important features of M&As, and these are most usefully addressed at the team level. The ideas of William Bridges (Chapter 3) provide a useful template for management activity during ending, the neutral zone and the new beginnings that occur during a merger or acquisition.

Managing endings

The endings are about saying goodbye to the old way of things. This might be specific ways of working, a familiar building, team mates, a high level of autonomy or some well-loved traditions. In the current era of belt-tightening and cost-cutting, there might be quite a lot of losses for people, similar to the effects of a restructuring exercise. (See Chapter 1 for more tips on handling redundancies.) Here is some advice for how managers can manage the ending phase (or how to get them to let go):

- Acknowledge that the old company is ending, or the old ways of doing things are ending.

- Give people time to grieve for the loss of familiar people if redundancies are made. Publish news of their progress in newsletters.

- Do something to mark the ending: for example have a team drink together specifically to acknowledge the last day of trading as the old company.

- Be respectful about the past. It is tempting to denigrate the old management team or the old ways of working to make the new company look more attractive. This will not work. It will just create resentment.

Managing the transition from old to new

This phase of a merger or acquisition, often known as integration, can be chaotic if it is not well managed. The 'barnyard behaviour' mentioned above, combined with high anxiety about the future, can lead to good people leaving and stress levels reaching all-time highs. Conflicts that are not nipped in the bud at this stage can lead to huge and permanent rifts between the two companies involved.

Tuckman's model of team development is useful to explain what goes on in a new, merged management team, or a newly merged sales team. We have added some suggestions on how to manage these phases; see Table 7.4.

Timing for this stage is also important. The integration stage should neither be squeezed into an impossible two-week period, nor be treated as an open-ended process that continues unaided for years. The need to squeeze this phase into a two-week period comes from management denial of the very existence of integration issues. Conversely, the need to let things take their course over time comes from a belief that time will

Table 7.4   How to manage the development of a merged team

Stage	Team activity	Advice for leaders
Forming	Confusion Uncertainty Assessing situation Testing ground rules Feeling out others Defining goals Getting acquainted Establishing rules	Be very clear about roles and responsibilities in the new company. Talk about where people have come from in terms of the structure, process and culture in their previous situation. Compare notes. Define key customers for the team and begin to agree new ground rules for how the team will work together.
Storming	Disagreement over priorities Struggle for leadership Tension Hostility Clique formation	Make time for team to discuss important issues. Be patient. Be clear on direction and purpose of the team. Nip conflict between cultures and people in the bud by talking to those involved.
Norming	Consensus Leadership accepted Trust established Standards set New stable roles Co-operation	Develop decision-making process. Maintain flexibility by reviewing goals and process.
Performing	Successful performance Flexible task roles Openness Helpfulness	Delegate more. Stretch people. Encourage innovation.

solve all the issues and they cannot be hurried. Therefore they are allowed to drag on and possibly get worse, and more entrenched.

Bridges offers advice about managing the integration phase that we have adapted to be directly useful for M&As:

- explain that the integration phase will be hard work and will need (and get) attention;

- set short-range goals and checkpoints;

- encourage experimentation and risk taking;

- encourage people to brainstorm with members of the new company to find answers to both old and new problems.

Managing beginnings

It is important to recognize when the timing is right to celebrate a new beginning. Managers need to be careful not to declare victory too soon. Here are some ideas for this phase:

- Be really clear about the purpose of the merger or acquisition, and keep coming back to this as your bedrock.

- Paint a vision of the future for you and your team, describing an attractive future for those listening. (ROCE or ROI just doesn't do it for most people!)

- Act as a role model by integrating well at your own level, and being seen to be doing so.

- Do something specific to celebrate a new beginning.

Managing yourself

There are many challenges ahead for managers as they enter a merger or acquisition. Managers may be uncertain about their own position, while attempting to reassure others about theirs. They may even be considering their options outside the organization while encouraging others to wait and see how things turn out.

Other difficulties include the overwhelming needs of team members for clarity, reassurance and management time. Managers find themselves repeating information again and again, and become frustrated with their team's inability to 'move on'. A glance at the Kubler-Ross curves pictured in Figure 7.2 will reveal that this problem comes from managers and their teams being out of 'sync' in terms of their emotional reactions. While the manager is accepting the situation and trying out new ideas, the team is going through shock, denial, anger and blame. This is quite a stark mismatch!

Devine (1999) offers a checklist for line managers:

- **Get involved.** Try to get in on the action and away from business as usual. Show you are capable of dealing with change.

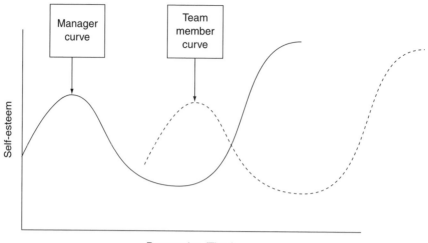

Figure 7.2   Change curve comparisons

- **Get informed.** Find out who is going up or down, especially among your sponsors or mentors. Have a 'replacement' boss you can turn to if your current one leaves.

- **Get to know people.** Network hard, get to know the people in the other company. Do not think of them as 'the enemy'.

- **Deal with your feelings.** Openly recognize feelings of anxiety and frustration. Form a support network and discuss these feelings with colleagues.

- **Actively manage your career.** Think carefully before moving function/ role at the time of a merger. You are remembered for your current job, whatever your past experience. Do not necessarily accept the first role that is offered to you. Decide what you would like to do, prepare your CV and work towards it – everything is up for grabs!

- **Identify success criteria.** Often performance criteria have changed or become unclear. Re-benchmark yourself by talking to people involved in the merger. Get informal feedback from subordinates, peers and bosses.

- **Be positive.** Be philosophical and objective about what is under your control. Do not beat yourself up – you can't win 'em all.

Handling difficult appointment and exit decisions

M&As often involve a restructuring process, which in turn involves managers in making difficult appointment and exit decisions. These decisions need to be fair, transparent, justified, swift and carried out with attention to people's dignity.

In one company that we know of, top management decided to reveal the newly merged company's structure chart in a formal town hall meeting of all staff. Those who did not appear on the chart had to make their own conclusions. You can imagine the resentment and lack of trust that this foolish and undignified process generated.

Devine advises:

- New appointments need to be seen to be fair. Try to ensure that selection criteria are objective, transparent and widely understood.

- Stick to company policy and processes. Do not take short-cuts as they are likely to backfire on you.

- Do not dither. This will cause resentment.

- Treat employees at every level with dignity.

Managing the organization

It is important to select and agree a change process that matches the challenges posed by the specific merger and acquisition. If the most important challenge is to achieve cost-cutting goals, then project management techniques can be applied and the changes made swiftly. This may mean the use of a task force to make recommendations, and the agreement of a linear process for delivering the cost-cutting goals. However, if the most important challenges are integration issues or cultural issues, then the ideas of both Bridges and Senge are relevant. Attention must be paid to managing endings, transitions and beginnings for specific teams involved in significant processes. Other teams may remain untouched.

We have used the Kotter model, introduced in Chapter 3, to illustrate the steps from initial news of the deal to full integration. This model is useful because it combines a range of different assumptions about change, so tackles the widest range of possible challenges:

1   **Establish a sense of urgency.** This is a tough balancing act for management. They must start to raise the issues that have led to the merger or acquisition without revealing the deal itself. For instance,

if the company is currently operating in a dwindling market, then managers should highlight the need to do something about this, without necessarily revealing any intentions to buy or to merge. People will be suspicious and resentful of a deal that does not make any sense. 'Why are we diversifying now? I thought the plan was to buy the competition!'

2   **Form a powerful guiding coalition.** Managers of both companies need to begin working together as soon as they can. They need to spend time together and build a bit of trust. When the deal is announced, managers will then be able to work together at speed.

3   **Create a new vision.** A top-level vision for the new company must be built by the new top management team. This vision will be used to guide the integration effort and to develop clear strategies for achieving this. The integration effort needs to be targeted on specific areas rather than be a blanket process, and clear timescales for implementation must be given.

   The new structure needs to be put quickly into place, a level at a time, ensuring that customers are well managed throughout. The new sales and customer service structure is therefore a priority. New values and ways of working should also be discussed and identified.

4   **Communicate the vision.** Kotter emphasizes the need to communicate at least 10 times the amount you expect to have to communicate. In addition, all the research about M&As indicates that it is impossible to over-communicate. Managers need to be creative with their communication strategies, and remember to work hard at getting the two companies to build relationships at all levels.

   The vision and accompanying strategies and new behaviours will need to be communicated in a variety of different ways: formal communications, role-modelling, recruitment and promotion decisions. The guiding coalition should be the first to role-model new behaviours.

5   **Empower others to act on the vision.** The management team now needs to focus on removing obstacles to change such as structures that are not working, or cultural issues, or non-integrated systems. At this stage people are encouraged to experiment with new relationships and new ways of doing things.

6   **Plan for and create short-term wins.** Managers should look for and advertise short-term visible improvements such as joint innovation

projects, or the day-to-day achievements of joint teams. Anything that demonstrates progress towards the initial aims of the merger or acquisition is newsworthy. It is important to reward people publicly for merger-related improvements.

7   **Consolidate improvements and produce still more change.** Top managers should make a point of promoting and rewarding those able to advocate and work towards the new vision. At this point it is important to energize the process of change with new joint projects, new resources and change agents.

8   **Institutionalize new approaches.** It is vital to ensure that people see the links between the merger or acquisition and success. If they have had to work hard to make this initiative happen, they need to see that it has all been worthwhile.

THE IMPORTANCE OF TRUST WHEN GOING THROUGH A MERGER

When we were acquired by ITSS we were full of trepidation. Our previous owners had stripped us of costs and then looked around for a buyer. We felt a bit used. So we were in no mood to start building trust.

ITSS kept calling this deal a merger, but we were hugely cynical about that. They had bought us after all. This was a case of vertical integration where a supplier buys its customer to gain access to primary clients and grow the business. We thought they would start to take our jobs and move the company to their own headquarters, around four hours down the motorway!

The whole thing came to a head one morning when some consultants were running an integration workshop for the new management team. ITSS were getting frustrated with our hostility. We were getting angry about their constant questioning about finances and account management and project costs. Someone from our company was brave enough to share his emotions.

The MD of ITSS, who is actually a pretty decent guy, sat down amidst us all and spoke quite calmly for about 10 minutes. He said, 'Look guys, I will do anything to make this company a success. Anything. But I need to know what I'm running here. I can't take that responsibility without knowing all the facts. I really want us to make this thing a success. But I need your help.'

After that we trusted him a bit more. Then things got better and better. That was four years ago. Things have improved every year since then. He kept his word, and that was really important to everyone.

Project leader, acquired company

SUMMARY

There are five main reasons for undertaking a merger or acquisition:

1   growth;

2   synergy;

3   diversification;

4   integration; and

5   deal doing.

Recent research indicates that five golden rules should be followed during mergers and acquisitions:

1   communicate constantly;

2   get the structure right;

3   tackle the cultural issues;

4   keep customers on board;

5   use a clear overall process.

Individuals can be managed through the process using the Kubler-Ross curve as a basis for understanding how people are likely to react to the changes. Teams can be managed through endings, transitions and new beginnings using the advice of Bridges. Tuckman's forming, storming, norming and performing process also lends understanding to the sequences of activities that leaders of new joint teams need to take their teams through.

Managers need to manage themselves well through an integration process. Roffey Park's advice is:

- get involved;

- get informed;

- get to know people;

- deal with your feelings;

- actively manage your career;

- identify success criteria;

- be positive.

Difficult appointment and exit decisions also need to be well managed using these principles:

- be fair;

- stick to the procedures;

- do not dither;

- remember people's dignity.

Kotter's model can be used to plan an M&A process as it combines several different assumptions about the change process, so providing adequate flexibility for the range of different purposes of merger or acquisition activity.

8

Culture and change

INTRODUCTION

An organization's culture can either catalyse or get in the way of change efforts. Indeed, people will often suggest that the culture of the organization itself needs to change, or be changed to allow the substantive changes to be successful.

However this is much trickier than merely having a plan to change the culture and then implementing that plan because culture is the invisible, unconscious all-pervading element within which everything else happens. From how the buildings are laid out to what we wear; from how meetings are run to how decisions are made; from how resources are allocated to what gets recognized and rewarded; from what projects turn out to be successful to which ones get derailed – culture is, classically, 'the way things are done around here'.

From an individual's perspective it is hard, if not impossible, to operate effectively counter to the prevailing culture. From the organization's perspective the prevailing culture shapes everything from the strategy to the way the business, and everyone in it, operates to achieve that strategy.

Kaplan and Norton (2004) state:

> Culture is perhaps the most complex and difficult dimension to understand and describe because it encompasses a wider range of behavioural territory

than the others… Executives generally believe that changes in strategy require basic changes in the way business is conducted at all levels of the organization, which means, of course, that people will need to develop new attitudes and behaviours – in other words, change their culture.

Many writers and researchers have itemized the importance of culture:

- Bain & Co's 2007 global survey of business leaders identified corporate culture to be as important as corporate strategy for business success. They also found that corporate culture had a significant impact on process improvements and decision making.

- Both Kotter and Heskett (1992) and Heck and Marcoulides (1993) found a significant correlation between organizational culture and performance.

- Hai (1986) saw culture as creating norms for acceptable behaviour and affecting innovation, decision making, communication, organizing, measuring success, rewarding achievement, worker motivation and goals.

- Hampden-Turner (1990) suggested culture reinforces ideas and feelings that are consistent with the corporation's beliefs.

- It influences the relationships with internal and external stakeholders (Hai, 1986).

- It has a powerful effect on individuals and performance (Kotter and Heskett, 1992).

These views support Barney's (1986) thesis that:

> A firm's culture can be a source of sustainable competitive advantage if that culture is valuable, rare, and imperfectly imitable. The sustained superior performance of firms like IBM, Hewlett-Packard, Procter and Gamble, and McDonald's may be, at least partly, a reflection of their organizational cultures.

Organizations exhibiting these attributes need to sustain them, whereas those who do not have these attributes can, of course, aim to build them. However (and here is the rub):

> Such efforts are typically imitable, and thus, at best, only the source of temporary superior performance. These firms must look elsewhere if they are to find ways to generate expected sustained superior financial performance.

This chapter is structured around answering the following questions:

- Perspectives on culture – What is culture, why is it so important to understand when managing change, and what are the different ways we can view and approach culture?

- Values, the key to understanding culture – what are values and what is the link between values, culture and the change process?

- Facilitating culture change – if we could change culture, how would we go about it?

- Shifting sands of culture – how do current business and societal trends impact the way we see culture?

- Summary of key principles of culture change – what are the key change management principles when dealing with culture?

PERSPECTIVES ON CULTURE

The purpose of this section is to explore what we mean by culture, look at some approaches to understanding culture, and establish why it is important when managing change.

What do we mean by culture?

Schein (1990) suggests that culture is:

> the pattern of basic assumptions that a given group has invented, discovered or developed in learning to cope with its problems of external adaptation and internal integration, and that have worked well enough to be considered valid and, therefore, to be taught to new members as the correct way to perceive, think, and feel in relation to those problems.

Although the popular notion that culture is 'the way we do things around here', we can see that the way things are done and the behaviours that happen are actually manifestations of something much deeper. Boonstra (2013) reinforces this by saying that one way of understanding culture is seeing it as the identity of the organization which is 'enduring, stable and difficult to influence'. He goes on to say that changing behaviours will not in itself change the culture. And wanting to change behaviours is quite difficult because when you do try you are 'tampering with the

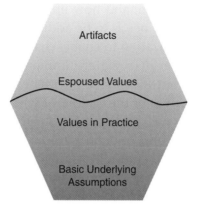

Figure 8.1 How values manifest

underlying convictions and the values and norms that give people something to hold on to'.

Boonstra, building on Schein, describes the basic assumptions as those that are below the levels of consciousness and are 'taken for granted'. They contain what we believe about the nature of reality, time and space, the nature of human nature, activity and relationships.

Manifesting with a greater level of awareness, but still below the surface, are the values that the organization and its people hold (values in practice). These are not necessarily the espoused values of the organization, but the values that are enacted by certain behaviours day in, day out. The outer layers of cultural artefacts are visible, though not necessarily understandable. They are the physical spaces, the technology, the behaviours, the outer manifestations of 'the way we do things around here'.

Schabracq (2007) postulates that Schein's outer layer could, with minimal adaptation, be conceived of as 'everyday reality' which is 'open to inspection, though usually nobody inspects them... the members of the organization do not pay much conscious attention to them... the norms are just experienced as self-evident parts of reality'.

Everyday reality is, of course, where work gets done, and where organizational functioning can be seen to be either moving the organization towards its chosen strategy or somehow getting in the way. And this is naturally self-reinforcing – the members within the organization pick up clues and cues as to how to behave from each other. They don't necessarily see these things as controlling mechanisms, but as Schabracq says:

> They are just automatically being acted upon... people continuously re-enact, reconstruct, recognize, represent and recite the forms and meanings of culture and abstain from other possibilities. People even recreate themselves.

Noting how processes happen, and how effective they are, will help us later on to understand what needs to be addressed, what levers need to be pulled within the organization to enable change to occur.

As Schabracq notes, because we are immersed in the culture it is often very hard to step outside of it to intervene within it! If, as change agents, we remind ourselves of the picture of what the strategic process might really look like, we will unknowingly or subconsciously be filtering our perceptions of the world and decision-making processes through a specific cultural lens (see Figure 8.2).

The discussions around the four organizational metaphors in the organizational change chapter and the five change paradigms in the

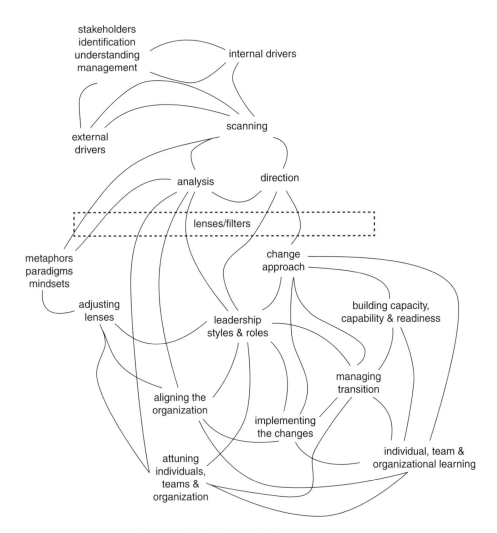

Figure 8.2 Strategic change process

change agent chapter will have alerted you to the need to become more conscious of both the way the organization is operating and also what your default position or perspective is. Making these things conscious enables the change agent not only to understand the organization on a deeper level but also to assist in the enabling of any culture shifts required.

HOW DO WE GET
A SPECIFIC CULTURE IN THE FIRST PLACE?

Schein (1999) suggests that there are six different ways in which culture evolves. Some of these can be influenced by leaders and some cannot:

1   a general evolution in which the organization naturally adapts to its environment;

2   a specific evolution of teams or sub-groups within the organization to their different environments;

3   a guided evolution resulting from cultural 'insights' on the part of leaders;

4   a guided evolution through encouraging teams to learn from each other, and empowering selected hybrids from sub-cultures that are better adapted to current realities;

5   a planned and managed culture change through creation of parallel systems of steering committees and project-oriented task forces;

6   a partial or total cultural destruction through new leadership that eliminates the carriers of the former culture (turnarounds, bankruptcies, etc).

Culture and managing change

Schein underscores the fact that organizations will not successfully change culture if they begin with that specific idea in mind. The starting point should always be the business issues that the organization faces. Indeed further research from Boonstra (2013), looking in depth over a two-year period at 19 organizations that had achieved successful strategic change, confirms this. 'Cultural change is not a goal in itself but is for the strategy of the business... not a single leader in the companies talks about cultural change explicitly'.

Schein is adamant that this sort of assessment cannot measure culture. In the same way that an identity card is not an individual, nor a country its credit rating, an organization is not just the results of a cultural audit. Cameron and Quinn (2011) suggest that 'one reason so many dimensions have been proposed is that organizational culture is extremely broad and inclusive in its scope. It comprises a complex, interrelated, comprehensive, and ambiguous set of factors'.

Cultural frameworks

Schein imagined culture as different levels or layers, going ever deeper into the core of an organization's identity – its visible structures, its strategies and values, and its underlying basic assumptions.

Deal and Kennedy (1999) also saw organizations in a multi-layered way. History lies at the core, leading to the development of values and beliefs which, in turn, create the rituals and ceremonies that add to the organization's infrastructure. These produce social cohesion and produce the heroes and stories that reinforce the culture. All these things contribute to and shape the way people behave, talk and think about the organization.

Other management researchers have tried to identify different ways to map and make sense of the manifestations of culture.

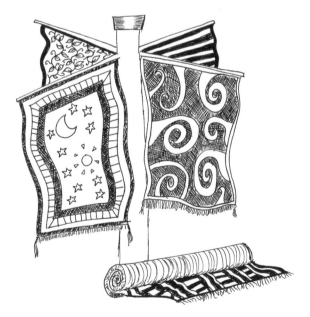

So, for example, both Harrison (1972) and Handy (1993) saw that you could categorize organizations by the way they centralized control or allowed more distributed authority on the one hand, and how formal or informal they were on the other. This led to a matrix with a profile of four cultures:

Table 8.1 Harrison and Handy's cultural dimensions

<table>
<tr>
<td rowspan="2">Centralization</td>
<td>High</td>
<td>**Task Culture**
Characterized by getting things done. Power and authority emanate from the ability to achieve the tasks in hand. What is rewarded is not necessarily position but task accomplishment, with systems and structures designed to enable that to happen. Indicative Organization: Adaptable, more service-oriented organizations, collaborative, problem-solving. Project management organizations and meritocracies often have a task culture.</td>
<td>**Role Culture**
Tries to fit the workings of the organization into clearly defined structures and roles. Accountabilities aligned to the role; each person in their role knows where they fit into the system. Indicative Organization: Bureaucracies; large businesses in relatively stable environments; traditional public sector bodies.</td>
</tr>
<tr>
<td>Low</td>
<td>**Person Culture**
Has the needs of the people central to its ethos. This might be at the expense of the overarching aims of the organization. Indicative Organization: Professional services, where individuals have knowledge and authority. Academic or professional associations or partnerships might display elements of the person culture, with more consensual decision-making and explicit displays of power shunned.</td>
<td>**Power Culture**
Decisions are based around the sources of power within the organization and are often centrally controlled. From entrepreneurial companies to organizations with strong charismatic leaders the operating paradigm is based around ensuring you have the necessary people 'on side' and have the power and authority to make decisions relatively quickly with few bureaucratic hindrances. Indicative Organization: Entrepreneurial businesses with a central powerful figure.</td>
</tr>
<tr>
<td></td>
<td></td>
<td>**Low**</td>
<td>**High**</td>
</tr>
<tr>
<td></td>
<td></td>
<td colspan="2">**Formalization**</td>
</tr>
</table>

Apart from the obvious insight people within organizations have when identifying where they and their organization are, a deeper mapping of the characteristics of any one of the four cultural types will yield valuable information as to whether the organization is indeed 'fit for purpose' to address external environmental challenges. It will also reveal the sorts of interventions, when it comes to change, that are most likely to be effective.

Likewise, as we saw in Chapter 5, Goffee and Jones (1998) teased out the differences in culture through looking at the degrees of Sociability and Solidarity within an organization. Sociability is the degree to which people are friendly with each other and work towards a social cohesion within the organization. Solidarity is in their words 'a measure of a community's ability to pursue shared objectives quickly and effectively, regardless of personal ties.'

Another popular framework is Cameron and Quinn's (2011) Competing Values Framework (also see Chapter 5). This framework arose from research into what makes organizations effective – and remember successful, longer-lived organizations have evolved their cultures in order to be effective in their strategic goals. Two major dimensions were derived from the analysis of effectiveness:

1 flexibility, discretion and dynamism as opposed to stability, order and control; and

2 internal orientation, integration and unity as opposed to external orientation, differentiation and rivalry.

This produces four quadrants:

- Clan – Flexible, Discretion, Internal Focus and Integration.

- Hierarchy – Stability and Control, Internal Focus and Integration.

- Adhocracy – Flexible, Discretion, External Focus and Differentiation.

- Market – Stability and Control, External Focus and Differentiation.

Cameron and Quinn saw these dimensions as creating tensions. How the organization holds these tensions makes manifest its unique culture. The desire for control on the one hand is always in tension with the desire for autonomy on the other. The resolution of this tension occurs for each organization in a different way and in a different place on the competing

Table 8.2   Cameron and Quinn's competing values framework

Flexibility & Discretion

	Clan eg Pixar Japanese companies	**Adhocracy** eg Google Amazon
	Hierarchy eg Ford, McDonald's Government departments	**Market** eg Philips Xerox

Internal Focus & Integration (left axis)   _External Focus & Differentiation_ (right axis)

Stability & Control

Source: Cameron & Quinn (2011)

values map. Each organization will therefore have a profile which, generally, spans across the dimensions and has elements of each quadrant within it.

As with all such frameworks, a number of questions arise:

- Is this cultural profile similar across all parts of the organization?

- If not, where are the major differences? Is there good reason for these differences, and if not, do we need to do anything?

- Is this profile the 'right' profile for the organization going forward?

- If not, how can we enact or stimulate change across the competing values framework?

For each of the quadrants Cameron and Quinn identify strategies, actions and leadership styles to shift an organization along the dimensions in its desired direction. So, for example, a government department identifying the need to be more externally focused and end-user responsive might set up an easily accessible call centre or 'neighbourhood shop' for advice giving. Likewise, a rapidly expanding start-up might need to build more of an infrastructure of systems and processes within its internal operations. Both Google and Amazon have had the challenges of being successful through having a culture of being flexible and externally focused but then needing to build an infrastructure and control systems.

In our experience, organizations can find cultural assessments or profiles extremely useful for a number of reasons:

- As with all frameworks they provide a way into understanding the world and making sense of some of the behaviours within the organization and how misalignments might occur.

- Whether warmly received or not, an organization's commitment to looking at culture can signal that there is a serious conversation about strategy and change happening.

- An important part of the strategy process is seeing whether the organization is fit for purpose, and any cultural diagnostic can help increase organizational self-awareness and suggest areas for evolution.

- It can generate discussions around how things are currently being done and what could be improved.

However, there are weaknesses. Remember Schein who says culture cannot be measured.

- The dimensions of the particular instrument may not be appropriate, relevant or comprehensive to this particular organization, in this particular situation and setting.

- They might not create any real depth of understanding and remain at a relatively surface level.

- They may dissect a phenomenon into discrete categories which actually, by definition, is a holistic concept.

- The instrument itself may not be very robust, in terms of published data on its validity (Sackmann 1991, Saffold 1988, Rousseau 1990).

VALUES – THE KEY TO UNDERSTANDING CULTURE

In the same way Freud (1899) saw that 'dreams are the royal road to the unconscious', values offer a way to really understand culture and change. They form the bridge between an organization's core identity and outward manifestations of behaviour.

Organizational values

Hofstede *et al* (1990) state that:

> The core of culture is formed by values, in the sense of broad, nonspecific feelings of good and evil, beautiful and ugly, normal and abnormal, rational and irrational – feelings that are often unconscious and rarely discussible, that can't be observed as such but are manifested in alternatives of behaviour.

We can define values as 'evaluative standards relating to work or the work environment' (Dose, 1997). Both Deal and Kennedy (1999) and Collins and Porras (1994) see organization values as a set of shared values.

The business dictionary (www.businessdictionary.com) defines values as:

> Important and lasting beliefs or ideals shared by the members of a culture about what is good or bad and desirable or undesirable. Values have major influence on a person's behaviour and attitude and serve as broad guidelines in all situations.

And Posner and Schmidt (1994) state that values are:

> A silent power for understanding interpersonal and organizational life. Because they are at the core of people's personality, values influence the choices they make, people they trust, the appeals they respond to, and the way they invest their time and energy. In turbulent times values give a sense of direction amid conflicting views and demands.

According to Schein, these values originated with the founders and leaders of the organization. And the values espoused were the ones which were enacted and led to the way of structuring the organization (in its broadest sense), which led to the behaviours that led to its continued success, which leads to those values being reinforced.

It is important to note that when organizations change their strategies and require a different way of doing things they may restate, refine, and reshape the set of values. These new values, as stated, suggested or directed by the leaders, are those that the organization should adopt. It is at this point that many staff and middle managers tend to express cynicism with senior managers. They recognize that an organization cannot simply change its values at will. If it could then, as we saw earlier with the work of Barney, there would be no competitive advantage, because other organizations would simply mimic them. However, if senior managers have gone through a rigorous strategic evaluation process, and have identified necessary shifts in their basic assumptions about the enterprise, the new espoused values can be seen as aspirational and indeed 'work in progress'.

> The senior managers of a financial services company were refreshing their values to deliver a world-class customer experience. A key value was Integrity – doing what you say you will do.
>
> The team did a self-assessment and came out with a 'score' of 7.8 out of 10. The chief operating officer was pleased with the result. As his coach, I said 'When it comes to Integrity, you either have it or you don't... 100 per cent or not at all'.
>
> After the team had worked up their new strategy (with everyone expressing total team commitment) they delivered it at a management conference. One of the team was heard to say he disagreed with it; he was asked to resign the next day.

Bourne and Jenkins (2013) have identified four useful organizational value types:

- Espoused – the values as stated by senior managers and appearing on the organization's website, posters on the wall and other written documentation.

- Attributed – how people might describe the organization's values, what they see as important to the organization.

- Shared – those values that members, perhaps in smaller units than the whole organization, see as the ones they have in common with each other.

- Aspirational – those values which, in an ideal world, staff and managers would like the organization to be embodying and to which they would like their behaviours to accord.

Espoused values carry considerable weight in organizations, but to consider them as a valid representation of the entirety of organizational values is problematic.

Attributed values therefore represent the history of the organization, but do not typically hold aspirations or intentions for the future.

The concept is also limited by the extent to which there can be any meaningful sense of shared values, particularly in larger organizations.

Representing the organization's values as an aggregation of the personal values of individual members is, however, clearly distinct from the espoused and attributed values forms.

In practical applications, Cameron and Quinn (2011) approach organizational culture change by assessing the gap between current, attributed values and future, aspirational values.

To summarize, organizations as social entities carry intentions for their future survival. Aspirational values are representations of these intentions held and so form a significant component of organizational values, but differ from espoused values by their location at the level of organizational members.

Bourne and Jenkins (2013)

It is only when the new strategy and the new way of doing things are seen to be successful that the espoused values are integrated into the basic assumptions of the organization.

Thornbury (2000), in her important values-driven work with KPMG in revitalizing their company culture, sees the core values as being at the centre of understanding culture. Espoused values are those that 'an organization claims to hold, or temporarily promotes to suit a business need... [but] will not have any influence on the organization's culture if they are espoused but not practised'.

On the other hand, core values for an organization are the 'timeless guiding principles for behaviour, decisions and actions'.

It is these core values that business researchers such as Deal and Kennedy, Peters and Waterman, and Collins and Porras have seen as giving a business competitive advantage. There is good evidence of a relationship between an organization having strong, identifiable values and corporate success. The difference between good and visionary or great companies is that the latter have core values that are not compromised by the vagaries of the marketplace, but remain fixed and enduring. (Stride 2011)

So having a clear vision, strategy and a set of core values leads to business success, and that is then reinforced in the evolution of the culture.

Do your values have to match the organization's?

Hofstede (1990) maintains that most values research is focused on the values of senior managers, not staff, who don't necessarily share the values of managers but enact their perception of the espoused working practices. Pruzan's (2001) research found that managers' espoused values may not even match the managers' own core individual values, let alone employees'. However, we do know that the values of leaders and senior management have a greater influence on organizational outcomes than those of other groups.

We also know that if there is an individual/organizational value fit there is likely to be greater employee commitment, in both times of stability and of change, which leads to less staff attrition and greater job satisfaction.

Schneider (1987) pointed out that people are attracted to organizations that enable them to achieve particular goals and outcomes. His attraction-selection-attrition (ASA) model states that members are attracted to, selected by, and removed from an organization on the basis of 'fit' with its orientation and characteristics. It is not the whole set of the individual's values that is relevant, but what we might call the values found in the work place. For example, there are no absolute differences in values between private or public sector workers, but there are significant differences in the values that workers bring to the fore in the workplace – advancement and prestige in the former, contribution to society in the latter (Lyons *et al* 2006).

In essence, we can see how an organization's culture forms through the ongoing business success of the enterprise, coupled with the 'winning formula' of the enacted behaviours and values of the senior leaders; initially through espoused values, but more sustainably through the core values and basic assumptions of the organization. People are attracted to and selected by the organization based on an individual and organizational values fit. Likewise they can be deselected by themselves or the organization if there is not a sufficient fit. The values fit can operate either at a deep level or with explicit or implicit agreement to the core or espoused values. Though in practice people may not share them but are merely following working practices – the surface manifestation of the values.

Values in times of change

The challenges when dealing with culture and values in times of change are:

- How do you articulate an authentic set of values which will underpin the organization's strategy?

- How do you embed those espoused values into the fabric of the organization?

- How do you manage the transition of individuals from bringing one set of values to work to a different set?

FACILITATING CULTURE CHANGE

This section looks at ways that cultural change can be approached using a number of frameworks and illustrations.

Two relatively accessible ways into seeing the components of cultural change are McKinsey's 7S model (which we looked at briefly in Chapter 3) and Johnson and Scholes' (1999) Cultural Web.

McKinsey's 7S

Organizational culture will be determined by the shape of each of the seven Ss and their interactions. It is a useful way of assessing the infrastructure of the organization as it is now, and what it needs to become in the future to maintain or attain a competitive advantage or sustained effective performance.

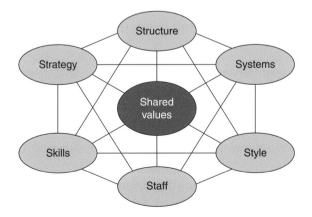

Figure 8.3   McKinsey 7S framework

The 7S categories are:

- Staff – important categories of people within the organization; the mix, diversity, retention, development and maximizing of their potential.

- Skills – distinctive capabilities, knowledge and experience of key people.

- Systems – processes, IT systems, HR systems, knowledge management systems.

- Style – management style and culture.

- Shared Values – guiding principles that make the organization what it is.

- Strategy – organizational goals and plan, use of resources.

- Structure – the organization chart, and how roles, responsibilities and accountabilities are distributed in furtherance of the strategy.

Strategy, Structure and Systems are the more tangible categories and therefore sometimes the ones that people concentrate on when managing change. If there are problems, managers often want to change the strategy, or upgrade the system or restructure. It is important to remember that these factors are all interconnected – if you change one aspect then that affects all the others. And they in turn interact with the external environment. Moving from the current to the intended culture is not just about changing the 'easier' factors but actually also about the whole system.

The framework can be used in a number of ways to help organize change:

a) flesh out the desired state and begin to design a programme of intervention that would achieve it; or

b) analyse the gap between the current reality and desired future state and design a process to bridge the gap.

Depending on the nature of the change you may choose one option or another. We show a real example from a social housing organization in Table 8.3.

For example, in looking at the shift in management style from an autocratic, centralist managerial style to a more authoritative, pace-setting style with distributed coaching leadership at a local level, clearly you

Table 8.3 Social housing 7S case study

7Ss	Before	After	Change Process
Strategy	To improve homes to modern standards whilst keeping rents stable through high quality standards of maintenance work and internal cost efficiency	To be a leading provider of high-quality affordable homes and services and to help create thriving and successful communities through achieving excellent customer- and community-focused services; delivering more new homes and maintaining robust businesses. This mission to be achieved by focus on growth through acquisition, internal development and diversification.	A major strategic shift resulting from a thorough review using PESTLE and SWOT and intensive stakeholder discussions.
Structure	Classical functional structure	Group of businesses with maximum autonomy with some shared central functions and corporate governance.	Discussions around what the most enabling structure would be to allow a more entrepreneurial culture.
Systems (IT, HR, Financial)	Uniform systems, policies and procedures	Enhanced systems for an expanding group of companies tailored to each company's needs, but compatible with group decision making and strategy.	Systems refreshed and renewed to be fit for purpose, both in terms of service delivery and also ensuring people were motivated to behave in a different way.

Table 8.3 *continued*

7Ss	Before	After	Change Process
Management Style	Autocratic, centralist style Managerial	Authoritative, pace setting with distributed coaching leadership at a local level.	The leadership behaviours needed to be aligned with a new way of doing things and compatible with values. Accent on modelling new behaviours.
Staff	Right staff in the right part of the hierarchy	Recruitment of staff to fit with new entrepreneurial ethos.	Communications with current staff to ensure they understood the new competencies and values were translated into behavioural indicators. New staff attracted by the new ethos. Some old staff left.
Skills	Right skills to do business as usual	Equip staff to operate in a more competitive environment that is constantly changing. Greater cross-group working and sharing best practice.	A staff and management development programme instigated to support and challenge all employees.
Shared Values	Central ethos of providing a good quality service to customers with a looked-after workforce	Customer-responsive, honest, open and true to their word and fair to all. Within this there is a strong emphasis on involving and responding to the needs of customers.	Discussions throughout the organization and with stakeholders to develop a set of shared values with behavioural indicators. Original values were built on rather than dismissed.

Source: adapted from Green (2007)

cannot wave a magic wand and all the managers start behaving in the new way. A structured management development programme – with options ranging from formal courses through to tailored on-site programmes to action learning sets and one-to-one coaching – would be realistic and appropriate. And of course the programme can be aligned, in time, with the structural changes that would allow and require more empowerment and distributed leadership. It can also be aligned with some of the systems changes that would allow a greater degree of autonomy in the new business units. In our experience, this is done by: agreeing a change agenda; setting up a myriad of small but powerful interventions (where leaders can lead or facilitate action); skilling people where required; then encouraging regular reviews of progress, and tough conversations about what's not shifting.

The systems themselves might be designed from a blank sheet of paper, with business analysts looking at key processes necessary for a group of independent operating companies with shared central services.

A dual approach might be taken to ensure that staff skills fit the desired state. A training needs analysis could be undertaken, looking at the desired competencies and identifying skills gaps in the existing staff. Training interventions could then be designed to raise the capabilities of those staff. In parallel, the HR department may wish to use a new set of behavioural competencies in their recruitment programmes.

So we can see how the 7 Ss can be used: first to diagnose the current internal state of the organization; second to articulate the desired future state; and third to start the process of working programmes of change.

Cultural web

Johnson and Scholes (1999) have designed what they call a cultural web, the elements of which make up the prevailing culture of an organization and which, if adjusted, can enable cultural change to occur in support of the organizational change initiatives.

At the centre of this web is what they call the *Paradigm*, an underlying set of assumptions embodying what the organization is all about – where it is going, how it is going to get there, and the core values to which it adheres.

The organization's *Control Systems* monitor and evaluate its operating performance. Some organizations will have tight control systems (for example, banks or publicly accountable operations); others will be looser (for example, start-ups or more entrepreneurial firms).

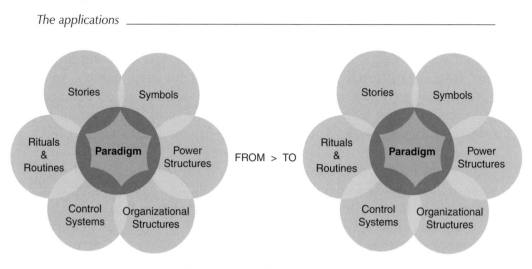

Figure 8.4 Cultural web

Organizational Structures will represent the hierarchical structure, lines of accountability and responsibility and communication and production flows.

Power Structures map out where power and authority lie in terms of decision making and mandate holding; whether power is centrally held or locally dispersed; whether leadership is located at the top of the organization, or whether it is distributed. And on what the power is based – whether it is position, role, expert power or personal charismatic power.

Symbols are artefacts or architecture that encapsulate what the organization values. These might include designs such as the corporate logo and uniform, and also include building design, office space and car parking space.

Rituals and Routines cover how the organization has come to organize and structure some of the things that it does – for example, the norm for organizational meetings, how reports are written and presented, how people are enfolded into the company, and how they leave.

Stories and Myths are what get chosen to be communicated formally and informally around the organization when describing significant events and personalities in its history, in its current situation or as part of its future strategy.

As the name implies, a web is very interconnected; one element will impact on others and be influenced in turn by them.

Table 8.4 illustrates an old cultural web compared to the preferred new one for a financial services organization.

Table 8.4 Cultural web case study – financial services

Element of the cultural web	Old Culture	New Culture	Change Process
Paradigm	Trustworthy Reliable 'Steady as she goes' Marketing led	Entrepreneurial Individual responsibility Joint accountability Sales driven	A new senior management team led a far-reaching strategic review to shift from a traditional centralist company to being 'fleet of foot'
Control Systems	Annual review Planning committee Financial reporting Strong and tight compliance culture	Business unit profit centres Core 'tight' controls and discretionary 'loose' controls Coaching culture	Decisions made to free up individual units to be autonomous without losing overall financial control
Organizational Structures	Functional Technical departments Pyramid	Separate business units Shared services Flatter organization	Shift from being internally focused with controlling ethos to external focus with flexibility
Power Structures	Managing director Credit board Director of finance Chief auditor	Chief operating officer Business unit MDs	With new control systems and organizational structure, local unit heads given responsibility and accountability
Symbols	Tower block as HQ Chauffeurs for executives Staff restaurant	New open plan building Atrium with break-out areas Riverside café	Together with the symbolism the new offices enabled greater face-to-face discussion across levels and 'silos'
Rituals and Routines	Board meetings Annual reports Summer party at the sports club	Quarterly reviews Business units 'doing their own thing'	Units quickly devised their own ways of running their business and creating their own identities
Stories and Myths	Historical anecdotes 'Who you know' not 'what you do' Gossip about the executive board Diary watching	Sales successes 'What you achieve' not 'how long you've been there' 'Sales success' stories	An element of rivalry sprang up between the units though the group had sufficient cohesion to keep this at a healthy level

Source: adapted from Green (2007)

Thornbury's approach at KPMG

As part of her work with KPMG in revitalizing their company culture, Jan Thornbury utilized a framework which placed the accent on uncovering values. She recognized that artefacts can generally be changed; although that in itself will not bring about any lasting change, nonetheless it does need to be done as part of the change. In one of the examples above, a fostering of cross-organizational co-operation and teamwork was enabled through the shift from a tower block to a much more open, lower building with a large open space where people could see each other and meet informally.

Using the 7S, it is possible to ask and answer questions such as 'what structures and systems do we need to move towards to enable the other shifts we are wanting?'

Behaviours are harder to shift than artefacts. They involve changing people, and as we have seen in Chapter 1, people will be going through a psychological process as well as some learning and survival anxieties at this time. Thornbury stresses the importance of having 'absolute commitment' from the leadership. In addition she recognizes that behaviour change 'requires focused initiatives and a high degree of sensitivity, patience and persistence'.

One of the key areas where people in organization become disaffected by change, and in particular cultural change (remembering that we needn't be calling it that), is around values. We often hear tales of employees and middle managers reacting cynically when a new set of values has been announced by top management because it feels as if the management believes the organization and its people can simply adopt a different set of values overnight.

This is why any espoused values articulated by senior management must be communicated and understood and their behavioural implications explained. Crucially, espoused values need to be role-modelled by those who have generated them. And the working practices associated with them need to be described so that individuals and teams have a clear understanding of how they are meant to behave.

For example, one of the authors assisted their client in identifying the values and developing the related behaviours necessary to deliver strategic success and organizational performance (Table 8.5).

The transition from espoused values to ensuring they are values in practice and therefore become core values is acknowledged to be a very slow process. Thornbury makes the point that identifying what is currently

Table 8.5 Values and behaviours case study

Value: integrity
Behaviours:
  Expressing views and opinions in an open, honest and constructive way.
  Consistently delivering on their promises and commitments.
  Taking accountability for decisions and actions.

Value: unity
Behaviours:
  Contributing enthusiastically to team goals, sharing and aligning own
    objectives with team(s).
  Supporting and encouraging players on their own team and other
    teams.
  Building personal success on team success and contributing to other
    teams' success.

Value: diversity
Behaviours:
  Treating diverse views, cultures and communities with respect.
  Learning from the variety of different cultures, countries, functions and
    teams within the organization.
  Acknowledging different approaches and seeking win–win solutions.

Value: performance with passion
Behaviours:
  Setting and exceeding stretching targets, individually and in teams.
  Demonstrating high levels of pacc, cncrgy and commitment in achieving
    goals.
  Finding new opportunities to improve their game and being courageous
    by trying them.

Value: celebration
Behaviours:
  Sharing success, recognizing and rewarding achievement of other
    players.
  Encouraging the celebration of success and building a 'success leads to
    more success' culture.
  Having a can-do mentality and encouraging others to do the same.

Value: learning
Behaviours:
  Being proactive in professional and personal development.
  Sharing learning and supporting the development of other players.
  Going outside the 'comfort zone', challenging the status quo, and
    learning from mistakes.

Primary embedding mechanisms

- What leaders pay attention to, measure, and control on a regular basis
- How leaders react to critical incidents and organizational crises
- How leaders allocate resources
- Deliberate role-modelling, teaching, and coaching by leaders
- How leaders allocate rewards and status
- How leaders recruit, select, promote and excommunicate

Secondary articulation and reinforcement mechanisms

- Organizational design and structure
- Organizational systems and procedures
- Rites and rituals of the organization
- Design of physical spaces, facades, buildings
- Stories about important events and people
- Formal statements of organizational philosophy, creeds and charters

Schein, E (2004)

As Schein notes, the six primary mechanisms 'are the major tools that leaders have available to them to teach their organizations how to perceive, think, feel, and behave based on their own conscious and unconscious convictions', whereas the secondary mechanisms tend to be cultural reinforcement tools, especially in newer organizations. They work to the extent that the primary mechanisms are in place and being done.

Aitken's research supports this view, and links it to the idea that leaders' communications and behaviours that support more non-hierarchical and more flexible cross-organizational patterns of co-operation, beginning with deliberate leadership role-modelling, will engender a culture more supportive of change. Aitken (2007) suggests the development of what he calls a 'leadership culture'. He defines it as:

> ... that amalgam of primary purpose, critical behaviours and essential personal values; uncovered, identified and agreed by the leaders as authentic and functional for their organization's culture (whole or part), which the leaders (formal and emergent) role-model through their everyday communications and actions.

The new head of organization development arrives in the car park on the first day in his new role and pulls up and throws away the sign that says 'Space reserved for senior management'.

Emerging embedding processes

Since the turn of the millennium there has been increasing interest in other, less traditional ways of influencing people and their behaviour. From the fields of behavioural science and behavioural economics, a number of authors (Gladwell (2000), Herrero (2008), Kahneman (2011) and Thaler and Sunstein (2009)) have suggested different mechanisms for shaping cultures.

Gladwell (2000), building on the Pareto principle that 80 per cent of the impact can be achieved by 20 per cent of the people, identified three key characteristics of people who were able to move a situation towards its final objective by reaching the 'tipping point' (which he defined as the moment of critical mass). Firstly, they needed to be excellent 'connectors' who had a flair for engaging and connecting with people and developing a network of connectivity, conversations and communication. They are able to achieve this 'ability to span many different worlds [through] some

combination of curiosity, self-confidence, sociability, and energy'. Secondly, as part of this connectivity and communication is their passion for being 'mavens' or information specialists, discovering information and disseminating it. This includes the desire to solve their own problems and help others in solving theirs – 'mavens are really information brokers, sharing and trading what they know'. The final characteristic is the 'salesperson' who is able to have influence and impact due to their presence.

Gladwell suggests that 'ideas and products and messages and behaviors spread like viruses' and that change agents should make effective use of this phenomenon. Likewise, Herrero (2008) sees that real change occurs in organizations through the concept of what he calls Viral Change™ which has a number of key principles including the central idea that what is required is behaviour change which will in turn lead to cultural change. These are not top-down or bottom-up centrally-controlled sets of behaviours. He suggests that it entails:

- the uncovering and articulation of a small set of non-negotiable behaviours to sustain the change goals;

- the identification of and reaching out to a small number of well-connected and influencing employees;

- the ongoing coaching and support to that community of champions; and

- the capturing of changes and tracking of progress via stories and other means.

www.thechalfontproject.com

Storytelling is a crucial element of this. As we have seen earlier in the chapter, the cultural web identifies that the stories that are told and retold help shape the culture. The stories that used to be told can be reduced whilst the stories that help frame and explain the new strategy can be accentuated.

Building on this, David Snowden (2005) emphasises that 'storytelling is a uniting and defining component of all communities. The quality of storytelling and its conformity or otherwise with desired corporate values is one measure of the overall health of an organization. Stories exist in all organizations; managed and purposeful storytelling provides a powerful mechanism for the disclosure of intellectual or knowledge assets in companies. It can also provide a non-intrusive, organic means of producing sustainable cultural change, conveying brands and values, and transferring complex tacit knowledge.

Thaler and Sunstein (2009) have popularized the concept of subtly changing the way that people behave through the use of a nudge, which 'is any aspect of the choice architecture that alters people's behaviour in a predictable way without forbidding any options or significantly changing their economic incentives. To count as a mere nudge, the intervention must be easy and cheap to avoid. Nudges are not mandates. Putting fruit at eye level counts as a nudge. Banning junk food does not.' Currently a number of national governments have taken to this idea, with, for example, the UK Government setting up a Behavioural Insights Team (see box below) which 'brings together ideas from a range of inter-related academic disciplines (behavioural economics, psychology, and social anthropology). These fields seek to understand how individuals take decisions in practice and how they are likely to respond to options. Their insights enable us to design policies or interventions that can encourage, support and enable people to make better choices for themselves and society.' This clearly has implications for how organizations can more subtly influence the way people move to a different way of behaving and the way they do things around here, most notably in developing effective health and safety cultures.

- Automatically enrolling individuals on to pension schemes has increased saving rates for those employed by large firms in the UK from 61 per cent to 83 per cent.
- Informing people who failed to pay their tax that most other people had already paid increased payment rates by over 5 percentage points.
- Encouraging jobseekers to actively commit to undertaking job search activities increased their chance of finding a new job.
- Prompting people to join the Organ Donor Register using reciprocity messages ('if you needed an organ, would you take one?') adds 100,000 people to the register in one year.

  http://www.behaviouralinsights.co.uk/

A key factor in all of these processes of inculcating culture change is communication, and of course, we have been witnessing a revolution in the way we are all communicating through social media. Never before has there been the ability to communicate across hierarchical levels, across organizational boundaries, using formal and informal, open and covert mechanisms. Euan Semple (2012) at the BBC was one of the first to introduce what have since become known as social media tools into a large, successful organization. He charts the emerging paradigm shift as both senior managers and employees across organizations see the liberating power of social media tools. Here are a few snippets from his groundbreaking book:

- Power is shifting from institutions and corporations to networks and individuals.

- Our new opportunities for connectedness will change how we see the world.

- Chaos needn't be the only alternative to our current way of controlling society.

- Networks intertwine with our more formal structures and help us to navigate the people in our organizations.

- Building networks that are large and diverse gives us more power – especially at work.

- Use the web to help people connect across geographical, political... and organizational barriers.

- If we can cross barriers and share problems we have a chance to work on them together.

- Communication has to not only pass on information but also to make people care about what is being conveyed.

- People learn best from each other and access to the real experiences of real people is one of the most effective ways to learn.

- Conversations aren't trivial. Culture is reinforced by shared conversations and understanding.

- Managers will be less able to rely on formal authority and will achieve influence through the quality of their relationships.

- Knowing all the answers is an increasingly impossible expectation.

Euan Semple (2012)

All of these emerging ideas around culture change sit most comfortably with the organism and flux and transformation metaphors and require a way of framing the nature of change and seeing culture as a system. We will look more closely at some of these concepts in the Complex Change chapter (Chapter 10).

SHIFTING SANDS OF CULTURE

The conventional wisdom is that culture is formed by the 'founding fathers' of an organization and that culture is underpinned by the values of those leaders with the behaviours derived from those values. In addition, traditionally, organizations have been seen to have one homogenous culture.

However, we are increasingly faced with a number of interesting questions that muddy the waters:

- How is organizational culture sustained when the organization has a presence in locations around the world?

- How do multi-cultural teams impact the organizational culture?

- With increasing gender equality at senior level, what impact is there on leaders' style and values?

- What is the effect of virtual teamwork on culture?

- How does remote working impact the sustaining of culture?

- In what ways do different generational values interact with organizational culture?

- How does an organization sustain its culture when outsourcing, entering shared service agreements, working in partnership or in a multi-agency setting?

- What is the impact of reducing job tenure and increasing mobility on an organization's culture?

- In what ways will the levelling effect of and capacity for communication across social media influence the way we address culture change?

In order to answer these questions it is worth returning to the discussions we had concerning values within an organization. Hofstede *et al* (1990) proposed that employees didn't necessarily share the values but 'a perception of working practices'. When contrasting national and organizational cultures he determined that 'cultural differences between nations are particularly found at the deepest level, the level of values. In comparison, cultural differences among organizations are principally identified at the level of practices. Practices are more tangible than values.'

Previously Meyerson and Martin (1987) had highlighted three particular ways we could see organizational culture:

- an Integration approach which suggested that there could indeed be one culture, shaped by the leadership which acted as a cohesive force;

- a Differentiation view which allowed for a number of sub-cultures within the organization which could at times be aligned and at other times in contradistinction; and

- an Ambiguity view where there are differences that cannot be reconciled so 'individuals share some viewpoints, disagree about some and are ignorant and indifferent to others'.

At times in this book we have suggested it is problematic whether change can be managed. We think it is even more so when it comes to culture. Can culture actually be managed, and indeed is there one distinct culture anyway? Our sense is that it is possible to nurture culture, and grow a unifying set of behaviours, but the process for doing this is complex!

SUMMARY OF KEY PRINCIPLES OF CULTURAL CHANGE

This is a summary of the key principles which we hope will help you to address the issues of culture change in your own organization.

Always link to the strategy

Use an iterative process to establish core cultural strengths whilst also focusing on the business strategy, organizational vision, mission and objectives to determine what organization capability or core competencies need to be developed. A clear vision and articulation of the values is often required to catalyse action, especially if it translates well into specific tasks.

The greater the clarity of focus the greater the chance one has of aligning people, processes, systems and structures to this end. It is no use if there are many initiatives that are not joined up, although that doesn't mean there has to be just one top-down plan. Many fires can be lit as long as there is an underlying coherence.

Build on core cultural strengths

Wherever possible, start from recognizing the existing culture is what it is and build on its strengths. Of course, there has to be a detailed analysis of all of the external factors, competitive position, stakeholder expectations and customer needs; but the decision on a new strategy is a result of the interplay between the detailed external and internal analysis, taking into account the existing values, attitudes and behaviours. Any changed strategy is chosen in relation to the strengths of the culture rather than the culture changed in relation to the strategy.

Shift mindsets, continually reinforce, sustain

The introduction of a 'foreign element' (see pp 35–38) into the organizational system is a good way of making change happen, be it external or internal. It needs to unlock and unblock energy to kick-start the process and also requires plans and processes in place to keep momentum going. Sometimes this may require an uncompromising attitude.

This continued momentum is critical, and needs to be sustained over a considerable period of time – so leadership resilience is also a key factor.

Senior management must be seen to be sponsoring, but with a growing number of people involved and energized. Viral change principles and Nudge philosophy can help.

Attend to stakeholder issues

Different stakeholders will have different experiences. Internal stakeholders need to create the behaviours which are likely to translate the espoused values into the core values, and this will be manifested by the experiences that external stakeholders have.

So for an organization to be successful in its strategy it needs to focus on enabling internal stakeholders to adopt the new way of working and be clear as to how this translates into the external stakeholders' experiences.

Remember that the how is as important as the what – role-modelling is key

Culture is about the way you do things around the organization. So if your organization has a set of core values you need to be managing the cultural change in line with these values.

Managers need to act as role models. They will need to model the new values but also support individuals and teams through a period of upheaval. This can be done through using some of the strategies outlined in the other chapters of this book.

Build on the old, and step into the new

If you want to shift the organization from one way of doing things to a new way of doing things then you will need to start to step into the new culture. Seek to retain and build on the current cultural strengths and begin to model aspects of the new culture – if you want a coaching culture then start coaching; if you want people to be empowered then start empowering! Look at how the structure, systems, skills and management style need to change to support the new culture.

With the changing landscape, ensure that the stories being told reflect the new or future realities.

Generate enabling mechanisms

It is important to generate enabling mechanisms such as reward systems and planning and performance management systems that support the objectives and preferred behaviours of the new culture. Processes and standards must support the desired behaviours. An organization cannot strive for a quality service, for instance, if the culture does not support people doing quality things.

Using one or more of the cultural tools mentioned in this chapter (for example, the competing values framework, the cultural web, the 7 Ss) can help guide you into the initiatives you need to be implementing.

Create a community of focused and flexible leaders

Organizations do not change by themselves – all five of the Change Leadership roles will be called for during a period of cultural change (see Chapter 4). However, it would be a mistake to believe that any one individual could carry this off by themselves. Chapter 4 also describes a number of ways that leadership can be distributed throughout the organization to make change happen.

Commitment to culture change cannot be developed by e-mail, or by memo alone. It has to be done face to face and in real time. Cultural change is achieved through action rather than words, so people need to see their managers doing it as well as talking about it.

Insist on collective ownership of the changes

One common trap is to make the HR department the owners of cultural change, while the CEO and the senior management team own the changes in business strategy. This type of functional decomposition of a change initiative is doomed to failure.

The greater the depth and breadth of people involved in diagnosing the current state, developing a vision of where the organization needs to be heading, and generating solutions to bridge the gap, then the more chance the organization has of gaining sufficient momentum for change.

When working across boundaries apply due diligence and make the implicit explicit

Whether the boundaries are departmental, functional, organizational, national, or generational, change agents will encounter cultural differences. These are grist to the mill for understanding and it is important to see how the difference plays out in thinking, feeling, behaving and communication within the relationship. By noticing, naming and attending to these phenomena we can consciously work more effectively across these boundaries.

When dealing with culture stand outside and use double and triple loop learning

Because we tend to be immersed within the culture when working with it, we need to develop mechanisms for being able to step outside of it in order to re-enter and make sense of it to intervene within it. Heifetz's injunction to get onto the balcony to see what is occurring within the system is good advice. Likewise, Argyris and Schon (1974) discuss ways we can learn at different levels:

- Single Loop Learning – where you respond in set ways according to the conscious or sub-conscious rules that that have been culturally determined.

- Double Loop Learning – this occurs when you take a step back and reflect upon whether the way you are responding is the most sensible way to respond. This involves looking at the process as well as the situation.

change are likely to be higher performing than those who struggle in this respect.

Projects are increasingly used as the preferred way of securing resources, building new products or services, making internal changes, and implementing new ways of working. They are also being used as part of larger programmes, designed to deliver wider strategic or transformational change, often including significant structure, process, behaviour and/or cultural change.

This chapter draws on a wide literature review combined with reflections on recent consulting and teaching experiences to answer the questions:

- What are projects and programmes supposed to achieve and how successful are they in doing this?

- How can a good balance between control and flexibility be achieved within project- and programme-led approaches?

- What new, flexible approaches are emerging (eg Agile and Scrum) and what are they delivering?

- How well is project and programme governance working and are project management offices (PMOs) adding value?

- What role are senior managers and business leaders playing, and how might this need to shift?

- What is the right place for change management and the change manager in the world of projects and programmes?

- How might project managers need to adapt, given the shifting context and the challenges ahead?

- What lies ahead for project managers and change managers given the rise of collaborative networks and the arrival of generation Z?

PROJECT MANAGEMENT TAKEN TO EXTREMES?

I'm all for using projects as a way of getting stuff done, but when our management team announced that the transformation programme would be managed through 83 different projects, my heart sank. Why can't we just have six or seven initiatives that everyone can get their heads around and contribute to? The rest of the work can flow from that...

Senior manager, retail business

UNDERSTANDING PROJECTS AND PROGRAMMES

A brief history of project management

To understand what project management is now, there is a huge amount of material to delve into regarding project management and its history. So while this definitely isn't the chapter to read if you want a full account of this, a little bit of history seems helpful in understanding its roots and subsequent development.

The concept of getting organized to complete big projects has existed for centuries, but only in the late 19th and early 20th centuries did people start devising and experimenting with scheduling tools. In the 1950s, the US Navy and Airforce started to talk about 'project management' and the term was then used to describe their approach to either big industrial projects, or technology projects. In the '60s and '70s professional bodies (eg PMI, the Project Management Institute) were established, and formal approaches to organize large-budget, schedule-driven initiatives became standard.

In the '80s, software tools were developed to make project management accessible on a desktop, and a project management 'body of knowledge' was published by PMI. In the '90s, PRINCE was formalized as a methodology. From 2000, Agile and Scrum approaches began to emerge, and PCs and notebooks started to run project management software. Then total cost management, an integrated programme management approach, was developed, in which portfolios of projects or programmes are in clear support of strategic or business objectives, designed to optimize assets.

The incorporation of organizational change as a key part of project management has become a topic of lively debate in the last 5–10 years or so, with the role of change manager becoming popular in a technology-led project environment only in the last few years. This role is now normally defined as someone who is responsible for transitioning individuals, teams and organizations to a future state, rather than someone who is responsible for monitoring change to the scope of a project.

Programme management is described by the UK's Association for Project Management (APM) as 'the coordinated management of projects and change management to achieve beneficial change'. Mike Hanford, Chief Methodologist for the IBM Summit, offers a more expansive definition in the box on the next page.

THE DIFFERENCE BETWEEN A PROJECT AND A PROGRAMME

Projects are typically governed by a simple management structure. The project manager is responsible for day-to-day direction, a senior IT executive integrates technology with business interests, and a business sponsor is accountable for ensuring that the deliverables align with business strategy.

Programmes require a more complex governing structure because they involve fundamental business change and expenditures with significant bottom-line impact. In fact, in some instances their outcomes determine whether the enterprise will survive as a viable commercial/governmental entity.

Mike Hanford, Chief Methodologist for the IBM Summit

What types of project are there?

It's important to be clear about the variability between different types of project, because the word 'project' covers a wide range of intentions and activities. (Note: in this chapter, when we refer to 'projects', this can normally be taken as a shorthand for both projects and programmes.)

Müller and Turner (2007) propose a tailored set of project 'attributes' drawn from Crawford, Hobbs and Turner (2005) which we have further edited (see box). We are using this list to set the scene for examining project success, and to suggest a way for enabling an 'attunement' between the type of project being tackled and the type of management and leadership required.

PROJECT ATTRIBUTES

Application area: Business change, IT product production, structural change, process change, research, construction project, organizational change (myriad others...) etc

Complexity level: Low, medium or high – depending on number of people involved, number of stakeholders, level of strategic importance, number of geographies involved, number of dependencies within the project – particularly on critical path, stability of context, nature of external dependencies, accessibility/explicability of functionality

Lifecycle stage: Feasibility, design and plan, implement/build, embed, commission, review, audit

Strategic importance: Reason for project: mandatory, repositioning, renewal
Centrality to operations: mission critical or not
Reputational risks: low, medium, high

Culture: Requires culture change to implement successfully
Involves engaging unfamiliar organizational/national cultures
Requires different factions/cultures to work together

Contract type: Fixed price, cost plus

adapted from Müller and Turner (2007)

What defines project success?

Westerveld and Gaya-Walters (2001) examined this topic in the context of an external project manager and team, and Müller and Turner (2007) extended this work. Our distilled version shows the simple success criteria that we've seen most often over the past five years, from the perspective of a business commissioning the project, whether internal or external:

1 meeting business performance, budget and timing criteria;

2 meeting user requirements as mapped out;

3 meeting external customer expectations (which may differ from 2 and 3);

4 meeting board expectations (which may differ from 1, 2 and 3);

5 end-user satisfaction;

6 internal project team satisfaction;

7 external project team satisfaction.

Of course, defining a comprehensive set of success criteria is hard to do in a real-life situation in which goal posts move and delays come from unpredictable sources. It's also highly probable that a mindset shift within key stakeholder bodies is vital to project success although this doesn't appear on the list of success criteria: an added complication is that every loyalty group has a different perspective on success.

CAUTION REGARDING SUCCESS STATISTICS!

Projects differ in size, uniqueness and complexity, thus the criteria for measuring success vary from project to project (Müller and Turner, 2007) making it unlikely that a universal set of project success criteria will be agreed (Westerveld, 2003). Individuals and stakeholders often will interpret project success in different ways (Cleland and Ireland, 2007; Lim and Mohamed, 1999). Furthermore, viewpoints about performance also vary across industries (Chan and Chan, 2004). Müller and Jugdev's (2012) study which focuses on the evolution of the project success literature over the last decade neatly summarizes this issue by asserting that it is a multi-dimensional and networked construct. They assert that perceptions of success and the relative importance of success dimensions differ 'by individual personality, nationality, project type, and contract type'.

Mir and Pinnington (2014)

Shenhar *et al* (2001) instead propose a four factor framework for reviewing success that includes both short- and long-term benefits and feels flexible and useful to us:

1   efficiency – meeting schedule and budget goals;

2   impact on customers – customer benefits and meeting customer needs;

3   business success – project benefits in commercial value and market share;

4   preparing for the future – creating new technological and operational infrastructure and market opportunities.

The relative contribution of project management

Professional project management bodies have spent the last 40 years claiming that good-quality project management, together with the use of tools and technologies results in successful projects. How true is this, what exactly is being measured, and what makes the difference?

Mir and Pinnington (2014) discovered via their recent research that 44.9 per cent of project successes in terms of overall performance can be explained by the contribution made by project management disciplines and effectiveness, which confirms various other studies named in their research. They investigated levels of performance by asking about the presence or absence of various enablers in the context of a recently completed project: leadership, planning, strategic linkage, stakeholder partnerships, staff training, lifecycle processes and KPIs. This implies that 55.1 per cent of project success variance depends on other factors – maybe such as the inherent risk, or the chosen contract type.

The management of KPIs was the most significant independent variable in the study. This indicates that the definition of a clear set of KPIs for any project, together with a method for tracking progress against them, is the most likely enabler to enhance the chances of success. Note that these KPIs are best defined in terms of multiple stakeholder success, and with both a short- and long-term perspective on benefits. Staff training, then quality of leadership, were the next most significant independent variables in the study.

THE IMPORTANCE OF PROJECT KPIS

It's very easy to get hooked into just getting on and delivering a product, particularly when there's a massive IT system to implement, but what matters is the value this system actually creates. Setting out and agreeing KPIs is a complex and painful exercise which people don't feel they have the time or energy for. I know from bitter experience! But it's very worthwhile – particularly when there are tricky decisions to made about where to invest time and money along the way.

Operations director, food company

PROJECT SUCCESS RATES

Despite Mir and Pinnington's positive findings for project management value, well-publicized statistics about extreme IT project overruns are often cited and tend to fill project sponsors with gloom and anxiety. This is particularly acute in the face of technology-led change provoked by

iv **Right investment, right impact**
Suggestion: Allocating the right amount of resource to tackling change management issues by understanding what will offer the best returns in terms of greater project success helps too.

In a similar vein, PWC's third global survey on the current state of project management (2012) which canvasses views from senior executives and practitioners, states that:

- 97 per cent of respondents agreed that project management is critical to business performance.

- 32.1 per cent desire higher maturity in their PM performance.

- When PM disciplines were used, quality standards, delivery of scope and benefit realization were all achieved in around 90 per cent of cases, but project schedules and budgets were still being missed 30 per cent of the time.

- Poor estimation at the planning stage continues to be the largest contributor to project failure.

- The adoption of portfolio management (or programme management) is not increasing, but where it is used it increases the chances of project success in terms of schedule, quality, scope, budget, time and business benefits.

- Efficient and effective communication strategies increase the project's chance of success, with a 17 per cent greater chance of hitting budget.

- 34 per cent of respondents employ 'Agile PM' approaches, though not in very mature ways, and find that these approaches contribute to increased efficiency and delivery performance.

SHORTCOMINGS OF PROJECT MANAGEMENT APPROACHES

Although our literature review indicates that project management approaches are working reasonably well to deliver business results when employed with sufficient skill and rigour, there are still serious short-comings that we believe require attention in today's more challenging context. These are explored below.

Moving away from 'old management ideas'

'Rethinking Project Management' was a UK Government-funded research network comprising academics and practitioners, meeting between March 2004 and January 2006. Its aim was 'to come up with a research agenda aimed at extending and enriching mainstream project management ideas in relation to the developing practice'.

This group met to address the prevailing sense that there had been significant growth in project work across all sectors, growing complexity in projects and programmes of increasing strategic importance to organizations, but still many projects were failing or giving poor results. There was also a sense that the bodies of knowledge being promoted by various professional institutions were based on 'old management ideas' and even 'stuck in a 1960s timewarp'.

The final report by Winter and Smith (2006) and the subsequent dedicated issue of the _International Journal of Project Management_ make very interesting and rich reading. One of the key 'outputs' was a provocative agenda for future research, set out as a 'From → To' map in Table 9.2.

Table 9.2 'Rethinking Project Management' report, from-to summary

FROM	TO
The lifecyde theory of projects	Frameworks and models that illuminate complexity
Mechanistic process models	Frameworks for understanding social and political processes
Product creation	Value creation
Narrow conceptualization of projects	Broader conceptualization of projects
Trained technicians	Reflective practitioners

Source: Winter and Smith (2006)

Below is a summary of the suggestions for future research and exploration based on this agenda:

i   _Devise new frameworks and models that illuminate complexity_
    The lifecycle model implies a linear development track eg Initiate, Plan, Organize, Control, Handover. However, there are many cases of projects where there are: ill-defined goals; multiple stakeholders with very different perspectives and level of buy-in; a number of

untested technical solutions to consider which require collaboration and negotiation as you progress.

– rather than a series of up-front plans.

ii *Identify new frameworks for understanding social and political processes*
Projects are often thought of as a mechanism for marshalling effort in a purely instrumental way ie to achieve stated goals, whereas there are often many complex agendas and interests connected to the success (or otherwise) of a project. If this can be better understood, then measures of success might be more accurate!

This might mean moving from projects as a linear sequence of tasks which constitute an apolitical production process, towards using concepts and images which focus on social interaction to understand how the work gets done.

iii *Move towards value creation*
The move from a narrower focus on concepts and methodologies for product creation, towards concepts and frameworks for value creation is seen as vital for the 21st century. Taking the example of the 2012 London Olympic Games, looking at this project with a focus on 'product creation' is very different from looking at it as a project with a 'value creation' focus.

iv *Create a broader conceptualization of projects*
Projects are now so much more than 'IT projects', the narrow conceptualization that often prevails. This is only a small part of the implementation of a new, more effective way of working. Examples offered of broader projects are: urban regeneration programmes, community development projects, social enterprise projects etc. Moving from single discipline projects with well-defined objectives to multi-purpose projects, open to renegotiation throughout, is seen as an important next step.

v *Envisage project managers as reflective practitioners*
A 21st-century project manager needs to do much more than follow detailed procedures and techniques, and do things 'by the book'. He or she needs to create clarity out of ambiguity, be able to tolerate ambiguity, lead by influence in increasingly complex contexts – rather than simply relying on hierarchical control. This means that project managers need to be reflective practitioners who can learn and adapt as they go, rather than trained technicians who expect others to fall in line with their methods.

> *If a project manager starts off by believing that he or she can run things exactly the way they were run in the last project, they're doomed to failure. These days project managers need to be savvy about context and willing to build partnerships with the guys in the business. Project Management discipline and a focus on delivery is hugely important of course, don't get me wrong, but an intelligent, flexible approach is absolutely vital.*
>
> CEO, financial services company

Managing uncertainty

The 'Rethinking Project Management' discussions described above draw attention to the difficulties that traditional project models and conceptualizations encounter when the degree of complexity and emergence that exists in many organizations is factored in.

Project tools and techniques are designed to contain ambiguities within a 'certain enough' plan, and to ensure as much as possible is done to meet the plan and deliver the key outcomes. Thus project managers often see their role as legitimizing the plan and playing down uncertainty. On the one hand, this helpfully reduces anxieties by illustrating how well things are being managed and controlled. On the other hand, it can be part of an extremely unhelpful process of denial of the real situation. To compound this, a project manager may contribute to a damaging climate of unreality and non-learning, if believing that his/her job is to 'do things right' according to a defined way forward, rather than reflecting, learning and adapting as things progress.

In the Atkinson, Crawford and Ward (2006) paper on fundamental uncertainties in projects and the scope of project management, the authors assert that there is a need to recognize that many project contexts are characterized by very high, difficult to quantify levels of uncertainty where management flexibility and tolerance of vagueness are necessary. Although project management can certainly be thought of as an approach to managing uncertainty via planning, milestones and change control there is definitely more to consider here.

The paper suggests three ways in which project managers can focus more explicitly on uncertainty management:

i the definition of clear performance criteria and accompanying objectives at project inception;

ii the management of tradeoffs between different performance criteria;

iii ownership and management of specific sources of uncertainty.

Table 9.3 Hard and soft projects – a framework for analysis

HARD										SOFT	
Goals/objectives clearly defined	0									10	Goals/objectives highly ambiguously defined
Physical artefact	0									10	Abstract concept
Only quantitative measures	0									10	Only qualitative measures
Not subject to external influences	0									10	Highly subject to external influences
Refinement of single solution	0									10	Exploration of many alternative solutions
Expert practitioner, no stakeholder participation	0									10	Facilitative practitioner, high stakeholder involvement
Values technical performance and efficiency, manages by monitoring and control	0									10	Values relationships, culture and meaning manages by negotiation and discussion

Source: Crawford and Pollack (2004)

Crawford and Pollack (2004) have identified a useful set of criteria to enable the grading of a project, or cluster of projects, according to a set of hard/soft criteria that represent the degree of uncertainty involved. Thus different approaches to project management can be selected according to the project type. These appear in Table 9.3.

For a project at the soft end of this spectrum, it is proposed that the following project management capabilities and skills are required:

- 'sense-making' activities;

- the ability to formulate qualitative success measures and sensitive performance management frameworks;

- the ability to build trust between different parties.

Change challenges

The change challenge for most projects is how to bridge the gap between the envisioned product, and a collection of busy stakeholders and users with a variety of starting points, perceptions and needs.

Traditionally this gap is bridged via change-oriented activities such as:

- readiness assessments to identify skills and awareness gaps;
- sponsorship from senior managers to support increased engagement;
- building awareness of the need for change through good quality communications;
- deepening skills and knowledge to support change through education and training;
- helping employees to transition through 1:1 coaching;
- using methods to sustain progress such as measures of success and rewards.

However, in more complex, softer settings the following are also likely to be required in our view:

- convening stakeholder groups to make sense of progress, build mutual trust and agree ways forward;
- discussing possible trade-offs between agreed performance criteria in the light of progress/new information;
- presenting and discussing project progress at management meetings and negotiating particular forms of line-leader support;
- agreeing timetables for various forms of stakeholder/user involvement/product 'socializing' eg via definition/testing/review/training activities.

Much work has been done to professionalize project change work. The role of 'change manager' and the disciplines of 'change management' have been identified and promoted by organizations such as Prosci, CMI, ACMP and APMG as well as others.

A wide range of change management training programmes is available across the globe. These 3–5 day programmes, in our experience, are often much appreciated by participants as they offer a good grounding in how people respond to change together with helpful frameworks for making sense of this territory in an organizational setting.

For example, Prosci's ADKAR framework (see *www.prosci.com*) is used widely, and offers change managers a way of directing change efforts using an outcome-oriented approach such that stakeholders/users are empowered to change.

Prosci defines change management as:

> ... the application of a structured process and set of tools for leading the people side of change to achieve a desired outcome. Change management emphasizes the 'people side' of change and targets leadership within all levels of an organization including executives, senior leaders, middle managers and line supervisors. When change management is done well, people feel engaged in the change process and work collectively towards a common objective, realizing benefits and delivering results.

...and their three-phase model is summarized as follows:

- preparing for change;

- managing change;

- reinforcing change.

Another challenge that arises when 'soft' projects are being considered is that traditional approaches to change tend to assume that the desired outcomes of change are reasonably predictable, and can be broadly mapped out from the start. However our recent experience of digital and/or strategic transformation projects (which tend to require Agile approaches (see below) and continuous, rapid experimentation) is that a more flexible and organic approach to change is necessary where products are piloted, and new behaviours are 'grown' through complex forms of engagement. This type of change work is likely to require not only skilled 'change facilitators', but also organizational leaders who are highly visible in guiding the process as things evolve.

BALANCING FLEXIBITY WITH CONTROL

Drawing on the 'Rethinking Project Management' conclusions and the PWC survey data earlier in this chapter, we believe that managing the uncertainty of softer, more complex, projects requires a balanced approach that has at least some of the basic disciplines and controls of a project managed environment, and yet is flexible enough to deal with variable goals, unpredictable external influences and multiple inputs along the way.

It is helpful to link back to some theory at this point. In Chapter 3, we set out four different metaphors for the change process, and in Chapter 4 identified how each is associated with a different type of leadership. If you turn back, you'll see that two of these metaphors are particularly relevant when discussing flexibility and control. The machine metaphor, aligned with control, requires traditional project management approaches such as goal setting, monitoring and controlling. The flux and transformation metaphor, aligned with flexibility and emergence, requires a more facilitative form of leadership that sets out governing principles, enables connectivity and amplifies issues.

Thus getting the right balance between these two elements requires a deft and subtle mix of two quite different leadership approaches. This suggests that project managers must develop more sophisticated leadership skills, and the ability to work with new models and frameworks that include complexity and ambiguity, if required to manage complex, strategic change projects. This resonates with the recommendations for future research set out in the 'Rethinking Project Management' report.

Alternatively, project managers and business leaders may need to work more closely with change managers – or perhaps in-house HR or OD professionals – to ensure that more attention is given to activities such as agreeing the right performance framework and convening the right conversations at the right time as work progresses.

Dealing with risk

When dealing with risk, project managers tend to rely on risk management plans and risk registers, but this is not the same as accepting and working with the uncertainties already threaded into a project.

> Quite often, the management of uncertainty through risk identification and assumptions becomes a box-ticking exercise which appears to be a case of applying mechanistic techniques to difficult-to-manage areas, without actually discussing them properly. The list gets looked at in rather a mechanical way on a monthly basis, but the issues are generally not properly addressed until they hit you between the eyes!
>
> Senior project manager, 'Big Four' management consultancy

Ward and Chapman (2003) say that this is because the term 'risk' encourages a threat perspective and tends to focus on negative 'events', whereas a focus on uncertainty allows potentially welcome effects to be considered as well as things that might go wrong. They add that uncertainty management is about 'identifying and managing the many sources of uncertainty that give rise to and shape our perception of threats and opportunities. It implies exploring and understanding the origins of project uncertainty before seeking to manage it, with no preconceptions of what is desirable or undesirable.'

In our experience, there is a temptation for less experienced project managers to name risks as a way of silently passing the buck to business leaders regarding potential problem areas, without discussing what the risk or uncertainty actually is. This is where the relationship between the project manager and business leader(s) becomes critical, as these risks may represent an opportunity, or something that requires attention from both parties.

Delivering on time!

Does disciplined project management control actually support on-time delivery? Or is this approach somehow counter-productive, particularly in high-complexity contexts? Although some of the classic data regarding project overruns has perhaps been exaggerated, it is still the case that many organizations struggle to complete projects to schedule and budget.

So what goes wrong? Is this failure down to unpredictable events and changing circumstances, and the impossibility of estimating how long something is going to take, given the unknowns at the start of a project? Or can some of this be managed better?

In our experience, some of the problem is down to knee-jerk reactions and unproductive 'pushing', usually from senior management, and outside of project control. Eden *et al* (2000) note that efforts to accelerate project progress after a period of considerable disruption or delay, or in an attempt to finish ahead of schedule for some reason, can be counter-productive and actually cause more disruption and delay. They also point out that effort spent addressing delays and disruptions could often be better used to stop and understand what's actually happening.

IT PROJECT DELIVERY PROBLEMS

The programme of change was based around the introduction of a big IT system and there were all sorts of demands and quibbles from different parts of the organization to be worked through, which was taking time and effort. Then senior management started to get nervous about deadlines and decided to force an early go-live date to help focus peoples' minds. This triggered a panic as the project manager set about reducing the scope of the initial delivery and forcing all the unresolved issues into the next phase. The whole programme ended up taking much longer to complete that initially planned, and I'm sure the forced deadline at the start didn't help.

Team manager, utilities company

The pros and cons of improvising

Improvisational approaches were labelled back in the 1950s and '60s as 'bad project management' or an organizational dysfunction, but are now seen as vital, for responding to and dealing with high levels of uncertainty and pressure to deliver on time, particularly in a project context.

Improvisation can refer to anything that doesn't go according to the plan, ie when the plan doesn't quite match reality, and rather than re-plan you 'improvise' a way through. The capacity to do this in a controlled way and do it well can enhance an organization's effectiveness, and even their speed-to-market amidst turbulence and rapid technological innovation and development.

Another useful definition of improvisation is 'making meaningful decisions within a limited timescale without optimum information and resources'. Collapsing complex processes into a faster, more streamlined approach is another type of improvisation. Lehrer (2000) states that there are some 'high dynamism' environments where planning is rendered futile, and that the use of 'bricolage' (ie improvisations such as the fusing of planning and execution) is widespread in fast-moving commercial sectors.

Some commentators say, and we tend to agree, that Agile is not a project management methodology at all, but a useful product development methodology for software development projects, business change initiatives and other situations where the deliverables are relatively unknown at the start.

Agile teams may also incorporate the Scrum framework, which encourages self-organization and daily face-to-face meetings of the whole team. This approach challenges assumptions of sequential and segmented approaches to development. Effort is focused on responding quickly to changes and new discoveries. There is acceptance that the problem being tackled cannot be fully understood or mapped out ahead of time, and that the customer may well change his or her mind about certain aspects as work progresses.

The 2011 CHAOS Manifesto, published by the Standish Group, reports that the percentage of IT and software projects using an Agile approach has risen from 2 per cent in 2002 to 9 per cent in 2011. It seems to have become a remedy for software application projects, bringing three times the success rate of traditional waterfall approaches (spec, plan, execute, test etc).

Pikkarainen *et al* (2008) spotted some downsides to the use of Agile in a software development context. Although the impact on internal software development team communications and day-to-day problem-solving tends to be good (as long as tacit knowledge is not over-relied on), Agile approaches do not provide the right communication mechanisms to ensure that this is done well throughout the project when there are multiple stakeholders groups and multiple development teams involved. They suggest that a plan-driven mechanism for stakeholder interaction is more effective.

Ken Schwaber's book *Agile Project Management with Scrum* (2004) advocates the use of Agile and Scrum for 'urgent and critical' projects, particularly because it dramatically shortens the feedback loop between customer and developer. He says that when you're dealing with a market economy that changes all the time with technology that won't stand still, it's important to be able to learn through short cycles of discovery.

Schwaber also warns that those steeped in traditional management practices have to unlearn them in order the master the Scrum approach. He says there are no Gantt charts, no detailed work plans, no schedules.

Hut (2009) helpfully cites a number of realistic difficulties with implementing an Agile way of working in your organization:

- Agile working requires differently skilled people from the ones already employed by your organization.

- The degree of individual ownership and freedom needed for Agile methods to work implies quite a big cultural change for many organizations.

- Agile teams are restricted in size and tend to meet for 15 minutes a day – which restricts the contexts in which the method can work ie larger, more complex teams cannot work like this.

- The face-to-face part of Agile may be impractical due to other commitments and geographic constraints etc – although perhaps virtual methods can be used.

- Not everything in a project can be stuffed into short meetings without records. There still needs to be some attention given to budget, scope, risk management, planning and reporting. Agile simply offers a form of team management, which isn't a methodology.

- If the project is owned by a team rather than an individual, the reward system should reflect that this, rather than be individually oriented, as many are.

Working with stakeholders

Stakeholders are an increasingly important focus of project management activity, not just because of the pressures of reduced cycle-time and the need to get staff/users on board quickly, but also because project success is often measured in terms of multiple parameters; stakeholder input and opinion is critical to this. Stakeholder analysis is a familiar activity, traditionally done at the start of the project and resulting in an influencing plan that lasts for the duration of the project. However, the needs and interests of stakeholders in more complex settings tend to shift and change during the life of a project, and more attention may be needed to identify and manage these shifts.

Assudani and Kloppenborg (2010) say that most projects can benefit from periodic reassessments of stakeholders, and particularly those that are emergent and complex. Assessing their relative importance to project success helps the project manager to apportion the considerable time spent liaising with stakeholders. They recommend the following activities:

i   identify all stakeholders, determining which are most important;

ii   build relationships with the most important and manage their expectations as the project progresses;

iii   communicate effectively with all stakeholders.

They say that stakeholder analysis is of central importance in working out 'who counts', and suggest using Mitchell *et al*'s (1997) framework of power, legitimacy and urgency. They recommend that more than a 'front-end' analysis is done, and offer the lens of 'social network theory' which views social relationship in terms of 'actors' or 'nodes', and the relationships or 'ties' between them. This enables you to identify the actors with the most social capital. This in turn provides a way of identifying salient stakeholders, and project team 'influencers' at any one time during the project by encouraging project managers and project stakeholders to explore:

- who will be affected by the project outcomes and process;

- who they will ask for inputs to the project;

- who will they talk to about project-related activities to ensure the success of the project.

IMPROVING THE GOVERNANCE AND ORGANIZATIONAL LEADERSHIP OF PROJECTS

Project governance is a significant factor in any project or programme set-up, and its importance is emphasized in popular project management methodologies such as PRINCE2. Project management offices (PMOs) are still a commonly used method for augmenting the effectiveness of project governance, particularly in large organizations in both private and public sectors. These offices are typically responsible for anything from the provision of project management support functions to the direct management of a projects and programmes.

Are governance structures working in a way that supports project success and brings a good balance between control and emergence in complex, fast-moving contexts? Or are they, as some critics say, cumbersome to implement, and end up being rather inflexible, bureaucratic and out of touch with the realities of progress on the ground?

What shifts might then be made in the way projects are governed, led and managed to improve success rates, particularly where sustainable change is aspired to in a complex, uncertain context?

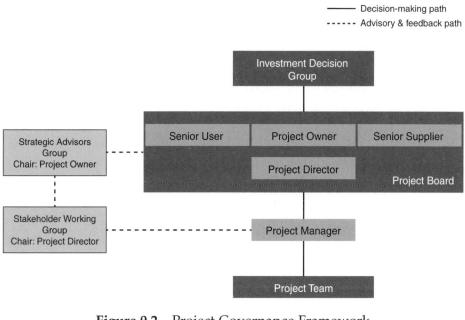

Figure 9.2 Project Governance Framework
Source: Garland (2009₂)

Project governance

In his book about governance (Garland, 2009) and his related article 'Developing A Governance Framework', Ross Garland states that although 'decision-making failure' appears to be one of the top 3–5 causes of project failure, project governance is still a haphazard affair with few established principles. This echoes our own experience of project governance as a topic that receives scant attention. Effort is more likely to be spent on the hunt for a good quality project manager, which many believe to be a more powerful determinant of a successful outcome.

Garland's proposes a structure for high-risk projects (see Figure 9.2) and asserts four helpful project governance principles:

- identify a single point of project accountability, rather than leaving this to a committee;

- ensure project governance is service delivery-focused – placing the business at the heart of the project;

- ensure separation of stakeholder management and project decision-making activities, ensuring that decision-making forums are not clogged with stakeholders;

- ensure separation of project governance and organizational governance structures, thus reducing the number of project decision layers.

However, he warns that the implementation of such a framework is a business change exercise in itself, and that the key issues are likely to include:

i   separating project governance from organizational governance, which is difficult;

ii   selecting a project board with enough experience;

iii ensuring that the 'customer' resources their part in project governance activities.

In our experience, organizations with mature structures and good quality leadership discipline find Garland's principles relatively straightforward to follow and implement, although there are clearly challenges in making some of this happen. However, where organizational structures are already poor, and leadership discipline and skills are weak or immature, there tend to be serious struggles with all three issues.

The role of project management offices

PWC's third global survey on the current state of project management (2012) reveals some interesting data on the use of PMOs:

- The majority of organizations never evaluate the effectiveness of the PMO.

- For those who do, it seems the longer PMOs are in place, the more effective they are in establishing standardized project management processes and controls – although this can take up to six years.

- Sixty-six per cent of surveyed organizations were using PMOs in 2012, a decline from 80 per cent in 2007. A hypothesis is offered that those who are not now using PMOs are using Agile methods instead and getting similar success rates.

- PMOs can be responsible for anything from project and programme administrative support support, to delivery management, right through to investment governance, so quite a range of activities are being discussed and evaluated here.

Professors Ward and Daniel (2012) explored the pros and cons of introducing a PMO structure, particularly within Information System (IS)-led change projects. Their research indicates that PMOs are increasingly being introduced in an attempt to improve overall control and co-ordination given the growing number and complexity of projects that organizations initiate to achieve strategic change.

Ward and Daniel found that the presence of a PMO actually 'reduces senior management satisfaction with IS project success, and has no overall effect on the success rates of those projects'. This appears to be due to senior management's increased knowledge of the inner workings of the project, particularly of what's not going to plan. The findings also suggest that it's 'more important for PMOs to be involved at the start and the review stage of projects, rather than in the ongoing monitoring ... where much of their current focus is'.

Unger, Gemunden and Aubry (2012) on the other hand, discerned positive effects of some aspects of PMO activity such as control and coordination, while emphasizing the need for clarity of function and reporting lines. Some PMOs end up either being ineffective, or being loathed by both the business and the project manager, as they perform something of an audit and 'policing' function for both.

So a mixed picture of PMOs' effectiveness is emerging. They seem to offer a high degree of visibility and security to senior leaders but don't always focus on the more 'value-adding' activities, such as supporting start-up or review stages. In our view, it's these activities that are likely to be particularly helpful in more uncertain and complex contexts.

The shifting role of project managers

In the initial set-up of a critical project, much emphasis tends to be put on the selection of the project manager. Are the appropriate qualities being sought, given the nature of the challenges he/she is likely to encounter?

The 'Rethinking Project Management' report (see page 345) indicates a need for project managers to move beyond being trained technicians to becoming reflective practitioners. The reports refers to the work of Fish and Coles (1998), who offer a framework (originally drawn up for healthcare professionals) outlining the shifts that project managers might need to make as they learn how to work effectively in softer, more complex settings:

CONCLUSION

Projects and programmes are seen and experienced as critical delivery mechanisms for improving business performance. However, as projects grow in complexity, there are questions about the effectiveness of aspects of this approach in delivering wide-scale, rapid, sustainable organizational change.

Over the last 5 to 10 years, change management has become an established adjunct to project management, such that increased attention is now given to the task of transitioning people from the current state to a desired future state. This combined approach can work well for relatively straight-forward projects and programmes, but may need to be revitalized in readiness for future challenges in a rapidly changing world, particularly where there is a high degree of uncertainty and/or multiple stakeholders.

The 'Rethinking Project Management' report suggests items to consider for meeting this challenge. These are: new frameworks for complexity; better understanding of social and political processes; a move toward value creation; broader conceptualization of projects; and more reflective project managers. More recent research indicates that the use of highly flexible design and implementation processes such as Agile is already increasing, with promising results.

The balance between flexibility and control will be key to running successful projects in the future, with issues of governance and leadership at the core. Suggestion for areas for attention and improvement are:

- Organizations need to set up project governance structures that i) separate project governance from organizational governance, ii) are overseen by a sufficiently experienced board and iii) include 'customer' representation able and willing to play their part well.

- Project managers need to broaden and deepen their capabilities if they are to deliver well in increasingly uncertain project contexts.

- Change managers require more authority to act, a more mature approach, greater facilitative skill and more familiarity with emergent processes, if they are to continue to be effective.

- Business leaders need to be given a clear brief, provide authoritative project sponsorship, including guidance for line-leaders as work progresses, and have the authority, motivation and time to carry out this important role.

- Project managers, change managers and business leaders must be clear about each others' roles, and prepared to build good-quality working relationships with each other.

Part Three

Emerging inquiries

You can tell whether a man is clever by his answers.
You can tell whether a man is wise by his questions.
Naguib Mahfouz (Nobel Prize Winner)

Although this book has the subtitle 'A *complete* guide to the models, tools and techniques of organizational change', that is, of course, not quite the case. Although we have attempted to include the majority of useful models, tools and techniques, there is still plenty more to ponder on and discover about how change happens and what enables people in organizations to give of their best when change is in the air.

Since the earlier editions were published we have been pursuing a number of our own inquiries into the nature of change, and we include two of these perspectives in Part Three. In Chapter 10 we explore complex change, identifying when change can be defined as 'complex' and uncovering theories, tools and leadership stances that can help in this situation. In Chapter 11, we explore the topic of leading change in uncertain times, which we hope will interest many readers who are grappling with the particular change challenges of 'these times'. In this chapter, we look at the impact of uncertainty on our working lives, explore the difficulties associated with decision making in an uncertain world and offer some skills and tools to support leaders faced with deep uncertainty.

Our hope is that these two chapters will stimulate your own further inquiry into these two fascinating and important topics.

10

Complex change

INTRODUCTION

Since the first edition of this book, some interesting new ideas have really started to take hold in the world of organizational development. Ideas on understanding organizations using complexity science and the notion of emergence rather than managed change are now being grasped and worked with by leaders and consultants alike. It is as though we are appreciating anew the possibility that not everything can be planned and controlled, and that even having a strong vision only gets you so far. Sometimes change happens in non-linear and chaotic ways, neither bottom-up nor top-down, and whether you believe in fate, the stars, the fundamentals of biology, or in the sheer randomness of life, one man or woman may really feel quite small in the face of it.

In Chapter 3 on organizational change, we discussed the metaphor of flux and transformation and briefly explored the assumptions that underpin this view of organizations. The flux and transformation metaphor could equally well be referred to as the complexity metaphor. Here, we explore this metaphor a bit further.

This chapter looks at a range of different approaches to understanding and dealing with complex organizational change. The key headings are:

- When is change complex?

- Understanding complexity science.

- Tools that support complex change processes.

- The role of leaders in complex change.

WHEN IS CHANGE COMPLEX?

It is easy to say when change is not complex. Installing a new phone system, or implementing a ready-made IT system, or organizing an office move are all the types of change activity that benefit from a well-planned, controlled approach. Any change that has a high 'technical' element to it lends itself to more linear methods. Although these changes may be complicated, they do tend to happen more easily if the details can be organized efficiently.

Restructuring programmes, cultural change initiatives, outsourcing, mergers, acquisitions and strategic-led change, especially when a large number of people are involved, can all be seen as complex change. These are changes that involve so many individuals, layers of activity, areas of focus and so many factors that cannot be pre-thought out that there will be a need for people to struggle and argue and work their way through to an unpredictable outcome.

The advantages of understanding the concept of complexity are many. Managers in today's organizations are often trained to think in purely analytical, rational ways. We are taught to see things independently rather than inter-dependently. Current mainstream management thinking is generally based on a mixture of cognitive psychology – which focuses on motivational goals and behaviour – together with scientific methods designed to map out and organize tasks, such as process engineering or project management. These disciplines do not leave much space for the possibility of complexity; the possibility that a contained 'muddle' may well sort itself out given the right conditions.

When managers begin to appreciate how complex processes work, they can release themselves from too much over-managing and begin to think about the different needs they should be fulfilling as leaders who encourage healthy, creative change to emerge.

UNDERSTANDING HOW COMPLEXITY SCIENCE APPLIES TO ORGANIZATIONAL CHANGE

Complexity science has been drawn from the scientific world and applied to organizations in an attempt to understand and explain the behaviour of large systems. There is no formal definition of what complexity science means in an organizational context, nor indeed how it is best applied to organizations.

In this discipline, large systems are often referred to as *complex adaptive systems*. Complex adaptive systems are made up of multiple inter-connected elements, and have the capacity to change and learn from experience. Complexity science is a collection of theories that seek to explain how these systems work. This branch of science is eclectic and draws its ideas from many other areas of science, for example the fields of neurology and microbiology. Examples of such large complex systems are communities, the stock market, the human body's immune system and the brain.

One of the most intriguing features of complex adaptive systems for those who study them in the context of human social organization, is their capacity to produce coherence, continuity and transformation in the absence of any external blueprint or nominated designer. The control of a complex adaptive system is highly dispersed and decentralized, and the whole system's behaviour appears to arise from competition and co-operation among the local agents in the system, coupled with sensitivity to amplifying or dampening feedback. Even if a major part of the system is out of action, the system continues to function. A good example of this in the field of biology is the human brain.

At the Santa Fe Institute in New Mexico, where scientists have studied the behaviour of computer-simulated complex networks for some time, the following six characteristics of a complex system were identified:

1   there is no central control;

2   there is an inherent underlying structure within the system;

3   there is feedback in the system;

4   there is nonlinearity – things do not happen in a cause and effect manner;

5   emergence is an outcome of the system – this happens without planned intent;

6   the system is non-reducible. This means that you cannot understand the system's behaviour by looking at one part. It is necessary to instead look at a representative slice of all of the parts.

Eric Dent of George Washington University (1999) proposed that our whole world view is beginning to shift from a rational to an emerging one. It is as if our 'technical' rational reactions to political or social situations are not working any more. For example, use of catalytic converters in cars represents our increased concern for the environment. However, the effects in parts of Africa where the platinum to produce these converters is mined are very negative. People are being moved out of their homelands, health and safety is not being carefully attended to, and workers are losing their lives through avoidable accidents due to the commercial drive for production. Our approach isn't holistic; it's partial. And we are worried about it. Dent says we have to shift our thinking if we are to be successful. He produced a helpful chart that illustrates the shifts required; the highlights are shown in Table 10.1. Dent (1999) sees the list on the right as an extension of the list on the left, rather than replacing it.

Table 10.1   World view descriptors

Traditional world view	Emerging world view
Reductionism	Holism
Linear causality	Mutual causality
Objective reality	Perspectival reality
Observer outside the observation	Observer in the observation
'Survival of the fittest'	Adaptive self-organization
Focus on discrete entities	Focus on relationships between entities
Linear relationships	Non-linear relationships
– marginal increases	– critical mass thresholds
Either/or thinking	Polarity thinking
Focus on directives	Focus on feedback
Newtonian physics perspectives	Quantum physics perspectives
– influence occurs as direct result of force exerted from one person to another	– influence occurs through iterative, non-linear feedback
– the world is predictable	– the world is novel
Focus on pace	Focus on patterns
Focus on results or outcomes	Focus on ongoing behaviour

Capra (1982) explains why we now need to see the world in different ways:

> Modern science has come to realize that all scientific theories are approximations to the true nature of reality, and that each theory is valid for a certain range of phenomena. Beyond this range it no longer gives a satisfactory description of nature, and new theories have to be found to replace the old one, or rather to extend it by improving the approximation.

Systemic views of organizations, such as the concept of the learning organization promoted by Senge (1993) owe much to the influence of complexity science. The four basic assumptions that Konigswieser and Hillebrand (2005) identify in their book about systemic consultancy provide a useful translation of the principles of complexity for use in organizational work:

- Organizations do not function like trivial machines. They do not simply work at the push of a button and can therefore neither be controlled directly nor completely understood.

- They constantly reproduce themselves through communication, are in a state of permanent change and continually create new order structures in the form of retained stories, recorded successes and agreed perceptions, patterns and expectations.

- This self-image gains intensity in the 'sense constructs' and views of the world projected as models from inside the system to the environment. Internal order structures, sense constructs and images of the world create security and stability within the organization, yet at the same time obstruct its ability to react to changes in a dynamic, rapidly changing environment.

- Organizations can learn from their environment not only in times of crisis and pressure, but also proactively by assuming an active and creative role in reshaping themselves and their respective environments.

There are some important principles and ideas embedded within complexity science that are useful for managers and consultants who are tackling organizational change issues:

- self-organization and emergence;
- rules of interaction;

- attractors;

- power relations;

- forms of communicating;

- polarities and the management of paradox;

- feedback.

Each of these is described and explained below, together with its significance for organizational change.

Self-organization and emergence

The principle of self-organization is central to complexity science. The belief behind this principle is that we live in a universe that seeks organization. Patterns and structures emerge that are not planned or pre-designed. Old structures disappear and new ones come into being. Change is happening all the time. Individuals within a system who aren't capable of change may eventually disappear.

In the biological sciences there are some good examples of self-organization working extremely efficiently. Bacteria, for example, operate as a global super-organism, able to swap genes and 'understand' and absorb each others' learning. No single bacterium has the knowledge of the whole, or understands how everything works. The bacteria, instead of being all-knowing, are superb at learning from each other, very quickly and efficiently. This is why bacteria that are resistant to antibiotics develop so quickly. In this type of system model the world knows how to create itself: as individuals we are simply partners in the process, not the ones responsible for it.

Patricia Shaw (2002) explains the parameters of self-organization by referring to an experiment performed by scientists at the Santa Fe Institute. The scientists modelled a large complex system using a lot of digital agents. Their experiments illustrated that low connectivity, low diversity and sluggish interaction between agents tended to result in stable, frozen or 'stuck' patterns of interaction. Conversely, high connectivity, high diversity and intensive interaction between agents results in disorder with no visible patterns arising. However, when the parameters were at certain critical values, the behaviour produced order and disorder at the same time. Langton (1992) has dubbed the phenomenon of complex networks interacting in such conditions as being 'at the edge of chaos', as the patterns produced were neither wholly random nor wholly repetitive. We can transfer this idea to the domain of human interaction, but must wonder who controls the parameters, if anyone does.

In economics, the market economy is said to be a self-organizing process. Some economists say that central economic planning, ie what will be produced by whom and how profits will be distributed, disturbs the efficiency of self-organizing markets. Others say that the propensity of individuals to pursue self-interest can be so damaging that governments must intervene and control the economy via taxation. The latter is an argument for a more controlled approach.

In human social interaction, techniques such as open space, future search (see later in this chapter), production cells and self-managed teams all use the principle of self-organization.

Rules of interaction

Complex adaptive systems self-organize and evolve over time using simple local rules that result in global complex behaviour. However, the system works without the rules of a central authority governing behaviour. Local rules are changed as experience accumulates. In a human system, these might be limits on activity or altered social norms. In human social systems these rules are not necessarily explicit and people are not always aware of them. Local rules exist in peoples' heads.

Change occurs when either the local rules change, or the pattern of connectedness changes across the global system. Stacey (2001) argues that this happens in the absence of an external blueprint. If we transfer this thinking to large complex organizations, this means that the traditional role of directors and senior managers who together may aspire to directly influence local behaviour, is unlikely to have the desired effect, and may end up stifling creative and healthy change. It may be that the essential cultural paradigm of the organization needs to shift from within.

Attractors

Systems in chaos appear to fall under the influence of different 'attractors'. Lorenz (in Gleick, 1987), the mathematician and meteorologist, showed how complex systems can combine order and

and putting a great deal of energy into making it work. The new way means more discussion and more engagement. However, old patterns of performance management and career progression rely on a reputation for 'toughness' and high personal achievement, so the polarity between 'toughness' and 'cooperation' starts to be an important one. This is where leaders who manage paradox well can be most useful. What elements of both toughness and cooperation are useful in the new order?

The necessity for either/or thinking is one of the great myths of Western culture. This occurs when two seeming opposites in any situation are seen as one 'good', one 'bad'. For instance, cooperation is 'good' and toughness 'bad'. This can easily lead to the assumption that 'I am right, and you are all wrong.' Either/or thinking demands that for something to be the 'right answer', there must be no contradictions. Combining options or blurring the boundaries is seen as illogical and muddled.

Once the seeming opposites are seen as a continuum, the polarization sets in. For instance, one director we work with sees 'teamworking' as the polar opposite of 'independent working'. This creates stagnation in his thinking. However, when the continuum is translated into a graph, the possibility that both of these may coexist, or that both contain both 'good' and 'bad' elements begins to be visible; see Figure 10.2.

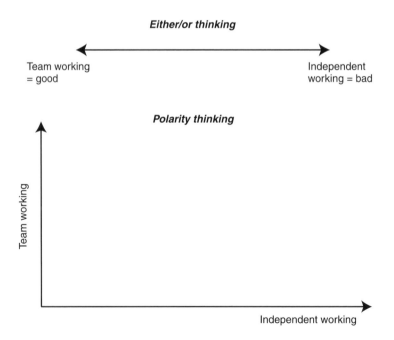

Figure 10.2 Moving from 'either/or' thinking to embrace 'polarity' thinking

Polarities are sets of opposites that cannot function well independently. The two sides of a polarity are interdependent, so one side cannot be 'right' or the 'solution' at the expense of the other. It seems that many of the current challenges within organizations are about managing polarities or paradoxes, rather than solving problems. So, for example, the argument about whether top-down or bottom-up change works best implies that one is right and the other is wrong. If these are seen as polarities that need to co-exist and both have their good points and bad points, it is possible to reframe the issues that might bring organizational stagnancy by creating positive new realities.

Feedback

One of the characteristics of a complex system is that feedback exists within it. The non-linear nature of change within a complex system means that linear cause and effect analyses do not work. Mutual causality is about understanding how change evolves through looping interactions, which can be modelled as positive and negative feedback loops. By doing this type of analysis it is possible to see where clusters of positive feedback loops create vicious circles, and where very small changes can lead to very significant outcomes. In organizations, delayed feedback or counter-responses may destabilize the system by eliciting exaggerated responses or behaviours.

Stacey (2001) refers to the interaction between agents in a complex system as 'gesture and response'. Within systems that are richly enough connected, and have enough difference within them, this self-organized interaction of gesture and response will produce both coherence and novelty.

STOP AND THINK!

Q 10.1 Think of an organization you know well. Taking Dent's theory of shifting from traditional to emerging world views (Table 10.1), discuss with a colleague how a shift in world view might change what happens in this organization.

Q 10.2 How would a greater belief in self-organization change your actions as a manager, coach or OD practitioner?

Q 10.3 Consider the paradoxes that exist in your own life as it shifts and changes, or those that exist in an organization you know that is going through a change process. How can these be managed well?

TOOLS THAT SUPPORT COMPLEX CHANGE

Storytelling

Storytelling is a type of sense making that helps us to shape our understanding of the complex goings-on in the world. People tell stories to share wisdom with each other, entertain each other, influence each other and help each other make sense of the world. Stories can be created collectively in the moment, or carefully crafted by individuals before they are told. Their essential logic is temporal. They generally move from the past to the present, and tend to open up possibilities for the future. So, paradoxically, stories are distinct ways of making sense of the past and showing how the past leads to the future, which in turn affects the present. Hearing a story may change how we view our current options, and the way we make sense of what has already happened.

There's a difference between telling a story and giving an example. A story has a plot, and characters and emotional and sensory detail. In a story you can examine both sides of an argument; a manager can tell a story in which a proposed change is simultaneously awful and exciting. This is more engaging and more real than an announcement that says: 'The change is coming. Stop moaning and get on with it.' A story can also help someone to walk in your shoes, to see things from your point of view. It can help others to see things they are not currently seeing.

Leaders can use storytelling to work with their teams to make sense of their own past, present and future, or to convey to their teams how they are making sense of it all. It is a way of communicating without oversimplifying. Instead of being used to convince others of a particular course of action, a story can be used to awaken sleeping wisdom and lead to good conversations about what to do next.

Shaw (2002) says of the practice of collective storytelling:

> The kind of storytelling I am alluding to is not that of completed tales but narrative-in-the-making. Rather than stating aims, objective, outcomes, roles as abstract generalities, people use a narrative mode. The starting point is often 'the story so far'. Someone recounts and at the same time accounts for or justifies the way they make sense of events and their own participation... As others associate and 'fill in' an increasingly complex patterned sense-making is co-created. This is an absorbing process because a person's identity in this situation is evolving at the same time. We are not 'just talking'. We are acting together to shape ourselves and our world.

Dialogue

Dialogue is a central tool for those interested in dealing with complexity. Dialogue is different from other forms of communication such as debate or discussion, or ordinary conversation. William Isaacs, who founded the MIT Dialogue Project, has been influential in bringing these ideas and practices into organizational settings. This way of talking pays particular attention to the meaning that unfolds when people communicate collectively.

Isaacs (1999) sees dialogue as not merely about talking but about taking action, and at its very best it includes meaning making and the expression of feelings and leads towards powerful action. Dialogue is about thinking together rather than thinking alone, and demands that we both let go of our own positional views and begin to face and hear about other people's experiences and realities.

Isaacs talks about 'choice points' in a conversation. A key choice point in a conversation that involves some deliberation is whether to either defend your own view or position, or suspend it and therefore listen without resistance. Defending usually leads to either productive analytical dialectic or unproductive verbal brawling. Suspending is more likely to lead to an exploration of the deeper questions, a new framing of key issues and the possibility of reaching collective, refreshing new insights.

Whole system work

Increasingly, organizations and public bodies are seeing the need to bring whole systems together to tackle complex and messy issues with multiple stakeholders. Patricia Shaw (2002) talks about these sorts of events:

> Carefully designed and facilitator-led large group events are an increasingly popular example of 'intervention' into the ongoing processes of organizing. These are intensive interactive conferences intended to stimulate new forms of action to address ambitious change in complex situations. Participants are invited to identify issues and create self-managing small groups to generate proposals for future work. The result is a public plan of action.

Open space technology

Harrison Owen, the originator of open space technology, says that his ideas are probably as old as homo sapiens; it is just that modern-day wisdom has obscured our instincts and intuition about how gatherings of people can self-organize to find what is exciting and energizing, and then make things happen. Owen's (1997) ideas emerged when he began to notice that at a regular international symposium he used to attend, which used the traditional formal presentation of papers plus orchestrated panel discussions, the real excitement and energy used to burst out in the coffee breaks. He wondered if it were possible to make the symposium one big coffee break.

An open space session is typically a large gathering that is clearly focused on one topic, has no set agenda, no organizing committee and a small band of facilitators. The agenda is discovered by participants who wish to pursue topics posting these on a notice board, seeing who signs up and then running these various conversations simultaneously. People can move from one conversation to another, and a record of each discussion, with issues ranked and next steps identified for the critical issues, is given to every participant. It seems that open space represents Owen's belief that the one thing we spend our time doing so much of – organizing and seeking control – is not only unavailable but unnecessary.

When is it appropriate? It works well when there is a very pressing issue that needs to be sorted out yesterday, when there is a great deal of complexity, when there is conflict and when there is a lot of diversity in the people who need to get together to solve the issue.

There are four Principles and one Law of open space sessions. The four Principles are:

1   **Whoever comes are the right people** – people demonstrate that they care by showing up.

2   **Whatever happens is the only thing that could have** – this helps people to focus on the here and now, not what could have been or should have been.

3   **Whenever it starts is the right time** – creativity is not dictated by the clock.

4   **Whenever it's over, it's over** – don't waste time! When the conversation is finished, move on.

 The one Law is called 'the law of two feet', which means when you are no longer listening or contributing, move on to somewhere more to your liking. This is not just about pleasing yourself, but about taking

responsibility for your own learning rather than sulking or blaming others for not making things more stimulating. Owen says that the Principles and Law are not really what makes open space work; it's just that these statements free people up to do what they would do naturally, given a chance.

Future search

Future search is a way of conferencing that is underpinned by research by Weisbord and Janoff (1992) into the conditions under which diverse groups seemed to be able to cooperate. Previous work by North American and Australian social scientists was also highly influential. Future search involves many people getting together for a large planning meeting, and is based on principles that enable diverse groups to get together and cooperate, be very task-focused, and quickly translate their energies into action.

These principles are:

- get the 'whole system' in the room – inviting a cross-section of all parties who care about the issue;

- explore the 'whole elephant' before acting on a part – get everyone talking about the same big picture;

- put common ground and future focus at the centre, and treat conflicts as information rather than items to be 'sorted';

- encourage self-management and responsibility taking for action by participants.

The conditions for success are:

- encourage full attendance – discourage part-timers;

- meet under healthy conditions – with food and snacks, and adequate breaks;

- work across three days (sleep twice) – things need time to be absorbed;

- ask for voluntary public commitments to next steps before people leave.

Wheatley urges leaders to lead through vision, values and ethics. This does not mean crafting a single vision that shines so brightly that it has its own power, but co-creating a vision that permeates the organization and harnesses the organization's own self-organizing power. However, the difficulty for many leaders is that vision and values seem 'a bit soft' when compared to traditional forms of authority, and they may feel powerless and somehow naked without the familiar controlling mechanisms.

Wheatley also emphasizes the importance of developing a new relationship with information so that it is embraced for all its vibrant, living qualities. She notices an unhelpful habit in leaders. Rather than looking for small differences in the information we receive, often leaders seek certainty and notice only the big trends and large gaps. They may value quick, surface decisions over wiser, deeper ones. She says that leaders need to see information as nourishment rather than power, and keep the flow well stocked.

Wheatley goes on to say that in this world of chaos and complexity we appear to need leaders rather than bosses; people who assist their employees in embodying organizational values and carry a strong sense of purpose. Policies and procedures curtail creativity and end up failing to control as effectively as a strong sense of purpose and some clear, hard rules.

Scharmer (2000) is a great believer in self-organization too, but he also sees a more spiritual dimension to organizational or community endeavours. As we sense and intuit together, something sacred happens, and out of the space between us something new emerges.

Scharmer refers to leadership as 'sensing and actualizing emerging futures'. He identifies two important methods of learning that are both important for sustained organizational success. The first is to reflect on the past in a way that loosens our traditional views of what's happened. The second is to begin to sense and embody the emergent future as it appears out of the mist between us, instead of re-enacting past patterns. He talks about the processes of both 'letting go' and 'letting come', which leaders need to understand as the root of generative learning. This process is not about being polite, or getting involved in conflictual debate or dialectic. It involves true generative and reflective dialogue.

Scharmer sees the leader's role as creating the conditions that allow others to 'shift the place from which their system operates'. There is a sacred quality to Scharmer's work that takes us far beyond the focus on ordinary conversation which sits at the root of complex responsive process theory.

Presence is another important quality that those writing about the complex view of change encourage in leaders. Facilitators of emergence need to embody presence if they are to be truly tuned into the complexities of organizational life. This means being less preoccupied by the world of objectives and performance indicators, and more open to the subtle complexities of the world as they unfold in front of them; more present in the 'here and now' moment.

Senge *et al* (2005) talk about presence as having an even deeper quality such as 'grace', or what the Buddhists call 'cessation'. This definition of presence has a spiritual quality to it. They say that presence occurs when there is a quieting of the mind, and the normal boundaries between self and the world begin to melt away. For leaders this means being able to let go, surrender control and open themselves to the wider needs of the world. The authors of *Presence: Exploring profound change in people, organizations and society* provide a sentence on what this notion of presence means to each of them:

> Jaworski: 'A profound opening of the heart, carried into action.'
> Scharmer: 'Waking up together... by using the Self as a vehicle for bringing forth new worlds.'
> Flowers: 'It's the point where the fire of creation burns and enters the world through us.'
> Senge: 'We have no idea of our capacity to create the world anew.'

STOP AND THINK!

Q 10.4 How could you use open space technology or World Café to good effect in your organization or local community?

Q 10.5 Imagine yourself in a leadership role in your organization. Maybe you are in one already. What is your area's core purpose? What is the whole organization's core purpose? This needs to reflect some value that is being created in the world. What are the few simple principles that apply to work in your area? (Once you have these, it will form the foundation for your leadership.)

SUMMARY AND CONCLUSIONS

New thinking on how complexity science can be applied to organizational problems is developing fast and becoming more widely known and understood.

Small, simple or highly convergent change initiatives such as technology roll-outs are less complex, and less emergent, and therefore less likely to benefit from being seen through a complexity lens.

'Complex adaptive systems' is the name given to large systems by complexity scientists. These systems are self-organizing, have no external blueprint, and yet they still have the capacity to produce coherence, continuity and transformation.

Dent (1999) suggests that our whole world view is beginning to shift from the rational to the emerging world view. This is in tune with much thinking about our ability to see the world as complex and emergent, rather than linear, rational and controllable.

The important elements of complexity science that relate to organizational work are: self-organization and emergence, rules of interaction, attractors, power relations, forms of communicating, polarities, and the management of paradox and the role of feedback.

Systems thinking and complexity science have very different roots, and lead to very different assumptions about how change works.

Storytelling, dialogue, whole systems work, open space technology, future search and World Café are all tools that support complex change.

Leaders have a different role in complex change from the traditional organizing or controlling roles of managers. The new role may be referred to as 'facilitator of emergent change'. This means leading through vision, values and ethics. It also means creating generative and reflective dialogue, and being present in the 'here and now'.

11

Leading change in uncertain times

INTRODUCTION

The whole globe is shook up, so what are you going to do when things are falling apart? You're either going to become more fundamentalist and try to hold things together, or you're going to forsake the old ambitions and goals and live life as an experiment, making it up as you go along.

Pema Chodron (2001)

The inferno of the living is not something that will be: if there is one, it is what is already here, the inferno where we live every day, that we form by being together. There are two ways to escape suffering it. The first is easy for many: accept the inferno and become such a part of it that you can no longer see it. The second is risky and demands constant vigilance and apprehension: seek and learn to recognize who and what, in the midst of the inferno, are not inferno, then make them endure, give them space.

Marco Polo's words, in *La Citta Invisibli* by Italo Calvino

In Chapter 10 we outlined some of the ideas from complexity science that support leaders in conceptualizing and leading a way through the complex nature of many of today's leadership challenges. This chapter focuses more specifically on the challenges posed by increased uncertainty in our working lives, the effect this has on leaders and the led, how organizations are responding, and how leaders can best equip themselves to lead and manage change through uncertainty.

The chapter is organized under the following headings:

- the impact of uncertainty on our working lives;
- decision making in an uncertain world; and
- skills and tools to support leading change through uncertainty.

Political, economic and climate instability are all familiar elements of the global context that we're now working in. The conundrum is that although we know that very little is predictable and stable in today's world, many of the tools and techniques available for leading and managing have been devised to fit with an 'old' rational, mechanical world view. This assumes that difficult problems can be reduced and understood, rational answers found and long-term plans made; leaders are heroes with an extra dose of this masterful rationality.

Our working lives, personal lives and communities are also more fragmented and less predictable than they used to be. Many people's careers now encompass several different sub-careers, families are more widely spread geographically and communities have less cohesion around a local geographic focus.

Some organizations are responding to these challenges with totally new organizational forms that increase their capacity to adapt and innovate, and flex to new forms of business partnership and to people's shifting lifestyles, while others struggle to respond at all. Many are calling for a new world view in which we become more open to uncertainty and confusion, and more trusting of emergent processes. This means letting go of heroic plans that no longer seem valid, finding new ways of responding to the here and now and offering leadership that enables this.

As individuals, many of us have far less stability in our lives than our parents had, and we are having to find ways of developing new skills to manage ourselves and tell our stories in this uncertain and turbulent world so that we can lead fulfilling and ultimately satisfying lives.

This chapter describes key themes that support leaders to find answers to these dilemmas.

> _The volume of education continues to increase, yet so do pollution, exhaustion of resources, and the dangers of ecological catastrophe. If still more education is to save us, it would have to be education of a different kind: an education that takes us into the depth of things._
>
> E F Schumacher (1973)

THE IMPACT OF UNCERTAINTY ON OUR WORKING LIVES

In his dense but highly readable short book, _Liquid Times,_ Professor of Sociology Zygmunt Bauman (2007) suggests five sources of uncertainty in today's world that he says are leading us to be more fearful and 'self-focused' as individuals:

1   Social forms – the institutions, businesses and other organized entities that limit individual choice and guard behaviour – are not expected to keep their shape for long, and are unlikely to solidify before re-forming – so can no longer serve as fundamental frames of reference for human actions.

2   Power and politics are becoming separate. Newly emancipated global power bases are calling the shots while increasingly irrelevant local politics is left impotent in the face of people's real-life problems. Local politicians are now abandoning the functions they traditionally performed, leaving these to market forces.

3   Individuals feel increasingly vulnerable to the vagaries of the markets. The reduction of the welfare state's care for individuals in tough times encourages competitive attitudes and downgrades collaboration (unless it's a temporary strategy for individual success).

4   The collapse of long-term thinking, planning and acting is leading to a life experienced as a series of fragmented, possibly unrelated steps or 'projects', where dropping old habits can be more important for success than building on previous learnings.

> *I realized after the meeting that my anxiety had got the better of me. I just 'went for' a member of my team in open forum, just because he hadn't completed an action. I really humiliated him out of all proportion. And afterwards, I could see this was really to do with my own anxiety about the chaos and uncertainty the team was working in, and my inability to manage things as brilliantly as usual.*
>
> A senior project manager in the motor industry recognizes his anxieties

As touched on above, some leaders may decide to give up in the face of uncertainty, 'keep their heads down' and 'not make waves'. Robert Quinn (1996) encourages us to resist the lure of being a powerless victim or a passive observer in this uncertain world, as this type of detachment erodes our sense of meaning and leaves us looking at the world in superficial ways. He calls this a 'slow death of the self' and urges us instead to make deep changes in ourselves – which might for instance mean absorbing and role-modelling collaborative behaviours at a completely new level – and then bring that experience to the world. Quinn says that this is not a new dilemma, but one that leaders are now facing more often as the search for meaning and equilibrium is now more elusive than ever before.

Quinn also warns that most of us build our identity on our knowledge and competence, but that conversely, making a deep change – the type of change that many leaders are now seeking in their organizations – involves abandoning both and 'walking naked into the land of uncertainty', which means taking significant risks and stepping outside well-defined boundaries.

Blame, shame and disconnection

In times of great uncertainty, when leaders might be feeling somewhat confused and 'at sea', it's not only fear and a sense of loss of control that leaders have to contend with. Feelings of inadequacy and shame can also arise in the face of organizational or cultural pressure to appear 'strong' and 'in possession of all the answers'. These can be extremely painful, particularly in organizations where blame is habitually used as a way of dealing with mistakes, ie the guilty are sought out and named and swingeing decisions are made as a result.

Shame is an extremely uncomfortable and powerful feeling. Kaufman (1989) describes it as 'an inner torment... a sickness of the soul. Shame is a wound felt from the inside, dividing us from both ourselves and from one another.' Often experienced as a deficiency in comparison with others, through shame we feel a failure in our own eyes and those of others.

When experiencing this type of private shame, a leader's instinct is often to disconnect from others, possibly by blaming them, and to keep any feelings of 'stuckness', confusion or not knowing hidden, even though these are typical sensations and to be expected in uncertain and complex contexts. In this frame of mind, it can be almost impossible for leaders to reach out for help, or to experiment with new, risky ways of behaving, as seeking help is experienced as yet another sign of weakness or inadequacy.

However, the negative impact of shame in organizational settings can be reduced, suggests Cavicchia (2010), if leaders adopt a less 'reductionist' or 'blame-centred' approach to problem solving and decision making – which inevitably pits individuals against each other – and instead develop a more multi-layered, systemically-wise approach to understanding how things happen in complex settings. This allows everyone to play their part well, and no one individual to be named as 'to blame'.

Creativity, energy and personal development

It's important to note that uncertainty brings upsides as well as downsides. Uncertainty in organizations, given the right leadership and context, can also give rise to great creativity, energy and personal development.

In Chapter 4, we referred to William Bridges' concept of the 'neutral zone' as a place in between an ending and a beginning in an organizational change process, where people may become disoriented. Bridges (1991) describes this as a different and potentially creative phase where experiments can happen, and people can become innovative and enthusiastic, given the right focus. Bridges advocates creating temporary systems and structures during this time, setting short-term goals, strengthening the skills people need to get through and not promising high levels of productivity. Creativity can be boosted by stepping back and asking key questions about the way things are done. It can also be boosted by supporting the rebuilding of connections between people and acknowledging that business as usual often deadens creativity.

This view is somewhat echoed by Day (2007), whose field research studying people's reactions to uncertainty and change in an organizational setting revealed a range of responses, from feelings of disorientation, to increased political activity, to painful emotions such as hostility, anger and fear, and also increased levels of creativity and enthusiasm. In all the organizations studied there were individuals and groups who were energized and excited about the change ahead. Where people were actively engaged in particular change challenges, there was evidence of creativity and innovation, and individuals were 'experimenting with new ways of working and enthusiastically applying their ideas in their work'. These individuals also reported that the challenges they were address-ing were stretching their capabilities and, while they experienced their contexts as 'difficult' or 'demanding', they were able to point to their own 'development and growth'.

So it seems that where leaders offer temporary structures, high levels of support, clear short-range goals and some easing of the pressure to deliver business as usual, creativity can flourish and good work gets done.

New organizational forms and ways of doing business

In Bauman's list of sources of instability he mentions that our organizations and institutions are in great flux. They are not expected to keep their shape for long and are unlikely to solidify before they begin to re-form. So what types of organizational forms are now emerging, how do they differ from traditional organizations and how do they actually work?

It is clear that there are new organizational forms emerging due to ex-treme competition, growing amounts of uncertainty in the global economy, unpredictable effects of global 'incidents', increasing importance of infor-mation, communication and technology, and the rise of social networking.

According to Child and McGrath (2001), these new forms share a set of features that contrast with the more traditional and familiar hierarchical, bureaucratic types of organizations. In Table 11.1, the differences are set out.

Two new types of organizational form that have attracted much interest from business people and academics over recent years are ambidextrous organizations and emergent organizations.

Ambidextrous organizations, as described by O'Reilly and Tushman (2004), separate their new 'exploratory' units from their traditional 'exploitative' ones, allowing different processes, structure and cultures, but maintain-ing tight links across these units at a senior level. This means that senior executives must develop the ability to understand and be sensitive to two different ways of operating. They must embrace both the rigorous cost-cutter and the free-thinking entrepreneur, and be able to be objective enough about both to make trade-offs between the two. In their later paper, O'Reilly and Tushman (2007) say that senior managers must also

Table 11.1 Common features of new organizational forms

	Hierarchical	New organizational forms
Goal setting	Top-down	Decentralized
Power	Concentrated	Distributed
Size of units	Large	Small
Leadership function	Control, monitoring	Guidance, conflict management
Vision	Dictated	Emergent
Structure	Formal hierarchy	Team and work-group structures
Primary unit of analysis	Firm	Network
Boundaries	Durable, clearly set	Permeable, fuzzy
Objective	Reliability, replicability	Flexibility
Regulation	Vertical	Horizontal
Assets	Linked to particular units	Independent of unit, shared
Role definition	Specialized, clear	Fuzzy, general
Uncertainty	Try to absorb	Try to adapt
Rights and duties	Permanent	Impermanent
Integrity	Rule-based	Relationship-based
Motivation	Efficiency	Innovation

Source: Child and McGrath, 2001

articulate a clear strategic intent that justifies the ambidextrous form as necessary for long-term survival and effectiveness. This is echoed by Bryson *et al* (2008), who examine the possibilities of and barriers to ambidexterity in public organizations, and conclude that effective strategic leadership is one of the strongest prerequisites for effective management of organizational dexterity.

It's important to add that research carried out by O'Reilly and Tushman indicates that companies using ambidextrous structures are nine times more likely to create breakthrough products and processes than those using other organizational structures – while sustaining or even improving their existing businesses.

Emergent organizations develop in the same way that living systems do. They evolve naturally and are not consciously directed, are extraordinarily decentralized and exist as open or boundary-less structures that shape themselves as they go. All features of the emergent organization such as decision processes, social relationships, meaning and culture are products of constant social negotiation and consensus building.

The rapid evolution of social networks and the accompanying growth in size, speed and utility of the internet have opened up all sorts of possibilities for emergence. The development of user communities, information communities and social communities has created new possibilities for businesses and new types of business models via Google, eBay, LinkedIn, Facebook, etc.

Examples of emergent, decentralized organizations are Wikipedia (see box) and YouTube. Brafman and Beckstrom's book *The Starfish and the Spider* (2006) explores the implications of the rise of such organizations. They use the analogy of the starfish which, in contrast to the spider, has a decentralized neural system that permits regeneration. The authors also explore the concept of the 'sweet spot'; an optimal mix of centralized and decentralized attributes.

Jimmy Wales, co-founder and promoter of on-line encyclopaedia Wikipedia talks about his emergent organization's growth:

The New York Times *website is a huge, enormous corporate operation with... I have no idea how many, hundreds of employees. We have exactly one employee, and that employee is our lead software developer. And he's only been our employee since January 2005, all the other growth was before that. So the servers are managed by a rag-tag band of volunteers, all the editing is done by volunteers.*

And the way that we're organized is not like any traditional organization you can imagine. People are always asking, 'Well, who's in charge of this?' or 'Who does that?' And the answer is: anybody who wants to pitch in. It's a very unusual and chaotic thing. We've got over 90 servers now in three locations. These are managed by volunteer system administrators who are online. I can go online any time of the day or night and see eight

> to 10 people waiting for me to ask a question or something, anything
> about the servers. You could never afford to do this in a company. You
> could never afford to have a standby crew of people 24 hours a day and
> do what we're doing at Wikipedia.
>
> http://www.ted.com/talks/jimmy_wales_on_the_birth_of_wikipedia.html

Brafman and Beckstrom list the capabilities and behaviours required by those 'catalysts' skilled at creating decentralized organizations. Perhaps we could see this as a new, emerging form of leadership:

- Genuine interest in others.

- Numerous loose connections rather than a small number of close connections.

- Skill at social mapping.

- Desire to help everyone they meet.

- The ability to help people help themselves by listening and understanding, rather than giving advice ('Meet people where they are').

- Emotional intelligence.

- Trust in others and in the decentralized network.

- Inspiration (to others).

- Tolerance for ambiguity.

- A hands-off approach. Catalysts do not interfere with, or try to control the behaviour of the contributing members of the decentralized organization.

- Ability to let go. After building up a decentralized organization, catalysts move on rather than trying to take control.

New careers and the need for 'managing oneself'

It isn't just leaders who are experiencing the challenges of rising levels of uncertainty and instability in the world. Changes in the way organizations are being set up, the types of jobs available and the emergence of new career patterns mean that the onus is increasingly on individuals to manage their own career paths, rather than rely on employers to do so.

The new careers of the 21st century are very different from the 'corporate climb' that people dreamed of until quite recently. Careers today tend to be more turbulent and lacking in stability, involving changes in employer, increased numbers of horizontal rather than vertical moves, changes in location and even changes in core occupation, although there is evidence that traditional one-company career paths still do exist.

Reitmann and Schneer (2008) say that the expectation within US organizations is that the employee will manage his or her own career, choosing companies that provide the right opportunities. They also note that the organization's role in managing the employee's career has become unclear, but suggest that companies that develop a reputation for helping employees to determine their best possible career path – inside or outside the organization – should end up with the best employees. They also say that organizations may need to accept that good workers may go elsewhere to gain new skills, and would be wise to leave the door open for employees to return.

What does it mean to manage your own career? Managing oneself means knowing oneself well, says Peter Drucker (1999). This means cultivating a deep understanding of yourself – not only what your strengths and weaknesses are, but also how you learn, how you work with others, what your values are, and where you can make the greatest contribution. He urges people to resist trying to change themselves, but rather to improve the way they perform and to avoid taking on work that they will not be able to do well. He also urges people to find organizations that match their values, or at least are compatible enough for them not to get frustrated and demotivated.

The short-term nature of many projects and jobs in the 21st century means that individuals need to be able to answer Drucker's question: 'Where and how can I achieve results that make a difference within the next year and a half?' They also need to understand their colleagues well, spotting their strengths, ways of working and values, and take responsibility for finding out what others are doing and how they are contributing.

There is criticism of some organizations for failing to support employees in adapting to these new self-managed career paths. Recent research on 'career resilience' by The Career Innovation Group (www.careerinnovation.com) in association with Creative Metier (www.creativemetier.com) indicates that constant change has left many employees in a 'career vacuum'. It seems that most organizations have not linked their strategic goals with practical support to help people to adapt to new skill and work requirements. The research cites some examples of 'excellence' where organizations are supporting their workers to equip themselves to thrive amidst constant change. They highlight three things that an organization can do:

1   Communicate today's realistic 'career deals' and provide a new kind of roadmap for careers.

2   Help everyone (not just top talent) to be resilient in their careers. That means blending online tools with encouragement to build their support network.

3   Support managers to develop their people. Career conversations are a vital way to raise engagement, and doing this regularly can build a resilient, change-ready workforce.

STOP AND THINK!

Q 11.1 What effects do you notice that increased uncertainty and instability in the world are having on:

- your life and the way you lead it?

- an organization you know well and the way leaders are leading it?

- your local community and how people are contributing to it?

Q 11.2 What might support those in the above situations, who appear to be fearful or anxious, to be able to focus on what needs to be done and contribute more effectively and responsibly?

DECISION MAKING IN AN UNCERTAIN WORLD

One of the most crucial and difficult tasks for leaders in uncertain times is decision making. When the goal posts are constantly shifting and changing, how is it possible to make good, confident decisions about what markets to target, what resources to commit, where to cut costs and what type of skills to develop to help you get there?

In this section we look at different ways of approaching the decision-making process according to the context. We explore both the lure of decisiveness and the difficulties of dithering, particularly in the political context, and investigate the impact of personality type on our ability to make good decisions. We also explain how leaders might benefit from acknowledging that regret is a healthy part of the decision-making process.

BUSINESS – A GAME OF SKILL, WITH A TWIST OF LUCK?

Is business like poker, a game of skill with a twist of luck... or is business a game of pure skill where, armed with the right information and the right 'laws' of management it is possible to manage your future success?
... to be able to make confident predictions about the future, the manager needs to be both managing in a world where causes have predictable effects, and where management theories have the status of scientific laws ... neither is the case.

(Blake, 2008)

Decision making and poker games

In his slim but informative book, *The Art of Decisions: How to manage in an uncertain world*, Chris Blake (2008) takes an extremely pragmatic view of how leaders need to learn to operate in an uncertain world. He notices our increasingly futile attempts as leaders to manage uncertainty, and says we can learn a lot from poker players who have to make quick, important and skilled judgements under conditions of uncertainty. Poker players refer to a 'bad beat', which is when you are odds-on to win but the cards turn against you. They dust themselves down, take stock, put it down to luck, and carry on.

Blake says that of course a recipe exists for making the perfect decision, but it's not practical when you are in the thick of intense business stress and pressure because it can take endless resource and a great deal of time to research something so thoroughly. Here's the recipe:

- know what you want – your goal;
- identify all the alternative courses of action;
- gather the information you need and then deduce all of the consequences of each course of action;
- select the course of action that best meets your goals.

Blake says that in business, just as in a poker game, time and resources are limited. You can't make the perfect decision and it can be counter-productive to try. At some point, you have to stop searching and start deciding – and this means using your intuition and judgement. He warns that leaders shouldn't be surprised if their goals change. They are never simple and the process of deciding will help you uncover goals that may not have been explicit. His top tip is to sample at least a third of the field before committing to the 'best you have seen'.

FOCUSED EXECUTIVE DECISION MAKING IN ACTION

In one global financial services company, senior level investment/ resource decisions are made on the basis of two slides only, presented by a senior executive at the monthly meeting, within a strict 20-minute slot for discussion. The presenter must produce evidence that he or she has had off-line conversations with key stakeholders and secured their buy-in. A decision is made by the CEO there and then.

A framework for decision making

Recent practical research into decision-making patterns indicates that wise executives tailor their decision-making approach to the type of situation being faced. Snowden and Boone (2007) advocate a decision-making framework that distinguishes between four different contexts. They suggest a different leadership response for each context and alert leaders to danger signals and potential inappropriate reactions:

- The first is the *simple context,* characterized by stability and clear cause and effect relationships. An example of this would be a mistake made in connection with a payment process, such as the customer paying the wrong amount. This requires straightforward management and monitoring. Leaders assess the facts of the situation, categorize them and then respond based on previous experience. Possible pitfall: mistaking a complex problem for a simple one.

- The second is the *complicated context,* which may contain multiple right answers, and tends to require expertise to analyse the facts and recommend the best response. An example of this is choosing an

IT system for a specific purpose. Possible pitfall: getting stuck in the analysis phase.

- The third is the *complex context* in which there are no right answers, although instructive patterns may emerge through experimentation. Leaders are required to patiently allow the path forward to reveal itself through increased levels of interaction and communication and by using methods that generate ideas. An example of this is the problem of setting prices in volatile and changing market conditions. Possible pitfalls: desire for acceleration or falling back into command and control.

- The fourth is the *chaotic context* in which only turbulence exists and searching for the right answers would be pointless. Leaders are required to act quickly to restore enough order. An example of this is a flood in the office or a power cut. Possible pitfalls: leaders apply a command and control approach longer than needed, and can become legendary in their capacity to turn things around and are protected by some followers from the truth.

Snowden and Boone say that in a time of increased uncertainty leaders will be called upon to act against their instincts. Faced with a wide variety of decision-making scenarios they will need to be able to change leadership style flexibly – knowing when to share power and when to wield it alone, when to look at the wisdom of the group and when to take their own counsel, when to use expert advice and when to open things up for discussion.

In our experience, due to the anxiety connected with the feeling of not knowing the answer, leaders often find themselves mistaking a complex context for a complicated context, and trying to solve unknown issues with so-called expert advice. A typical example of this is the setting up of a programme office to drive forward, monitor and control a series of discrete 'change projects'. At best, with the necessary discussion and high-quality interaction, this can catalyse healthy, productive activity. At worst this approach consumes much expert project management resources and leadership attention, but there's a sense of ticking boxes and 'going through the motions' rather than making real, fundamental progress.

The lure of decisiveness and the difficulties of dithering

The quality of decisiveness, ie bold and timely decision making, is seen by many in the UK and the United States as an extremely attractive leadership quality, particularly in our political leaders, and particularly in times of uncertainty. Decisiveness is seen as strong, and its polar opposite, dithering, is seen as weak. Sometimes it's as if we prefer to see our leaders deciding something – anything at all – rather than being seen to dither.

A recent example of this concerns President Barack Obama and the public's shifting view of his capacity to lead on military decisions. Many criticized his apparent dithering over the issue of whether to send more troops to Afghanistan in 2009 (see box), but when US special forces shot dead Osama Bin Laden in Abbottabad in 2011, his bold decisiveness was celebrated. Stephen Hess, one of the United States' most respected commentators on the White House, said that this would change the dynamics of US politics: 'It's going to be very hard for Republicans to use any more that label of weak and indecisive.'

PRESIDENT OBAMA – CAREFUL OR DITHERING?

Only 17 percent of Americans saw President Barack Obama as a strong and decisive military leader, according to a Reuters/Ipsos poll taken after the United States and its allies began bombing Libya in 2011.

Nearly half of those polled view Obama as a cautious and consultative commander-in-chief and more than a third see him as indecisive in military action.

Obama was widely criticized in 2009 for his months-long consultations with senior aides and military chiefs on whether to send more troops to Afghanistan. Critics called it dithering, but he said such a big decision required careful deliberation. He eventually dispatched 30,000 more troops.

But Obama is facing mounting discontent among opposition Republicans and from within his own Democratic Party over the fuzzy aims of the US-led mission in Libya and the lack of a clearly spelled-out exit strategy for US forces.

Reuters report, March 2011, pre-Abbottabad

At the time of writing, Prime Minister David Cameron's coalition government in the UK is also being criticized for its poor decision making, in this case for a series of policy 'u-turns' ranging from the trivial to the significant. Cameron's supporters see these moves as government responsiveness and courageous, up-front honesty. Others interpret them as incompetence and the sign of a government losing its grip.

This societal bias towards decisiveness makes it extremely difficult for leaders in highly uncertain or complex environments to make good, timely decisions in the right way. Leaders need to be able to resist caving in to external pressure to decide something prematurely. They might need to first hear the views of other stakeholders, or to take a small action and wait and observe how things work out. It's also difficult, when the spotlight is on you, to know exactly when to stop considering and consulting and observing and to get on and decide. For some, the anticipated pain of the 'u-turn' or 'getting it wrong' justifies endless delays. Hence the lure of dithering!

The general call for decisive leadership may also place organizational leaders under pressure to decide things on behalf of their teams rather than to allow people to struggle in productive ways, and then perhaps make mistakes and learn or innovate. This is yet another complication for leaders facing uncertainty. They need to identify which elements of the work that they can and must be clear and decisive about, and in which parts it makes more sense for others to find their way. This can be seen as 'drawing a line in the sand' to indicate 'here's where I'm clear and there's no discussion, and here's where I need you to engage and work things out'. See the skill of 'framing' later in this chapter.

Similarly, in today's flatter, more matrix-oriented organizations, decision making is complex and demands an ever-widening range of skills. Leaders need to find ways of working with peers and/or stakeholders, over whom they have no clear authority and possibly with whom they have no clear agreement, in a shifting and uncertain context. They also need to develop strong, clear partnerships based on joint goals, despite temptations to either work out a decisive individual strategy and set about 'strongly influencing' others to play along, or to stay out of partnership altogether for fear of the unmanageable complexity that might need to be confronted.

Decision making and personality

What makes a good decision maker? How is it possible, in times of uncertainty, to:

- Recognize the type of decision in front of you and respond appropriately?

- Walk the precarious tightrope between knee-jerk decisiveness and the paralysis of too much analysis and discussion?

- Come up with a sufficiently good decision?

Is personality type a key factor in being able to do this well? Do some personality types make better decision makers than others and, if so, what are they able to do that others might learn from? Research into this topic has used the Myers-Briggs Type Indicator™ (MBTI™) as a basis for looking at the impact of personality type on decision-making success (see Chapter 1 for more information on the MBTI™).

According to Jung, whose theory of personality underpins the Myers-Briggs Type Indicator™, every individual has a set of personality preferences in the way they take in information and come to conclusions. The theory says that every individual acquires data to make a decision using two methods – sensing and intuition, with a preference for one method over the other. A sensing (S) individual prefers hard data and 'here and now' specifics, while an intuitive individual (N) prefers to look at possibilities and patterns, and 'what might be'. Similarly, every individual, after acquiring the data to make a decision, comes to a conclusion using two methods – thinking and feeling, with a preference for one method over the other. Thinking (T) stresses logical and formal reasoning, while feeling (F) considers the decision in personal terms, and relates to the values of those affected.

Research undertaken by Paul Nutt (1993) indicates that leaders who have access to all four modes of understanding associated with decision making (S, N, T and F) are likely to be more successful decision makers over the longer term, and more immune to the distractions of uncertainty and ambiguity. Nutt's research indicates that organizational success may be influenced by the style of the organization's top executives. When making strategic choices in a context of high ambiguity and uncertainty, the top level decision maker who has a balanced perspective that stems from good quality access to S, N, T and F modes of understanding is more apt to seek change and transformation, thus enabling the organization to thrive. His research shows that this fully flexible decision-making style is rare, appearing in only 7.9 per cent of top executives in the study, and no middle managers. Over-use of the data-processing modes of sensing (S) and thinking (T) were linked to conservatism and lack of risk taking, and therefore lack of tolerance for ambiguity and uncertainty.

Patricia Hedges (1993) offers helpful tips for those trying to develop their 'shadow' modes of understanding, ie the modes of understanding that are not their first preference; see Table 11.2.

Table 11.2   How to develop 'shadow' modes of understanding

Developing sensing for intuitives (S)	Developing intuition for sensers (N)	Developing thinking for feelers (T)	Developing feeling for thinkers (F)
Try to improve your eye for detail. You might compare what you notice with an 'S' friend.	If you have a 'hunch' see if you can follow it up and take notice of it.	See if you can stand outside and watch a situation instead of feeling involved in it.	Before disagreeing with people, be sure to consider their opinions and points of view.
Accept that established methods for doing things generally work.	When studying something, try to see the thing as a whole.	Even if it means disagreeing with someone, stick to your beliefs and convictions.	Find ways of giving specific appreciation to others by praising them verbally.
Good ideas may come to nothing if you fail to take small and precise details into account.	Try doing a job in an unusual way. It may not work, but you are likely to learn something.	Try to be less personally concerned in the day-to-day circumstances that occur. Many of these may not really involve you.	Try to develop some close relationships and be willing to spend time and patience nurturing them.

Source: adapted from Hedges (1993)

Learning to deal with regret

In this section we've been looking at approaches that support leaders to make good decisions in times of uncertainty. However, the whole mindset we use when making a decision is important too.

We've observed that leadership time is often devoted to coming up with the 'successful strategy', the 'brilliant decision', or the 'best practice approach', as if it were possible in every given context to come up with the 'right' solution. The assumption is that if the right solution is found, and the right level of commitment is applied, this will be followed by harmonious patterns, correct actions, brilliant outcomes and all other solutions will have been proved wrong. This assumption leads to 'righteousness', which Nevis (1998) says is one of the great barriers to organizational change, and labels it the 'enemy of regret'.

'RIGHTEOUSNESS' AT WORK IN A PUBLIC SECTOR DEPARTMENT

Once the decision was made to reorganize, senior leaders became weirdly evangelistic about the new matrix structure. Rather than being open to the problems it was throwing up and willing to co-create solutions, they just blamed the middle managers for not being able to make it work.

I had to go to the lengths of commissioning consultants to audit the effectiveness of the new structure and feed back the findings before they would really listen and begin to understand their part in making this work.

HR director

Why is regret important in leadership? Every strategy or policy carries with it some benefit and some cost, so leaders make choices between imperfect solutions, thus rejecting some options that have benefits, and selecting an option that has some costs. Nevis suggests that if leaders are aware and accepting of this, they experience the joy and the sadness of making the decision, and any regrets are acknowledged and felt in that moment. This makes them better, more effective leaders in an uncertain, pluralistic environment. If not, this leads to righteous adherence to a particular choice, and increases the possibility that defensive projections such as blaming others and seeing alternatives or changes in approach as 'wrong' will take place.

When a leader takes action out of righteousness, the action stands out as being forceful and provocative in nature, which is qualitatively different from a grounded and well-supported decision. Righteousness is more brittle; leaders with a righteous attitude about a particular decision are likely to be anxiously defensive about it.

Nevis refers to major business decisions as 'big acts', such as significant reductions in workforce, mergers and acquisitions, etc, which leaders often feel they have to carry out in a righteous manner, perhaps because they have such huge consequences and are often heavily contested by others. The question is whether, after a 'big act', any kind of learning can take place as these actions unfold, ie does any new awareness emerge that might lead to a reshaping of the original assumptions, or does righteousness prevent this from happening? See the box for an example of Horta-Osório's initial righteousness, followed by a little trace of regret.

LLOYDS BANKING GROUP – 'BIG ACTS' IN ACTION... AND SMALL REGRETS

António Horta-Osório stamped his mark on Lloyds Banking Group on Thursday, cutting 15,000 jobs and pledging to revitalize the Halifax brand in an effort to help taxpayers make a profit on their £20bn investment in the bailed-out bank.

The Portuguese-born banker, who was lured from Spanish bank Santander, was at first unrepentant about the scale of the job cuts although later admitted: 'I do regret that we have to do this. I would prefer to put this bank back on its feet without reducing staff.'

But, he insisted the cuts were essential. 'We have to do this. This bank has lost money, it's losing money this year on an after-tax basis.

'We have to get this bank back on to its feet to support the UK economy and we have to pay taxpayers' money back,' he said.

The Guardian, June 2011

In an uncertain and complex world, those with a tendency towards righteousness and 'big acts' would be wise to consider other options. They may give up 'big acts' altogether and instead, through greater awareness, select smaller actions from which yet further awareness may unfold. For instance, a difficult situation might build up over time, culminating in a big leadership act such as laying off large numbers of staff. However, with greater awareness, smaller actions might have been chosen during the build up, such as reducing people's salaries, and greater learning may have emerged and a better result achieved in the long run. See the box for an example of this from KPMG.

KPMG'S 'SMALL' BUT SIGNIFICANT 'ACT'

Professional services firm KPMG is seeking to change the terms and conditions of staff employment contracts in case it needs to reduce the paid working week or send workers on sabbatical.

The groundbreaking HR initiative is designed to allow KPMG to request that employees who agree to the change can be required to work a four-day week or take between four and 12 weeks' sabbatical at 30 per cent of their pay.

Rachel Campbell, Head of People at KPMG, said that the scheme, called Flexible Futures, was introduced to ensure 'maximum flexibility to respond proactively and positively to any change in the market'.

The proposed change to the terms and conditions will last for 18 months, and the maximum salary loss in one year will be capped at 20 per cent. The firm will continue to provide full benefits throughout that period.

KPMG is the first of the 'big four' global accountancy firms to ask staff to cut back their hours, in the hope of staving off redundancies. The move follows 300 voluntary redundancies at rival firm Deloitte as a result of slower demand for services across the sector. A spokeswoman there said there were currently no plans for further redundancies or to put in place measures such as short-time working.

People Management, 29 January 2009

Another possibility is for leaders to find ways of being more open to changes of approach following a 'big act'. This means keeping a close watch on progress following their decision, being prepared to listen to feedback, and staying open to the possibility of changing tack in some way.

STOP AND THINK!

Q 11.3 Think of a major decision that you had to make recently. Reflect on the way you made the decision and identify which of the four modes of understanding you used to make that decision (sensing, intuition, thinking and/or feeling). If you used one or two modes less, explain how you might improve your modes of understanding and therefore your decision-making.

Q 11.4 Identify a 'big act' that a senior manager initiated in your organization recently (see Nevis's definition above). How might this have been approached as a series of smaller actions and what impact, positive or negative, might this have had on the organization in the long term?

SKILLS AND TOOLS TO SUPPORT LEADING CHANGE THROUGH UNCERTAINTY

A change leadership pathway

In uncertain times, linear models of the change process such as Kotter's eight steps (see Chapter 3) don't serve leaders particularly well. They tend to imply a predictable sequence of events in which vision and strategy can be decided up front, leading to a plan that sets out key measures, which then dictates front-line activities. Models of the change process that acknowledge uncertainty and complexity and enable leaders to find their way through transition, dealing with whatever emerges as they go, are significantly harder to find.

One of the authors, as part of her recent consulting work in support of more emergent forms of change, has co-developed a useful pathway for guiding leaders through the change process. This is not intended to be a programmatic solution to modelling the stages of change, but rather a loose, organic guide – with potentially overlapping stages – that is used to support leaders who are facing considerable change (see www.integralchange.co.uk).

The key stages of this pathway (see Figure 11.1) are:

- *Deepening Commitment*: leaders work with their teams and stakeholders to develop a deep sense of purpose that will guide their collective intent through the process of change. This might involve top team away-days, sharing ambitions and concerns, identifying critical success factors and key obstacles and mapping out the journey ahead.

- *Aligning Strategy*: a compelling vision and high-level plan are agreed that are clear enough to elicit interest, but not so detailed that others can't engage with them and play their part. This might involve naming the 'top five' strategic priorities in an attractive, engaging way.

- *Focusing Action*: leaders focus on connecting key people and agendas, both internally and externally, communicating constantly and inspiring through words. This might involve an interactive launch event, or some lively, engaging cascades.

- *Growing Capability*: people in key roles are supported to step up through skill-building exercises and coaching. High-performing teams are developed. This might involve one-to-one development

Figure 11.1   The change leadership pathway

conversations, targeted skill-boosting sessions and tailor-made team-building interventions.

- *Clarifying Progress*: results are measured simply and elegantly, successes and difficulties are clarified, and new processes are implemented with increased vigour. This might involve rigorous review processes, careful tracking of progress, increased focus on accountability and leaders role-modelling accountability-taking.

Skills for leading through uncertainty

In today's climate of urgency, high stakes and uncertainty, the traditional leadership skills of analytical problem solving, crisp decision making, immaculate forward planning and the articulation of a clear direction are no longer as useful as they were, and can in fact get in the way of success.

New leadership skills and practices are required. In this section we set out the top five skills that we find ourselves, in our consultancy roles, supporting leaders to develop as they step up to the challenges of leading significant change.

Presence and 'deep listening'

The concept of 'presence', and the notion that it is a fundamental leadership skill, was introduced to the business world by Senge *et al* (2005) in the book of the same name. The authors see presence as a core capacity for leaders faced with uncertainty. They say it involves 'deep listening', which means being open beyond our preconceptions and historical ways of making sense. This allows leaders to operate from a deeper sense of purpose. It also means letting go of old identities and the need to control – two of the very things that are so difficult to let go of in times of change and uncertainty.

At a basic level, presence means being alert and aware to whatever is happening right here and now, with the fundamental belief that the whole is entirely present in any of its parts so it's always worth paying attention! A difficulty with this principle for many leaders begins with the challenge of truly listening and this begins with noticing how you are listening now. As others talk, we tend to experience feelings and reactions, which come in a flood of images and perceptions triggered by our memories of and anxieties about whoever is talking and whatever they are talking about. Learning how to be 'present' involves being able to allow these inner voices and thoughts to arrive, not get too caught up in them, and to somehow quieten the mind, to allow for the possibility that something new or fresh might arrive. This is quite difficult for most of us, so a leader has reached quite an advanced state of maturity when he or she is able to do it well.

A first step is to practise listening in a non-anxious way. This means slowing down and being much more aware of your thinking and listening. It also means heading into the difficult areas – for you and for the speaker/s – using open questions and keeping an open heart. The challenge is to look for evidence that disconfirms your point of view rather than just confirms it, and to really try to understand and hear what others' perceptions are, no matter how irritating or off the mark they seem to be. The principle here is that once you understand how others have formulated their perceptions and how they are reacting, you will have a richer sense of what's going on with any change process, and it will ultimately make your next change leadership move much clearer.

The importance of 'framing'

When there is much uncertainty around and there are many significant changes to be made, the leadership skill of 'framing' becomes extremely important. This is a guiding rather than a controlling way of leading, so is well-adapted to times of uncertainty. When a leader is 'framing,' he or she defines a clear context or operating space for others to step into. This can mean painting a picture that illustrates the change destination and holding this frame clearly and consistently so that others can engage with it and 'fill it in'. It can also mean setting out the broad phases of change and key milestones so that others can get a sense of how this process is going to feel.

It is important to note that recent research has demonstrated that the use of 'framing' is strongly correlated with success in most change contexts (Rowland and Higgs, 2008). However it's an element of leading that is often absent from change management training programmes, and hasn't made it into common parlance yet!

This skill also embraces the ability to communicate immediate goals, purpose and vision in an engaging way, let people know how things are unfolding and nurture a clear organizational or team identity and culture.

Framing skills are particularly helpful when there's a great deal of uncertainty swirling around. When teams have a sense of what they're there to do, and a sense of who they are, this gives people a 'place to stand' and a way of anchoring decisions and next steps. Thus leaders who

DISTRIBUTION MD FRAMES THE CHALLENGES AHEAD

The MD of a distribution business found a way of framing the challenge ahead for his sales team that transformed their level of engagement.

He was concerned that some members of the team had become quite demotivated and had got into the habit of promising much but delivering little. Even though the market was tough, he knew that they were missing opportunities and sensed that they had the ability do much better.

At the opening of the sales department's two-day conference, the MD slowly and carefully told them the story of the last six months, setting out the figures and telling them about the conversations he was having with his boss, and being clear – but not alarmist – about the concerns this was raising at higher levels about the future of the organization. His presentation culminated in the phrase: 'So you see my jam tomorrow story is wearing a bit thin now, and so is yours.' He then expressed his support for the measures his sales director was putting in place to help improve performance and urged the team to bring their best to the two days.

This well-thought-through piece of framing helped the team to understand and take responsibility for their results and the impact this was having on the whole business, and to engage more fully in tackling the challenges ahead.

can help organizations to develop their sense of purpose and identity are very useful in uncertain times.

In times of flux and therefore increased anxiety, leaders need to increase their use of framing skills in their regular group and individual meetings with team members and stakeholders. This means introducing the purpose and context of meetings with much more care than usual, and ensuring that meeting agendas are particularly well-managed. This may mean something as simple as re-framing the session if an important topic overruns. When people are anxious, they need help from leaders in understanding what's important for them to focus on and what's not. Framing also means sticking to regular meetings and one-to-ones rather than cancelling them and collapsing into a chaotic, unpredictable meetings schedule, which simply leads to more anxiety.

There is also much off-line, informal framing work to be done by leaders in the midst of a change process. For instance, when people involved with a change are seeing an issue in an unhelpful way, leaders may need to re-frame the issue so that people are more able to approach it constructively. Similarly, when significant obstacles to change do arise, the leader needs to take responsibility for framing these obstacles so that people can see and understand the issues and begin to test out and agree possible ways forward.

Developing the capacity to 'contain'

The constant requirement to deliver change in uncertain times is a highly stressful business for leaders. They must absorb pressure and anxiety from their boss, make imperfect decisions that can feel risky and 'out of control', listen to and respond to the anxieties and worries of those around them, and deal with their own emotional ups and downs. To lead well within this swirling cocktail of emotions, leaders need to become skilled at 'containing'.

In the psychodynamic world, 'containment' means providing a holding environment where anxieties can be safely worked through and processed in a healthy way. For leaders, this means being confident and calm even in challenging situations, and having an ability to make difficult conversations 'ok'. It also means practising high-quality dialogue skills such as advocacy and inquiry (Isaacs, 1999), particularly in a group or team setting. In times of uncertainty and change, it's particularly valuable to give people the opportunity to air problems and express worries in a safe, well-bounded environment, rather than let them leak out in other ways. Some leaders feel tempted to suppress this kind of conversation, perhaps to give the impression that everything is 'under control'.

Containing also means being clear with people about priorities, explaining exactly what you can and can't do about an issue and being clear about when significant issues will be resolved. It also involves being disciplined in recognizing and managing your own emotions and, if necessary, channelling your frustrations into 'tough conversations' with the appropriate people rather than letting them spill over into grumbling, or cynicism, or other destructive activities.

THE MD OF A UTILITIES COMPANY PROVIDES CONTAINMENT TO THE TEAM

A large utilities company was facing the possibility of a significant merger, but much had still to be explored and decided before the merger could go ahead. This was provoking all sorts of anxieties and concerns in the 80-strong extended leadership team about how to make key decisions, whether to recruit, what to tell staff, etc.

At the regular quarterly leadership conference the MD made a point of putting aside two hours for questions about the merger. He let the group know, 'I will answer all your questions as honestly as I can. Some questions I won't be able to answer, but I'll tell you why not. For your part, you need to ensure that when I say something is confidential that it stays in this room. We have two hours together today, and I am more than happy to stay beyond that if there are still questions that need answering.'

In this way he provided a container or holding space for his extended team to have their worries heard and acknowledged and their questions answered. This session lowered the levels of anxiety in the room, built trust, and helped leaders to decide what their focus needed to be over the coming weeks.

A difficulty for leaders who are required to develop containing skills is that it is remarkably hard to do this when you are feeling anxious yourself! This is why it's absolutely crucial that leaders of change develop their own container to support themselves as they work through or let go of their own anxieties, which may be considerable. This means finding ways of acknowledging and perhaps skillfully sharing these anxieties and emotions rather than suppressing them.

All the successful senior change leaders we have worked with over the years have developed ways of regularly switching off from work and letting go of leadership activity. It seems that this is one of the most fundamental keys to being a successful leader of significant change. They have all found ways to create peaceful spaces for themselves that allow good-quality processing of anxieties, doubts and ideas. This might involve gardening, cycling, walking, running, yoga, meditation or, in one case, mucking out cows (see box). Whatever it is, it tends to be a regular, highly valued, well-guarded space.

FINDING THE CONTAINER WITHIN

A marketing director with a high-pressure, highly stressful job in a global FMCG company found a unique way of regularly processing her own emotions. Every Friday evening, after a week of global travelling and high-powered meetings, she would come home to the farm that her husband owned and ran, and he would tell her to get her wellies on and give her an unpleasant, mucky job to do, like cleaning out the cow shed. She said she really relished this time, as somehow when she pulled her boots on and trudged out into the mud – often in the dark – all the pressures of the week would subside, complex issues would swirl and settle, and insights would begin to emerge in an almost effortless way.

(See Chapter 5 for more explanation of 'containing from the Change Agent perspective.)

Negative capability

When decisions are complex and there is pressure for pace and delivery, leaders often find themselves driving progress and trying to demonstrate achievement, even if it may be more effective to create space for further thinking and struggling, and to wait patiently for a solution to emerge. It can be very difficult for leaders to decide whether to deliberately hold off from active intervention or to 'get stuck in' more actively.

'Negative capability' can be described as the ability to receptively support teams and individuals to continue to think and struggle in challenging situations, by holding or 'containing' a situation or context. 'Positive capability' is the more familiar face of leadership, which features decisive, active interventions based on knowing. In a paper on emergent change, Robertson (2005) describes negative capability as the negating of habitual patterns of pressured action. This 'negating' allows the creative process its own rhythm and prevents premature closure. He goes on to say that negative capability is a combination of the ability to resist the inappropriate pressure for solutions and the capacity to hold the creative tension. He warns it takes considerable skill for a leader to remain detached enough to know not only how but also when to act, especially when there is a great deal of focus on the bottom line. It's important to note that it's not just the boss, colleagues or stakeholders who pile on the pressure – leaders may also be putting a lot of pressure on themselves to perform.

Practising self-care

Long, drawn-out change processes tend to cause stress in many leaders and may ultimately lead to burn-out. French (2001) refers to the tendency for change to cause anxiety and uncertainty, even if the 'technical aspects' such as the change process itself and the required roles and procedures are well managed. As a result of these high levels of anxiety, French notices that leaders have a tendency to 'disperse' energy into a range of avoidance tactics to deflect themselves from their concerns about the task, as opposed to staying with the issues and demonstrating the capacity to contain.

This perhaps explains why many leaders sometimes seem to go into 'hyperdrive', indulging in demonstrations of not very productive or thoughtful 'positive capability' (see above) and then eventually burning out. Containing, also mentioned above, is an excellent antidote to this. By becoming their own containers, leaders can find ways of looking after themselves well.

Senge _et al_ (2005) cites the ancient idea that 'with power comes wisdom', and says that to become a leader in the 21st century one needs to be dedicated to developing a capacity for delayed gratification, seeing longer-term effects of actions and achieving quietness of mind. This really means getting involved in quiet, dedicated, personal work, possibly involving practices such as meditation or tai-chi, which many leaders are unfamiliar with and might see as rather alien. Others, however, are becoming more interested in this type of development and how it might support them to be more peaceful, compassionate and strong in their work and in their personal lives.

At a much more basic level, things such as getting enough sleep, taking regular exercise, eating healthily, avoiding too much alcohol, as well as finding time to connect with the unchanging aspects of your life that really matter to you such as family, music, community, etc are all important in enabling leaders to take care of themselves and support themselves through times of stress, change and uncertainty.

STOP AND THINK!

Q 11.5 Interview five senior leaders in your organization (or observe them from afar if that's easier) and find out how they might mark themselves out of 10 on each of the above five skills for leading through uncertainty. What conclusions do you draw about the type of development needed to support these leaders as they tackle the challenges ahead of them?

Q 11.6 And how would you rate yourself? What development might you need?

SUMMARY AND CONCLUSIONS

The impact of uncertainty on our working lives:

- We are leading more fragmented lives and living in a world that has more instability and uncertainty than ever before. The current sources of uncertainty and shifts in our global systems being experienced are leading us to be more fearful about our future and possibly more 'self-focused'.

- Even though high levels of uncertainty provoke fear, anxiety and a sense of loss, those in leadership positions must face their own fears and find ways to enable people in their organizations to co-create new ways forward, and to let go of old habits and identities.

- Less blame-centred approaches to problem solving and a more multi-layered way of understanding how things happen in organizations will support leaders in feeling less ashamed about 'not knowing all the answers' and being more able to either reach out for help or experiment with new, more connected ways of behaving.

- Uncertainty and change can also provoke active engagement, enthusiasm and highly creative responses from people. This appears to happen when there is a temporary structure accompanied by short-term goals.

- New organizational forms are emerging in this highly uncertain and extremely competitive context, including 'ambidextrous' and 'emergent' organizations. Ambidextrous organizations survive by separating their 'exploratory' units from their 'exploitative' ones, and need senior managers who can lead strategically and understand both sides. 'Emergent' organizations evolve naturally, are not consciously directed and are catalysed by those skilled at creating decentralized organizations.

- In the 21st century people are expected to manage their own careers by cultivating a deep understanding of themselves and by working on improving their own performance. There is criticism that some organizations are not supporting employees enough to adapt to this new era.

Decision making in an uncertain world:

- Decision making can be seen, like poker, as a game of skill with a twist of luck, rather than an exact science.

- Snowden and Boone (2007) offer a framework to help leaders to identify the decision-making context and select the right approach.

- In the United States and the UK, decisiveness is associated with leadership strength and dithering is seen as weak. Political leaders are more often criticized for dithering and 'u-turns' than they are for making clear decisions. A balance needs to be struck between sensing, analysing, discussing and 'getting on and deciding'.

- Leaders also need to be clear about which decisions they need to make themselves and which it is important for their teams to struggle with. In a matrix organization, some decision making may be better done in partnership with stakeholders rather than in isolation.

- Research by Nutt (1993) indicates that successful top executives include all four Myers-Briggs modes of understanding in their decision-making style. This appears to help them to overcome the distractions of ambiguity and uncertainty.

- Leaders make choices between imperfect solutions and need to accept this. Righteous adherence to a particular choice leads to inflexibility, blaming and a lack of learning. Learning to experience the joy and sadness – and regret – of decision making helps leaders to be more effective in an uncertain, pluralistic environment. This may also mean either giving up 'big acts' and choosing smaller actions that lead to greater learning and a more successful outcome, or being more open to a change of tack following a 'big act'.

Skills and tools to support leading change through uncertainty:

- The change leadership pathway (www.integralchange.co.uk) is a loose, organic guide to support leaders facing complex change challenges. The key stages are:

  - deepening commitment;

  - aligning strategy;

  - focusing action;

  - growing capability;

  - clarifying progress.

- Five important skills for leading change through uncertainty are proposed:

  - *Presence and 'deep listening':* being alert to whatever is happening here and now, and truly listening.

  - *Framing:* defining a clear context or operating space for others to step into.

  - *Containing:* being confident and non-anxious even in challenging situations and providing a bounded space for others to air their anxieties, both one-to-one and in group settings; developing a container 'within' to process own anxieties.

  - *Negative capability:* being able to resist the urge to act, or drive self or others to come up with a quick solution, and instead to hold the creative tension.

  - *Practising self-care:* looking after oneself physically and mentally, being one's own 'container' and developing deeper skills that enable a quietening of the mind.

Conclusion

So what did we set out to do, and what did we achieve here? We wanted to write a book that allowed leaders of all persuasions to dip into the rich casket of theory on change, and to come out with their own jewels of learning. We most of all wanted to help to create the time and space for people to reflect on the changes facing them in the past, now and in the future by making the theory accessible, asking the right questions and providing practical glimpses of our experiences. We hope all of this will stimulate new thoughts and new connections and would urge you to get in touch if you'd like to exchange views.

And having come this far together we would like to leave you with a Sufi tale:

Two sides of a river
Nasrudin sat on a river bank
when someone shouted to him
from the opposite side:
'Hey! How do I get across?'
'You are across!' Nasrudin shouted back.

HOW TO GET IN TOUCH WITH THE AUTHORS OF THIS BOOK

Comments

We are interested in hearing from you if you have enjoyed the book or if you have any suggestions or ideas that would improve it. Please send your thoughts to us via the contact details below. Since the first edition we have heard from many people around the world offering us their experiences and their ideas – as well as sending gratefully received appreciation for our endeavours. So thank you and please do stay in touch!

Credits

We have made strenuous efforts to get in touch with and acknowledge those responsible for the ideas and theories contained in this book. However, we realize that we may have unintentionally neglected to mention some people. If you are aware of any piece of work contained here that has not been properly credited, please do let us know so that we can make amends in future editions of this book.

Coaching and consultancy

If you would like any information about our coaching and consultancy work in connection with managing change and leadership development, we would be delighted to hear from you.

Esther:
Website: www.integralchange.co.uk
E-mail: esther@integralchange.co.uk

Mike:
Website: www.transitionalspace.co.uk
E-mail: mike@transitionalspace.co.uk

References

Adams, J, Hayes, J and Hopson, B (1976) *Transitions: Understanding and managing personal change*, Martin Robertson, London

Aiello, R J and Watkins, M D (2000) The fine art of friendly acquisition, *Harvard Business Review*, Nov–Dec, pp 101–07

Aitken, P (2007) Walking the talk: the nature and role of leadership culture within organisation cultures, *Journal of General Management*, **32** (4), pp 17–37

Argyris, C (1990) *Overcoming Organizational Defenses – Facilitating organizational learning*, Allyn and Bacon, Boston, MA

Argyris, C and Schon, D (1974) *Theory in Practice: Increasing professional effectiveness*, Jossey-Bass, Oxford

Armenakis, A, Holt, D, Feild, H and Harris, S (2007) Readiness for organizational change: the systematic development of a scale, *The Journal of Applied Behavioural Science*, **43** (2), pp 232–55

Ashkenas, R N, Demonaco, L J and Francis, S C (1998) Making the deal real, *Harvard Business Review*, Jan–Feb, pp 165–78

Assudani, R and Kloppenborg, T J (2010) Managing stakeholders for project management success: An emergent model of stakeholders, *Journal of General Management*, **35** (3)

Atkinson, R, Crawford, L and Ward, S (2006) Fundamental uncertainties in projects and the scope of project management, *International Journal of Project Management*, **24** (5), pp 687–98

Bain & Co (2007) Bain's global 2007 management tools and trends survey, *Strategy & Leadership*, **35** (5), pp 9–16

Balogun, J (2003) From blaming the middle to harnessing its potential: Creating change intermediaries, *British Journal of Management*, **14**, pp 69–83

Balogun, J and Hope Hailey, V (2004) *Exploring Strategic Change*, 2nd edn, FT/Prentice Hall, Harlow

Bandler, R and Grinder, J (1979) *Frogs into Princes*, Real People Press, Utah

Barney, J (1986) Strategic factor markets: expectations, luck, and business strategy, *Management Science*, **32** (10)

Barthel, E (2011) Building relationships and working in teams across cultures, in (eds) K Kruckeberg and W Amann, *Leadership and Personal Development: A toolbox for the 21st century professional*, Information Age Publishing, Charlotte, NC

Basset, T and Brunning, H (1994) The ins and outs of consultancy, *The Journal of Practice and Staff Development*, **4** (1)

Bauman, Z (2007) *Liquid Times: Living in an age of uncertainty*, Polity Press, Cambridge

Beck, A (1970) Cognitive therapy: nature of relationship to behaviour therapy, *Behaviour Therapy*, **1**, pp 184–200

Beckhard, R and Gleicher, D (1969) *Organization Development: Strategies and Models*, Addison-Wesley, Reading

Beckhard, R F and Harris, R T (1987) *Organizational Transitions: Managing complex change*, Addison-Wesley, Reading, MA

Beer, M and Nohria, N (2000) Cracking the code of change, *Harvard Business Review*, May–June, pp 133–41

Belbin, M (1981) *Management Teams: Why they succeed or fail*, Butterworth-Heinemann, London

Bell, B and Kozlowski, S (2002) A typology of virtual teams: implications for effective leadership, *Group and Organization Management*, March, pp 14–49

Bell, D (1997) *Reason and Passion*, Karnac, London

Bennis, W (1994) *On Becoming a Leader*, Addison-Wesley, Reading, MA

Berry, L and Parasuraman, A (1991) *Marketing Services: Competing through quality*, Free Press, New York

Binney, G (1992) *Making Quality Work: Lessons from europe's leading companies*, Economist Intelligence Unit, London

Bion, W R (1961) *Experiences in Groups and Other Papers*, Tavistock, London

Blake, C (2008) *The Art of Decisions: How to manage in an uncertain world*, Prentice Hall, Harlow

Block, P (2000) *Flawless Consulting*, 2nd edn, Pfeiffer, San Francisco, CA

Boonstra, J (2004) _Dynamics of Organizational Change and Learning_, Jossey Bass Wiley, San Francisco, CA

Boonstra, J (2013) _Cultural Change and Leadership in Organizations: A Practical Guide to Successful Organizational Change_, Wiley, New Jersey

Bourne, H and Jenkins, M (2013) Organizational values: a dynamic perspective, _Organization Studies_, **34** (4)

Bowlby, J (1980) _Attachment and Loss_, Vol 3, Basic Books, New York

Bowlby, J (1988) _The Secure Base_, Basic Books, New York

Brafman, O and Beckstrom, R (2006) _The Starfish and the Spider: The unstoppable power of leaderless organizations_, Penguin, Harmondsworth

Bridges, W (1991) _Managing Transitions_, Perseus, Reading, MA

Bridges, W and Mitchell, S (2002) Leading transition: a new model for change, in (eds) F Hesselbein and R Johnston, _On Leading Change_, pp 47–59, Jossey-Bass, San Francisco, CA

Brown, J and Isaacs, D (2001) The World Café community, _The Systems Thinker_, **12** (5)

Brown, S L and Eisenhardt, K M (1995) Product development: past research, present findings, and future directions, _Academy of Management Review_, **20** (2), pp 343–78

Bryman, A (1992) _Charisma and Leadership in Organizations_, Sage, London

Bryson, J, Boal, K and Rainey, H (2008) 'Strategic Orientation and Ambidextrous Public Organizations', paper presented at the conference on Organizational Strategy, Structure and Process: A Reflection on the Research Perspective of Raymond Miles and Charles Snow

Buber, M (1961) _Tales of the Hasidim_, (2 volumes) Schocken, New York

Buchanan, D and Huczynski, A (1985) _Organizational Behaviour_, Prentice Hall, London

Bullock, R J and Batten, D (1985) It's just a phase we're going through, _Group and Organization Studies_, **10** (Dec), pp 383–412

Burns, T and Stalker, G M (1961) _The Management of Innovation_, Tavistock, London

Buus, I (2011) Leading in a virtual environment, in (eds) K Kruckeberg and W Amann, _Leadership and Personal Development: A toolbox for the 21st century professional_, Information Age Publishing, Charlotte, NC

Caldwell, R (2003) Models of change agency; a fourfold classification, _British Journal of Management_, **14** (2), pp 131–42

Cameron, E (2011) 'Hiding from uncertainty: Things leaders (and consultants) do' (working paper)

Cameron, E and Green, M (2008) *Making Sense of Leadership*, Kogan Page, London

Cameron, K S and Quinn, R E (2011) *Diagnosing and Changing Organizational Culture: Based on the competing values framework*, Jossey Bass Wiley, San Francisco, CA

Capra, F (1982) *The Turning Point*, Simon and Schuster, New York

Carey, D (2000) Lessons from master acquirers, *Harvard Business Review*, May–Jun, pp 145–54

Carnall, C A (1990) *Managing Change in Organizations*, Prentice Hall, London

Carr, N G (2003) IT doesn't matter, *Harvard Business Review*, May

Casey, D (1993) *Managing Learning in Organizations*, Open University Press, Buckingham

Cash, J I Jr, McFarlan, F W and McKenney, J (1992) *Corporate Information Systems Management: The issues facing senior executives*, 3rd edn, Irwin, Chicago, IL

Cavicchia, S (2010) Shame in the coaching relationship: reflections on organizational vulnerability, *Journal of Management Development*, **29** (10), pp 877–90

Chan, A P C and Chan, A P L (2004) Key performance indicators for measuring construction success, *Benchmarking: An International Journal*, **11** (2), pp 203–21

Change Tracking (accessed 2008) http://www.ctreconsulting.com/home.htm (accessed April 2008)

Cheung-Judge, L M-Y (2001) The self as an instrument – A cornerstone for the future of OD, *OD Practitioner*, **33** (3)

Cheung-Judge, L M-Y (2011) in (eds) L M-Y Cheung-Judge and L S Holbeche, *Organizational Development*, Kogan Page, London

Child, J and McGrath, R (2001) Organizations unfettered: organizational form in an information-intensive economy, *Academy of Management Journal*, **44** (6)

Chodron, P (2001) *The Places that Scare You: A guide to fearlessness in difficult times*, Shambala, Boston, MA

CIPD (accessed 2003) Organising for Success in the 21st Century [Online] www.cipd.org.uk

Cleland, D I and Ireland, L R (2007) *Project Management: Strategic design and implementation*, 5th ed, McGraw-Hill, New York

Cohen, S G and Bailey, D E (1997) What makes teams work: group effectiveness research from the shop floor to the executive suite, *Journal of Management*, 23, pp 239–90

Collins, J C and Porras, J I (1994) *Built to Last: Successful habits of visionary companies*, HarperBusiness, New York

Covey, S (1989) _The Seven Habits of Highly Effective People_, Simon and Schuster, London

Covey, S (1992) _Principle-centred Leadership_, Simon and Schuster, London

Crawford, L H, Hobbs, B and Turner, J R (2005) _Project Categorization Systems: Aligning capability with strategy for better results_, Project Management Institute, Newtown Square, Philadelphia

Crawford, L and Pollack, J (2004) Hard and soft projects: a framework for analysis, _International Journal for Project Management_, **22** (8), pp 645–53

Crosby, L and Johnson, S (2001) Branding and your CRM strategy, _Marketing Management_, Jul–Aug

Cummings, T G and Worley, C G (2009) _Organization Development and Change_, 9th edn, South-Western/Cengage Learning, Mason, OH

Czander, W and Eisold, K (2003) Psychoanalytic perspectives on organizational consulting: Transference and counter-transference, _Human Relations_, **56** (4)

Davenport, T H (1994) Saving IT's soul, _Harvard Business Review_, Mar–Apr, pp 11–27

Davenport, T H and Short, J E (1990) The new industrial engineering: information technology and business process redesign, _Sloan Management Review_, Summer

Day, A (2007) Living in uncertain times, _The Ashridge Journal_, Autumn

de Caluwé, L and Vermaak, H (2004) Change paradigms: an overview, _Organisation Development Journal_, **22** (4)

Deal, T and Kennedy, A (1999) _The New Corporate Cultures_, Texere, London

Dent, E (1999) Complexity science, a worldview shift, _Emergence: The Journal of Complexity in Management and Organizations_, **1** (4), pp 5–199

Devine, M (1999) _Mergers and Acquisitions: The Roffey Park mergers and acquisitions checklist_, Roffey Park Management Institute, West Sussex

Dose, J (1997) Work values: An integrative framework and illustrative application to organizational socialization, _Journal of Occupational and Organizational Psychology_, **70** (3), pp 219–40

Drucker, P (1999) Managing oneself, _Best of HBR, Harvard Business Review_, Boston

Eden, C, Williams, T, Ackermann, F and Howick, S (2000) The role of feedback dynamics in disruption and delay on the nature of disruption and delay in major projects, _Journal of the Operational Research Society_, **51** (3), pp 291–300

Egan, G (1994) _Working the Shadow Side: A guide to positive behind-the-scenes management_, Jossey Bass Wiley, San Francisco, CA

Ellis, A and Grieger, R (eds) (1977) _Handbook of Rational-Emotive Therapy_, Springer, New York

Evans, P (2000) Chapter 5 in (ed) S Chowdhury, *Management 21st Century: Someday we'll all manage this way*, FT/Prentice Hall, London

Fayol, H (1987) *General and Industrial Management: Henri Fayol's classic revised by Irwin Gray*, David S Lake Publishers, Belmont, CA

Feldmann, M L and Spratt, M F (1999) *Five Frogs on a Log*, Wiley, Chichester

Fish, D and Coles, C (1998) *Developing Professional Judgment in Health Care: Learning through the critical appreciation of practice*, Butterworth Heinmann, Oxford

French, R (2001) Negative capability: Managing the confusing uncertainties of change, *Journal of Organizational Change Management*, **14** (5), pp 480–89

Freud, S (1899) *The Interpretation of Dreams*, Basic Books, New York

Gardner, H (1996) *Leading Minds: An anatomy of leadership*, HarperCollins, London

Garland, R (2009) *Project Governance*, Kogan Page, London

Garland, R [accessed 20 November 2014] *Developing a Project Governance Framework* [online] http://www.aipm.com.au/documents/3g/garland_project_governance_paper.pdf

Gaughan, P A (2010) *Mergers, Acquisitions, and Corporate Restructurings*, Wiley, New York

Gladwell, M (2000) *The Tipping Point: How little things can make a big difference*, Little Brown, London

Glaser, R and Glaser, C (1992) *Team Effectiveness Profile*, King of Prussia, PA

Gleick, J (1987) *Chaos: Making a new science*, Penguin, New York

Goffee, R and Jones, G (1998) *The Character of a Corporation*, HarperCollins, London

Goleman, D (1998) *Working with Emotional Intelligence*, Bloomsbury, London

Goleman, D (2000) Leadership that gets results, *Harvard Business Review*, **78** (2), pp 78–90

Green, M (accessed 2001) What makes a premier performer? [online] www.transitionalspace.co.uk

Green, M (2007a) *Change Management Masterclass*, Kogan Page, London

Green, M (2007b) *Politicians and Personality*, IDeA, London

Greene, J and Grant, A M (2003) *Solution-focused Coaching*, Pearson Education, Harlow

Greene, W, Walls, G and Schrest, L (1994) Internal marketing: the key to external marketing success, *Journal of Services Marketing*, **8** (4), pp 5–13

Griffin, E (1991) *First Look at Communication Theory*, McGraw-Hill, New York

Hai, D M (ed) (1986) *Organizational Behavior: Experiences and cases*, West Publishing, St Paul, MN

Hailey, V H and Balogun, J (2002) Devising context sensitive approaches to change: the example of Glaxo Wellcome, *Long Range Planning*, **35** (2), pp 153–79

Hammer, M and Champy, J (1993) *Reengineering the Corporation: A manifesto for business revolution*, HarperBusiness, New York

Hampden-Turner, C (1990) *Creating Corporate Culture*, Addison-Wesley, Reading, MA

Handy, C (1993) *Understanding Organizations*, Penguin, Harmondsworth

Harrison, R (1972) Understanding Your Organisation's Character, *Harvard Business Review*, **50** (3), pp 119–28

Hawkins, P and Smith, N (2006) *Coaching, Mentoring and Organizational Consultancy: Supervision and development*, Open University Press, McGraw-Hill, Maidenhead

Heck, R and Marcoulides, G (1993) Organizational culture and performance: proposing and testing a model, *Organization Science*, **4** (2), pp 209–25

Hedges, P (1993) *Understanding your Personality*, Sheldon, London

Heifetz, R and Laurie, D (1997) The work of leadership, *Harvard Business Review*, **75** (1), pp 124–34

Heifetz, R and Linsky, M (2002) *Leadership on the Line*, Harvard Business School Press, Boston, MA

Henrik, R (1980) *The Psychotherapy Handbook*, New American Library, New York

Herrero, L (2008) *Viral Change: The Alternative to slow, painful and unsuccessful management of change in organisations*, meetingminds, Dubai

Herzberg, F (1968) One more time: how do you motivate employees?, *Harvard Business Review*, (Jan/Feb), pp 53–62

Hesselbein, F and Johnston, R (2002) *On Leading Change*, Jossey-Bass, San Francisco, CA

Higgs, M (2006) Course materials prepared for Henley Business School MBA

Higgs, M and Rowland, D (2005) All changes great and small, *Journal of Change Management*, **5** (2), pp 121–51

Hill, W F and Gruner, L (1973) A study of development in open and closed groups, *Small Group Behavior*, **4**, pp 355–82

Hirsh, S and Kummerow, J (2000) *Introduction to Type in Organisations*, Consulting Psychologists Press, Palo Alto, CA

Hofstede, G, Neujen, B, Ohayiv, D and Sanders, G (1990) Measuring organisational cultures: a qualitative and quantitative study across 20 cases, *Administrative Science Quarterly*, **35**, pp 286–316

Honey, P and Mumford, A (1992) *The Manual of Learning Styles*, 3rd edn, McGraw-Hill, Maidenhead

Hoyt, F and Beverlyn, K (1987) Services marketing: a conceptual model, *Journal of Midwest Marketing*, **2**, pp 195–99

Huber, N (2003) Hitting targets? The state of UK IT project management, *Computer Weekly*, [online] http://www.computerweekly.com/Articles/2003/11/05/198320/hitting-targets-the-state-of-uk-it-project-management.htm (accessed April 2008)

Huffington, C, Cole, C and Brunning, H (1997) *A Manual of Organizational Development: The psychology of change*, Karnac Books, London

Hut, P M (2009) various articles, www.pmhut.com

IBM Corporation [accessed 20 November 2014] *Making Change Work* [online] http://www-935.ibm.com/services/us/gbs/bus/pdf/gbe03100-usen-03-making-change-work.pdf

Isaacs, W (1999) *Dialogue and the Art of Thinking Together*, Random House, New York

Jaworski, B and Kohli, A (1993) Market orientation: antecedents and consequences, *Journal of Marketing*, **57** (Jul), pp 53–70

Johnson, G and Scholes, K (1999) *Exploring Corporate Strategy*, Prentice Hall, Harlow

Jones, J and Bearley, W L (1986) *Group Development Assessment*, King of Prussia, PA

Jorgensen, M and Molokken, K (2006) How large are software cost overruns? A review of the 1994 CHAOS report, *Information and Software Technology*, **48** (4), pp 297–301

Kahn, W A (2001) Holding environments at work, *The Journal of Applied Behavioral Science*, Sept, p 3

Kahneman, D (2011) *Thinking, Fast and Slow*, Macmillan, London

Kanter, R (2002) The enduring skills of change leaders, in (eds) F Hesselbein and R Johnston, *On Leading Change*, pp 47–59, Jossey-Bass, San Francisco, CA

Kaplan, R S and Norton, D P (2004) The Strategy Map: A guide to aligning intangible assets, *Strategy & Leadership*, **32** (5), pp 10–17

Kaufman, G (1989) *The Psychology of Shame: Theory and treatment of shame-based syndromes*, Springer, NY

Keidal, R W (1984) Baseball, football, and basketball: models for business, *Organizational Dynamics*, Winter

Kerr, S (1995) On the folly of rewarding A while hoping for B, *Academy of Management Executive*, **9** (1), pp 7–14

Kets De Vries, M F R (2001) *Struggling with the Demon: Perspectives on individual and organizational irrationality*, Psychosocial Press, Madison, CT

Klein, J (1987) *Our Need for Others*, Tavistock, London

Klonsky, M (2010) 'Discussing undiscussables: exercising adaptive leadership', Dissertation, Fielding Graduate University, Santa Barbara, CA

Kohli, A and Jaworski, B (1990) Marketing orientation: the construct, research propositions and managerial implication, *Journal of Marketing*, **54** (Apr), pp 1–18

Kolb, D (1984) *Experiential Learning*, Prentice Hall, New York

Konigswieser, R and Hillebrand, M (2005) *Systemic Consultancy in Organisations*, Carl-Auer-Systeme-Verlag, Germany

Kotter, J P (1990) What leaders really do, *Harvard Business Review*, **68** (3), pp 101–11

Kotter, J P (1995) Leading change: why transformation efforts fail, *Harvard Business Review*, **73** (2), pp 59–67

Kotter, J P (1996) *Leading Change*, Harvard Business School Press, Boston, MA

Kotter, J P (2006) Transformation, *Leadership Excellence*, **23** (1), p 14

Kotter, J P and Heskett, J (1992) *Corporate Culture and Performance*, Free Press, New York

Kubler-Ross, E (1969) *On Death and Dying*, Macmillan, New York

Kubr, M (1986) *Management Consulting: A guide to the profession*, International Labour Office, Geneva

Lacey, M (1995) Internal consulting: perspectives on the process of planned change, *Journal of Organizational Change Management*, **8** (3), pp 75–84

Langton, G C (1992) Life at the edge of chaos, in (eds) G C Langton, F J Doyne and S Rasmussen, *Artificial Life II (Santa Fe Institute Studies in the Science of Complexity Proceedings)*, 10, Addison-Wesley, Reading, MA

Larson, C and LaFasto, F (1989) *Teamwork: What must go right, what can go wrong*, Sage, Newbury Park, CA

Lehrer, M (2000) From Factor of Production to Autonomous Industry: The transformation of Germany's software sector, *Vierteljahreshefte für Wirtschaftsforschung*, **69** (4), pp 587–600

Lewin, K (1951, 1952) *Field Theory in Social Science*, Harper and Row, New York

Leybourne, S (2006) Improvisation within the project management of change: Some observations from UK financial services, *Journal of Change Management*, **6** (4), pp 365–81

Lim, C S and Mohamed, M Z (1999) Criteria of project success: An exploratory re-examination, *International Journal of Project Management*, **17** (4), pp 243–48

Lipman-Blumen, J (2002) The age of connective leadership, in (eds) F Hesselbein and R Johnston, *On Leading Change*, pp 89–101, Jossey-Bass, San Francisco, CA

Locke, E A and Latham, G P (1984) *Goal Setting: A motivational technique that works!*, Prentice Hall, Englewood Cliffs, NJ

Lyons, S T, Duxbury, L E and Higgins, C A (2006) A comparison of the values and commitment of private sector, public sector, and parapublic sector employees, *Public Administration Review*, **66** (4), pp 605–18

McCaulley, M (1975) How individual differences affect health care teams, *Health Team News*, **1** (8), pp 1–4

McGregor, D (1960) *The Human Side of Enterprise*, McGraw-Hill, Maidenhead

Marks and Mirvis (2001) Making mergers and acquisitions work, *Academy of Management Executive*, **15**, pp 80–94

Maslow, A (1970) *Motivation and Personality*, Harper & Row, New York

Mayo, E (1946) *The Human Problems of an Industrial Civilization*, Harvard Press, Boston

Mayo, E (1949) *Hawthorne and the Western Electric Company: The social problems of an industrial civilization*, Routledge, London

Meredith, J R and Mantel, S J Jr (2000) *Project Management: A managerial approach*, Wiley, New York

Meyerson, D and Martin, J (1987) Cultural change: an integration of three different views, *Journal of Management Studies*, **24** (6), pp 623–47

Miles, R E and Snow, C C (1984) Fit, failure and the hall of fame, *California Management Review*, **26** (3), pp 10–28

Miller, D (2002) Successful change leaders: What makes them? What do they do that is different?, *Journal of Change Management*, **2** (4), pp 359–68

Mir, F A and Pinnington, A H (2014) Exploring the value of project management: linking project management performance and project success, *International Journal of Project Management*, **32** (2), pp 202–17

Mitchell, R K, Bradley, R and Wood, D (1997) Toward a theory of stakeholder identification and salience: defining the principle of who and what really counts, *The Academy of Management Review*, **22** (4), pp 853–86

Modlin, H and Faris, M (1956) Group adaptation and interaction on psychiatric team practice, *Psychiatry*, **19**, pp 97–103

Mohrman, S A, Cohen, S G and Morhman, A M (1995) *Designing Team-based Organizations: New forms for knowledge work*, Jossey-Bass, San Francisco, CA

Molenaar, K, Brown, H, Caile, S and Smith, R (2002) Corporate culture, *Professional Safety*, July

Morgan, B B and Salas, E (1993) An analysis of team evolution and maturation, *Journal of General Psychology*, **120** (3), p 277

Morgan, B B, Glickman, A S, Woodward, E A, Blaiwes, A S and Salas, E (1986) *Measurement of Team Behaviors in a Navy Environment* (Tech Rep no 86-014), p 3, Naval Training Systems Center, Orlando, FL

Morgan, G (1986) *Images of Organization*, Sage, Thousand Oaks, CA

MORI poll [accessed 19 November 2014], *Investors in People UK Management Style* [online] http://www.ipsos-mori.com

Müller, R and Jugdev, K (2012) Critical success factors in projects: Pinto, Slevin and Prescott – the elucidation of project success, *International Journal of Managing Projects in Business*, **5** (4), pp 757–75

Müller, R and Turner, J R (2007) Matching the project manager's leadership style to project type, *International Journal of Project Management*, **25** (1), pp 21–32

Mumford, E and Beekman, G (1994) *Tools for Change and Progress*, CSG, Leiden

Nadler, D A and Tushman, M L (1997) in (ed) M B Nadler, *Competing by Design: The power of organizational architecture*, Oxford University Press, New York

Nevis, E (1998) *Organizational Consulting: A Gestalt approach*, Gestalt Institute of Cleveland Press, Ohio

Noer, D (1993) *Healing the Wounds: Overcoming the trauma of layoffs and revitalizing downsized organizations*, Jossey-Bass, San Francisco, CA

Nutt, P C (1993) Flexible decision styles and the choices of top executives, *Journal of Management Studies*, (30)

O'Neill, M (2000) *Executive Coaching with Backbone and Heart*, Jossey-Bass, San Francisco, CA

O'Reilly, C A and Tushman, M L (2004) The ambidextrous organization, *Harvard Business Review*, April

O'Reilly, C A and Tushman, M L (2007) Ambidexterity as a dynamic capability, *Harvard Business Review*, May

Obholzer, A and Roberts, V (eds) (1994) *The Unconscious at Work*, Routledge, London

Owen, H (1997) *Open Space Technology: A user's guide*, Berrett-Koehler, San Francisco, CA

Pascale, R (1990) *Managing on the Edge*, Penguin, Harmondsworth

Pavlov, I P (trans 1928) *Lectures on Conditioned Reflexes*, International, New York

Perls, F (1976) *The Gestalt Approach and Eyewitness to Therapy*, Bantam, New York

Perls, F, Hefferline, R and Goodman, P (1951) *Gestalt Therapy*, Dell, New York

Pfeifer, T and Schmitt, R (2005) Managing change: quality-oriented design of strategic change processes, *The TQM Magazine*, **17** (4), p 297

Pfeiffer, J (1992) *Managing with Power: Politics and influence in organizations*, Harvard Business School Press, Boston, MA

Pikkarainen *et al* [accessed 20 November 2014] The Impact of Agile Practice on Communication in Software Development [online] http://cs.gmu.edu/~offutt/classes/763/papers/pikkarainen2008.pdf

Porter, L and Tanner, S (1998) *Assessing Business Excellence*, Butterworth Heinemann, Oxford

Posner, B Z and Schmidt, W H (1994) Values congruence and differences between the interplay of personal and organizational value systems, *Journal of Business Ethics*, **12** (5), pp 341–47

Prochaska, J O, Norcross, J C and DiClemente, C C (2006) *Changing for Good*, Collins, New York

Prosci Benchmarking Report (2003, 2007) *Best Practices in Change Management*, www.prosci.com

Pruzan, P (2001) The question of organizational consciousness: can organizations have values, virtues and visions?, *Journal of Business Ethics*, **29** (3), pp 271–84

Pugh, D S (ed) (1990) *Organization Theory*, Penguin, Harmondsworth

PWC [accessed 20 November 2014] The Third Global Survey on the Current State of Project Management [online] http://www.pmi.org/~/media/PDF/RCP/PwC_PPPM_Trends_2012.ashx

Quinn, J (1980) *Strategies for Change: Logical incrementalism*, Irwin, New York

Quinn, R (1996) *Deep Change: Discovering the leader within*, Jossey-Bass, San Francisco, CA

Reitmann, R and Schneer, J A (2008) Enabling the new careers of the 21st century, *Organization Management Journal*, **5**, pp 17–28

Roberto, M and Levesque, L (2005) The art of making change initiatives stick, *Sloan Management Review*, Summer

Robertson, C (2005) Working with emergent change in organizations, *Organizations and People*, **12** (4)

Rogers, C (1967) *On Becoming a Person*, Constable, London

Rokeach, M (1968) *Benefits, Attitudes and Values*, Jossey-Bass, San Francisco, CA

Rokeach, M (1973) *The Nature of Human Values*, Free Press, New York

Rousseau, D M (1990) Assessing Organizational Culture: The case for multiple methods, in *Organizational Climate and Culture*, Jossey-Bass, San Francisco

Rowan, J (1983) *The Reality Game*, Routledge and Kegan Paul, London

Rowland, D and Higgs, M (2008) *Sustaining Change: Leadership that works*, Wiley, Chichester

Royce, W (1998) *Software Project Management*, Addison Wesley, Reading, MA

Sackmann, S (1991) *Cultural Knowledge in Organizations*, Sage, London

Saffold, G (1988) Culture traits, strength, and organizational performance: moving beyond 'strong' culture, *Academy of Management Review*, **13**, pp 546–58

Satir, V, Banmen, J, Gerber, J and Gomori, M (1991) *The Satir Model: Family therapy and beyond*, Science and Behavior Books, Paolo Alto, CA

Sauer, C and Yetton, P W (1997) *Steps to the Future: Fresh thinking on the management of IT-based organizational transformation*, Jossey-Bass, San Francisco, CA

Schabracq, M J (2007) *Changing Organizational Culture*: The change agent's guidebook, Wiley, New Jersey

Scharmer, O (2000) 'Presencing: Using self as gate for the coming-into-presence of the future', paper for conference on knowledge and innovation, May 25–26, Helsinki

Scharmer, O (2007) *Theory U: Leading from the future as it emerges*, Berrett-Koehler, San Francisco, CA

Schein, E (1988) *Process Consultation*, 2nd edn, Prentice Hall, London

Schein, E (1990) Organizational culture, *American Psychologist*, **45** (2)

Schein, E (1992) *Organizational Culture and Leadership*, 2nd edn, Jossey-Bass, San Francisco, CA

Schein, E (1999) *Corporate Culture Survival Guide*, Jossey-Bass, San Francisco, CA

Schein, E (2004) *Organizational Culture and Leadership*, 3rd ed, Jossey-Bass, California

Schein, E and Bennis, W (1965) *Personal and Organizational Change through Group Methods*, Wiley, New York

Schneider, B (1987) The People Make The Place, *Personnel Psychology*, **32**, pp 437–53

Schumacher, E F (1973) *Small is Beautiful: Economics as if people mattered*, Blond and Briggs, London

Schutz, W (1982) *Elements of Encounter*, Irvington, New York

Schwaber, K (2004) *Agile Project Management with Scrum*, Microsoft Press, United States

Scott Peck, M (1990) *The Different Drum: Community-making and peace,* Arrow, London

Scoular, A (2011) *FT Guide to Business Coaching,* Pearson, Harlow

Selden, L and Colvin, G (2003) M&A needn't be a loser's game, *Harvard Business Review,* June, pp 70–79

Semple, E (2012) *Organizations Don't Tweet, People Do: A manager's guide to the social web,* Wiley, New Jersey

Senge, P (1993) *The Fifth Discipline,* Century Business, London

Senge, P, Keliner, A, Roberts, C, Ross, R, Roth, G and Smith, B (1999) *The Dance of Change,* Nicholas Brealey, London

Senge, P, Scharmer, O, Jaworski, J and Flowers, B S (2005) *Presence: Exploring profound change in people, organizations and society,* Nicholas Brealey, London

Shaw, P (2002) *Changing Conversations in Organizations,* Routledge, London

Shein, E (1969) *Process Consultation: Its role in organization development,* Addison Wesley, Reading, MA

Shenhar, A, Dvir, D, Levy, O and Maltz, A C (2001) Project success: a multi-dimensional strategic concept, *Long Range Planning,* **34** (6), pp 699–725

Sirken, H L, Keenan, P and Jackson, A (2005) The hard side of change management, *Harvard Business Review,* Oct

Skinner, B F (1953) *Science and Human Behaviour,* Macmillan, London

Snowden, D and Boone, M (2007) A leader's framework for decision making, *Harvard Business Review,* November

Snowden, D [accessed 19 November 2014], *Story Telling: An old skill in a new context* [online] http://cognitive-edge.com/uploads/articles/10_Storytellling1_-_Old_Skill_New_Context_.pdf

St John of the Cross (2003) *Dark Night of the Soul,* Riverhead Books, New York

Stacey, R D (1993) *Strategic Management and Organisational Dynamics,* Pitman, London

Stacey, R D (2001) *Complex Responsive Processes in Organizations: Learning and knowledge creation,* Routledge, London

Stanford, N (2010) *Corporate Culture: Getting it right,* Wiley, New Jersey

Stride, H (2011) *The relationship between values and commitment: a study of supporters and staff in the charity sector,* Thesis, Henley Business School

Sundstrom, E, de Meuse, K P and Futrell, D (1990) Work teams: applications and effectiveness, *American Psychologist,* **45**, pp 120–33

Taylor, F W (1911) *The Principles of Scientific Management,* Harper & Brothers, New York

Thaler, R and Sunstein, C (2009) *Nudge: Improving decisions about health, wealth, and happiness*, Penguin, London

The Standish Group [accessed 20 November 2014] *CHAOS Manifesto 2013* [online] http://www.versionone.com/assets/img/files/CHAOSManifesto2013.pdf

Thompson, J (2001) *Strategic Management*, Thomson, London

Thornbury, J (2000) *Living Culture: A values-driven approach to revitalising your company culture*, Random House, New York

Todnem, R (2007) Ready or not, *Journal of Change Management*, **7** (1), pp 3–11

Tolbert, M A R and Hanafin, J (2006) Use of self in OD consulting: what matters is presence, ch 4 in *The NTL Handbook of Organization Development and Change*, Jossey Bass Wiley, San Francisco, CA

Townsend, A M, DeMarie, S M and Hendrickson, A R (1998) Virtual teams: technology and the workplace of the future, *Academy of Management Executive*, **12**, pp 17–29

Trompenaars, F and Hampden-Turner, C (1997) *Riding the Waves of Culture: Understanding cultural diversity in business*, Nicholas Brealey, London

Tuckman, B (1965) Development sequences in small groups, *Psychological Bulletin*, **63**, pp 384–99

Turquet, P M (1974) Leadership: the individual and the group, in (eds) A D Colman and M H Geller, *Group Relations Reader 2*, pp 71–87, A K Rice Institute, Washington, DC

Unger, B N, Gemunden, H G and Aubry, M (2012) The three roles of a portfolio management office, *International Journal of Project Management*, **30** (5), pp 608–20

Ward, J and Daniel, E M [accessed 20 November 2014] *The Role Of Project Management Offices (PMOS) in IS Project Success And Management Satisfaction* [online] http://oro.open.ac.uk/33995/2/246D196E.pdf

Ward, S and Chapman, C (2003) Transforming project risk management into uncertainty management, *International Journal of Project Management*, **21** (2), pp 97–105

Wasmer, D and Bruner, G (1991) Using organizational culture to design internal marketing strategies, *Journal of Services Marketing*, **5** (1)

Weinberg, G (1997) *Quality Software Management: Volume 4, anticipating change*, Dorset House, New York

Weisbord, M R and Janoff, S (1992) *Future Search: An action guide to finding common ground in organizations and communities*, Berrett-Koehler, San Francisco, CA

Westerveld, E (2003) The Project Excellence Model: linking success criteria and critical success factors, *International Journal of Project Management*, **21** (6), pp 411–18

Westerveld, E and Gaya-Walters, D (2001) *Het Verbeteren van uw Projector-ganisatie: Het project excellence model in de praktijk*, Kluwer, Dementen

Wheatley, M (1999) *Leadership and the New Science*, Berrett Koehler, San Francisco, CA

Wheatley, M (2007) *Finding Our Way: Leadership for an uncertain time*, Berrett-Koehler, San Francisco, CA

Wheatley, M and Kellner-Rogers, M (1999) What do we measure and why? Questions about the uses of measurement, *Journal for Strategic Performance Measurement*, June

Whelan-Berry, K and Gordon, J (2000) Effective organizational change: new insights from multi-level analysis of the organizational change process, *Academy of Management Proceedings*, p 1

Whittaker, J (1970) Models of group development: implications for social group work practice, *Social Science Review*, **44** (3)

Wind, J Y and Main, J (1998) *Driving Change*, Kogan Page, London

Winnicott, D (1960) The theory of the parent-infant relationship, *International Journal of Psychoanalysis*, **41**, pp 585–95

Winnicott, D (1965) *The Maturational Processes and the Facilitating Environment*, International University Press, New York

Winter, M and Smith, C [accessed 20 November 2014] *Rethinking Project Management – Final report* [online] http://www.ronrosenhead.co.uk/wp-content/rethinking-project-management1.pdf

www.behaviouralinsights.co.uk [accessed 21st September 2014]

www.thechalfontproject.com [accessed 21st September 2014]

INDEX